THE NEW ENCYCLOPEDIA OF THE HUMAN BODY

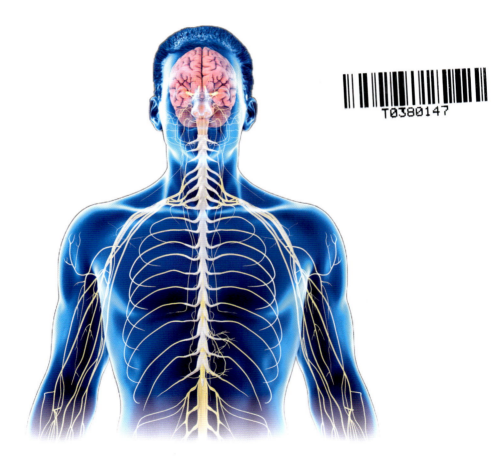

Clare Hibbert, Tom Jackson, Claudia Martin,
Kevin Pettman, and Giles Sparrow

ARCTURUS

Picture Credits:
Key: b-bottom, t-top, c-centre, l-left, r-right

Alamy: 32br superclic, 54–55 PCN Black, 60–61 Neil Overy/Gallo Images, 94bl Charles Bertram/Associated Press, 108bl Digital Image Library, 150–151 Yuri Arcurs, 150bl Associated Press, 206–207 Westend61 GmbH, 210c Nolan Wynne, 212c mkarco, 214b imageBROKER, 220c Chris Willson, 220b Alfonso de Tomas, 227l X3A Collection, 228–229 Daria Artemenko, 234–235 Visuals Stock, 235br Sue Ogrocki/Associated Press; **Bibliothèque Interuniversitaire de Santé, France:** 20bl Bichat; **Getty Images:** 40–41 Digital Vision, 46–47 Viktor Drachev, 64–65 Westend61, 68c, 68bl Sebastian Kaulitzki, 123tl ullstein bild Dtl., 125bl Heritage Images, 130–131 Callista Images, 136–137 Smith Collection/Gado, 164–165 Amelie-Benoist/BSIP, 174–175 andrear, 190–191 Images by Tang Ming Tung, 216c Steve Debenport; **Library of Congress:** 144bl Harris and Ewing, 192bl George Grantham Bain Collection, 219bl; **Lorraine Inglis:** 66b; **Martin Sanders:** 238–249; **Nanokick Technologies:** 45bl; **NASA:** 196cr; **National Library of Medicine, USA:** 19br, 131bl, 133tl; **National Museum of American History, USA:** 84bl; **National Portrait Gallery, UK:** 234bl; **New York Academy of Medicine, USA:** 23tl; **Rambam Institute:** 80bl Blaisio Ugolino; **Science Photo Library:** 11cr Christian Darkin, 12–13 John Bavosi, 18–19 Kateryna Kon, 20–21 Innerspace Imaging, 24–25 Gwen Shockey, 26–27 Jacopin/BSIP, 28–29 Power and Syred, 30–31 Clouds Hill Imaging Ltd, 42b Steve Gschmeissner, 44–45 SGI, 44b Microscape, 58cl Profs. PM Motta, KR Porter, & PM Andrews, 62c John Bavosi, 70, 71l Sebastian Kaulitzki, 72cr KH Fung, 74c Leonello Calvetti, 76–77 KH Fung, 76c Carol & Mike Werner, 80–81 Pixologicstudio, 80cr Steve Gschmeissner, 85 KH Fung, 86–87 Zephyr, 88–89 Francis Leroy, Biocosmos, 90–91, 164bc Thomas Deerinck, NCMIR, 99cr Prof P Motta/Dept of Anatomy/University "La Sapienza", Italy, 100bl Ziad M. El-Zaatari, 118–119 KH Fung, 119br Steve Gschmeissner, 120tr David M Martin, 120–121 Springer Medizin, 122–123 Frank Fox, 123br Asklepios Medical Atlas, 124–125 SEM, 124cl Simone Alexowski, 126–127 KH Fung, 127t Microscape, 142–143 Russell Kightley, 144–145 KTSDesign, 152–153 Zephyr, 153tr Mauro Fermariello, 161, 207t Zephyr, 166cr, 168–169 Kemoal/BSIP, 166bl Geoff Tompkinson, 176br, 178c Fernando da Cunha, 180c Henning Dalhoff, 192 Science Photo, 207cr Prof P Motta/Dept of Anatomy/University "La Sapienza", Italy, 227br Sheila Terry, 230–231 Amelie-Benoist/BSIP, 232br Universal History Archive/UIG; **Shutterstock:** 1, 50br, 68tr, 155l Sebastian Kaulitzki, 3tl Yakobchuk Vasyl, 3tr, 24cr Orla, 3bl Lu Yago, 4tl, 150cr Maryna Olyak, 4tr, 96–97, 132–133, 173bc Prostock-studio, 4bl, 154 Life Science, 5tl, 108–109, 192–193, 194bl, 202r New Africa, 5tr, 223tl Canaryluc, 5bc, 203l Ljupko Smokovski, 6–7 Masonjar, 6br John Bill, 7tl YanLev, 7c Wallenrock, 7br, 83tr, 170bl, 208–209, 211bc, 218b Monkey Business Images, 8–9 jaojormami and others, 10–11 tonkid, 10c therormb, 10bl Georgios Kolidas/C Cook, 11tr, 147tl, 184r BlueRingMedia, 12bl, 14–15, 16–17, 24br, 52c, 120bl, 136c, 136cb, 185br Kateryna Kon, 13r Tomacco, 14b Amadeu Blasco, 15tc rblfmr, 16b, 18l, 30c, 47br, 56l, 73cr, 78cl, 82cr, 88cr, 90bl, 95tr, 118cr, 143cr, 152bl, 160cr, 164cr, 187b Designua, 17c, 78br, 114tr Aldona Griskeviciene, 17cr molekuulbe, 20cl, 41tl udaix, 21tr Anna Jurkovska, 22–23, 182bl, 217tr Dean Drobot, 22tr racobovt, 23br StevenK, 27tl Akif Kutlu, 27cr nicemonkey, 27b Raimundo79, 28c, 29tr, 30bl Dee-sign, 32–33c WHYFRAME, 32cl, 53b, 130b Vector Mine, 34–35 DisobeyArt, 34c Lyubov Levitskaya, 35tc, 124br ART-ur, 36–37 David Havel, 36c, 190br Lapina, 36bl Mazur Travel, 37tl Everett Collection, 38–39 sportoakimirka and others, 40cl kaling2100, 40bl, 48bl Everett Historical, 42cr, 157cr sciencepics, 43 Potapov Alexander, 45clt, 112–113, 214–215, 218–219 Rawpixel.com, 46bl Kjpargeter, 47tl Alex Mit, 48–49 design36, 48c Artemidapsy, 49br Anton Nalivayko, 50–51 oneinchpunch, 50c stihii, 52–53 Gleb Usovich, 54c Samo Trebizan, 54bl art4stock, 55cr, 82–83 Maxisport, 56–57 karuka, 56cr, 56br sruilk, 57tl, 58cc, 204c, 205tl Pikovit, 58–59 javarman, 58bl New Vibe, 59tr Vector Tradition, 60cr zuper_electracat, 60bl iobann, 62bl Lermot, 63cr Irira Bg, 64cl Amparo Garcia, 64br Pomezz, 65tl Crop3D, 66–67c CandyRetriever, 66br EugeneEdge, 66bl Kvitka Fabian, 68–69 insta_photos, 69bl Twinkle picture, 71br Anusorn Nakdee, 72–73 Alex Brylov, 74–75 Merla, 74bl Nadia Buravleva, 75b, 84tr, 114b, 146c, 210b Alila Medical Media, 76br Arturs Budkevics, 78–79 ako photography, 79bl Morphart Creation, 80tr NelaR, 84cr Quetzalcoatl1, 86l Olga Bolbot, 87tr Tridsanu Thopet, 87bl Neveshkin Nikolay, 88c somersault1824, 90cr, 190c Sakurra, 91bl Nicolas Primola, 92–93 BaLL LunLa, 92cl Leszek Glasner, 93c Drp8, 94–95 Peakstock, 94c tolem929, 98–99 DavidTB, 98l jacksparrow007, 100–101 windmoon, 101cr metamorworks, 102–103c ifong, 103cr hmardinal, 104–105 06photo, 104c Alexey Smolyanyy, 105cr David Cohen 156, 106–107 Dream79, 106c, 108c, 110c Olena758, 106br Jiri Hera, 107bl ibreakstock, 109cr Viktoriia Hnatiuk, 110–111 nadianb, 110bl Olga Miltsova, 111tl G.S. Dixit, 112cl Art Syslik, 112br, 115bl, 144c Ph-HY, 116–117 Syda Productions, 116c Oleksandr Dripsyak, 116bl, 198c stockshoppe, 117tl hobbit, 118bl elenabsl, 120cr bitt24, 122b, 164cr, 206cr Tefi, 126b Andrea Danti, 127bl Rose Rodianova, 128–129 goffkein.pro, 128c Marochkina Anastasiia, 128bl Eduards Normaals, 129br Jose Luis Calvo, 130c La Gorda, 132cl DenisFilm, 132br YG Studio, 136t jezpr, 136bl Suz7, 137tl Marcel311, 138–139c Darryl Fonseka, 138cl Elena Istomina, 138b Jaitham, 140–141 PERO studio, 140cl, 176–177 PeopleImages.com, 140br beton studio, 141bl OMIA silhouettes, 142cl Timonina, 142bl Sai Tha, 145b Tomsickova Tatyana, 146–147 PR Image Factory, 146bl Inspiring, 148–149 Andrey Popov, 148cl Amarita, 148cr Igor Klyakinh, 148bc PRILL, 149bl ArtDemidova, 151bc Sorapop Udomsn, 152c Alexandr Chytil, 155r ramcreations, 156bl Johan Swanepoel, 158cr Tongstocker, 158b Sky Antonio, 159 Nacha Petchdawong, 160cl rauf pessel, 160bl Robert Voight, 162–163, 226cr MriMan, 162c Vasilisa Tsoy, 163cr Levent Konuk, 164br Juan Gaertner, 166–167 Rido, 168–169c Mr science, 170–171 Daisy Daisy, 170cr, 172c, 174c decade 3D - anatomy online, 171bl buteo, 172–173 Victor Joly, 172bl ilusmedical, 174bl dore art, 175bc Yanya, 176cr J Sue, 177tl Dietmar Temps, 178–179 Fizkes, 179tl Gladskikh Tatiana, 180–181 Nattapol StudiO, 180bl Irin Fierce, 181tr Khosro, 182–183 Joana Lopes, 182cr Alexander_P, 184–185 icealex, 186–187 Pixel-Shot, 186c Anuwat Meereewee, 186bl Peter Hermes Furian, 188–189 Andrii Zastrozhnov, 189bl, 224–225, 228bl Photoroyalty, 192cl Maxx-Studio, 193br miha de, 194–195 DGLimages, 194c, 216bl, 221bl Macrovector, 195bc Subbotina Anna, 197 AJP, 197br sihasakprachum, 198–199 Don Mammoser, 199b Cookie Studio, 200–201 Zdenka Darula, 200c Tsomka, 200bl Maquiladora, 201cr Shutterstock, 202–203 Proonty, 203r beeboys, 204–205 Vane Nunes, 204bl gritsalak karalak, 206bl Timonina, 208c Designer Things, 208b GagliardiImages, 209l Semmick Photo, 210–211 Fakhrul Najmi, 212–213 Olesia Bilkei, 213cr michae jung, 214c tammykayphoto, 216–217 Rob Crandall, 218cr IVASHstudio, 220–221 Yavuz Sariyildiz, 222–223 design_bazaar, 222bl Yakobchuk Viacheslav, 223br PanuShot, 224c M_V, 225cr Odua Images, 226c Semnic, 226cr Monet3k, 226bl Ververidis Vasilis, 228c Art_Photo, 230c Okrasyuk, 231bl Dmitry Kalinovsky, 232c chaiyawat chaidet, 233 Robert Przybysz, 234c Deborah Asamoah, 236l Karelnoppe, 236br Body Stock, 237br Armando; **US Information Agency:** 25tl; **Wellcome Collection:** 43tl, 61tl, 67bl, 82bl, 101tl, 129tl, 139br, 157tl, 159tl, 183bll Lippiatt, 183blr John Caswell Smith, 184bl, 230bl; **Wikimedia Commons:** 15bl The History of Biology de Erik Nordenskiöld, Ed. Knopf, 1928, 17bl Maurice-Quentin de La Tour/Bavarian State Painting Collections, 31bl Smithsonian Institution/Science Service, restored by Adam Cuerden, 33tr Unknown Author, 34bll Bianca Fioretti of Hallbauer & Fioretti, 34bl Duncan Hall and The Royal Society, 51bl Advanced Microscopy Group/paultmoon, 52bl Museo di Palazzo Poggi, 72bl MSM Takrouri & M Khalaf, 77tl J Solis Cohen, 88bl Popular Science Monthly (vol. 58), 92bl Georg Paul Busch/The Lancet, 99bl Journal of Chemical Education, 102br George Chalmers/The James Lind Library, 113bl Wielka Encyklopedia Powszechna PWN, 162bl Mark Dow, Brain Development Lab, University of Oregon, USA, 163bl Clark University/Garrondo, 166tl www.ilportaledelsud.org, 178bl Spotlight Health Aspen Ideas Festival, 188bll, 188bl The Royal Society, 191tl Umami Information Center/Google Arts and Culture, 196bl, 212bl, 215tl Sarah-Jayne Blakemore, UCL/Shamus O'Reilly, 198bl DBCLS/BodyParts3D, 224bl Imperial War Museum, 229bl Weltrundschau zu Reclams Universum 1902, 233bl Biographical Memoirs of the National Academy of Sciences (vol. 40).

Front cover and back cover images: Shutterstock.

This edition published in 2025 by Arcturus Publishing Limited
26/27 Bickels Yard, 151–153 Bermondsey Street,
London SE1 3HA

Copyright © Arcturus Holdings Limited

All rights reserved. No part of this publication may be reproduced, stored in a retrieval system, or transmitted, in any form or by any means, electronic, mechanical, photocopying, recording or otherwise, without prior written permission in accordance with the provisions of the Copyright Act 1956 (as amended). Any person or persons who do any unauthorised act in relation to this publication may be liable to criminal prosecution and civil claims for damages.

ISBN: 978-1-3988-5632-5
CH012693US
Supplier 29, Date 0325, PI 00010029

Printed in China

Authors: Clare Hibbert, Tom Jackson, Claudia Martin, Kevin Pettman, and Giles Sparrow
Designers: Lorraine Inglis and Amy McSimpson
Consultants: Anne Rooney, Dr. Mandy Hartley, Dr. Kristina Routh

A note on large numbers:

1 million	1,000,000
1 billion	1,000,000,000
1 trillion	1,000,000,000,000
1 quadrillion	1,000,000,000,000,000
1 quintillion	1,000,000,000,000,000,000
1 sextillion	1,000,000,000,000,000,000,000
1 septillion	1,000,000,000,000,000,000,000,000

Contents

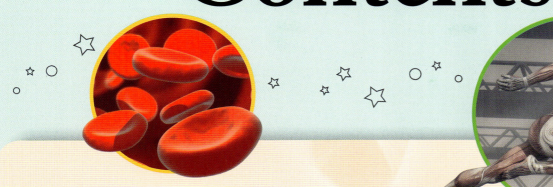

INTRODUCTION — 6

CHAPTER 1: Building a Body — 8

BODY CHEMISTRY — 10
CELLS — 12
RESPIRATION — 14
CELL MEMBRANES — 16
MITOSIS — 18
TISSUES — 20
ORGANS — 22
ORGAN SYSTEMS — 24
GENES AND DNA — 26
CHROMOSOMES — 28
MEIOSIS — 30
GENOTYPES AND PHENOTYPES — 32
UNIQUE YOU — 34
IN THE FAMILY — 36

CHAPTER 2: Body Structure — 38

THE SKELETON — 40
OUR BONES — 42
HOW BONES GROW — 44
JOINTS — 46
MUSCLES — 48
MOVEMENT — 50
BRAIN TO MUSCLES — 52
EXERCISING MUSCLES — 54
INVOLUNTARY MUSCLES — 56
HAIR — 58
NAILS — 60
SKIN — 62
CARING FOR SKIN — 64
HOMEOSTASIS — 66
SPARE PARTS — 68

CHAPTER 3: Lungs and Heart — 70

OXYGEN FOR LIFE — 72
BREATHING — 74
INSIDE THE LUNGS — 76
ALVEOLI — 78
BLOOD VESSELS — 80
CIRCULATION — 82
THE HEART — 84
HEART CYCLE — 86
BLOOD — 88
RED BLOOD CELLS — 90
EXERCISING — 92
HEART HEALTH — 94

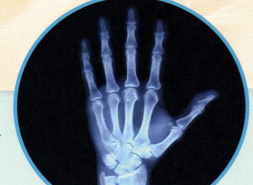

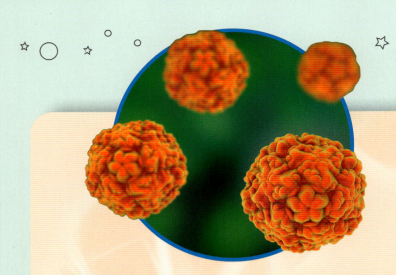

CHAPTER 4:
Digestive System — 96

EATING FOR ENERGY	98
THE DIGESTIVE PROCESS	100
A BALANCED DIET	102
SPECIAL DIETS	104
CARBOHYDRATE	106
PROTEIN	108
FAT	110
VITAMINS AND MINERALS	112
INSIDE THE MOUTH	114
TEETH	116
MOUTH TO STOMACH	118
THE INTESTINES	120
ABSORBING NUTRIENTS	122
APPENDIX	124
LIVER	126
PANCREAS	128
KIDNEYS	130
BLADDER	132

CHAPTER 5:
Defending the Body — 134

GERM WARFARE	136
VIRUSES	138
RAPID RESPONSE	140
WHITE BLOOD CELLS	142
ANTIBODIES	144
LYMPHATIC SYSTEM	146
ALLERGIES	148
SUFFERING THE SYMPTOMS	150
BODY REPAIRS	152

CHAPTER 6:
Brain and Senses — 154

IN CONTROL	156
CONSCIOUSNESS	158
INSIDE THE BRAIN	160
MAPPING THE BRAIN	162
BRAIN CELLS	164
CEREBRUM	166
LOBES	168
CORPUS CALLOSUM	170
CEREBELLUM	172
BRAINSTEM	174
MEMORY	176

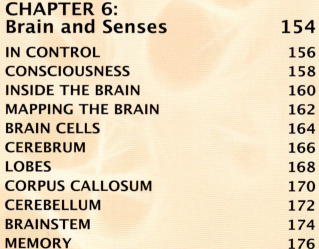
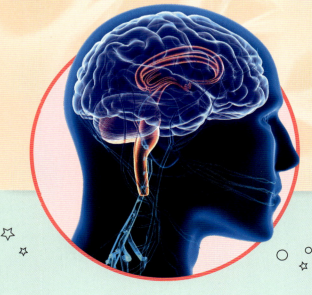

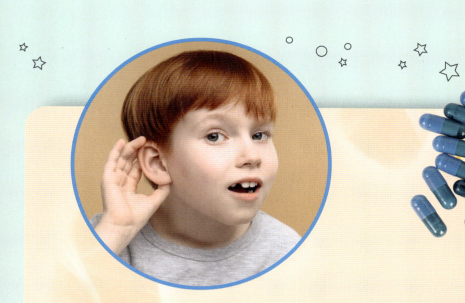
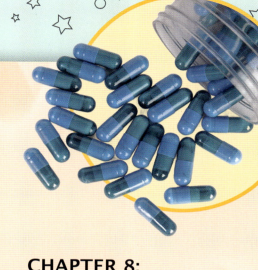

EMOTIONS	178
SLEEP	180
HORMONES	182
NERVOUS SYSTEM	184
SIGHT	186
SMELL	188
TASTE	190
HEARING	192
TOUCH	194
BALANCE AND COORDINATION	196
LANGUAGE AND COMMUNICATION	198
LIVING MINDFULLY	200

CHAPTER 7:
Stages of Life　　202

DIFFERENT BODIES	204
LIFE BEGINS	206
PREGNANCY	208
BIRTH AND BABY	210
CHILDHOOD MILESTONES	212
ADOLESCENCE	214
ADULTHOOD	216
FAMILY LIFE	218
OLD AGE	220

CHAPTER 8:
Medicine　　222

MEDICATIONS	224
STUDYING ANATOMY	226
SURGERY	228
REPLACEMENT PARTS	230
BLOOD MEDICINE	232
VACCINATIONS	234

CHAPTER 9:
Health and Fitness Primer　　236

THE FORCE OF FITNESS	238
ON THE MENU	240
ENERGY BOOST	242
SLEEP TALKING	244
TIMELINE OF DISCOVERIES	246
IN THE FUTURE	248
GLOSSARY	250
INDEX	254

Introduction

Great thinkers have argued for thousands of years about what humans are. Like all animals, we have an amazing body that has changed over time. We also have special abilities that make us stand out from other animals.

Worldwide Family

Today there are more than 8 billion humans on Earth. We belong to one species, but we do not all look the same. Over thousands of years, our bodies slowly adapted to suit different environments, because humans with useful characteristics were most likely to survive and reproduce.

Black or white, tall or short … we are diverse, but we all belong to one species: *Homo sapiens*.

In the Animal Kingdom

Scientists organize living things into groups with shared characteristics. Our body has a backbone, so we are vertebrates. We breathe air, have hair, and produce milk to feed our babies, so we are mammals. Our intelligence, flexible fingers and toes, fingernails, and forward-facing eyes place us with the primates. Being large and tailless makes us great apes.

Human babies need more looking after than other mammal babies. Foals walk minutes after they are born, but humans cannot do that for months.

Super Senses

Our understanding of the world around us comes from our senses of sight, hearing, smell, taste, and touch. Extra senses make us aware of hot and cold, pain, balance and gravity, and where our body is in relation to everything else. Our brain uses all this sense data to respond usefully to our surroundings.

This spearfisher relies on senses to know where his limbs are, find a fish, and fire his spear accurately.

Hands Free

Humans are the only primates that walk upright all the time. This frees up our hands to use tools, carry things, and communicate with each other by drawing, writing, and even texting.

Our fingers and thumbs work together so we can hold things precisely.

Intelligence

Human intelligence is driven by the brain's processing power. We can solve problems, plan ahead, learn and remember, feel emotions, and much more. Other animals show some of these mental abilities—but even the smartest ones do not match humans in all these areas.

Sharing books is one way humans pass on knowledge.

Chapter 1

Building a Body

Your body is like a machine that is revving up and raring to go! But it is more amazing than a car or a plane. Just think of all the incredible things your body can do: ride a bicycle, solve puzzles, learn songs. But, like a car or a plane, your body is made of small parts that come together to form one extraordinary whole!

Same Ingredients

Your body is special because it is different from anyone else's body. But at the same time, it is made from the same basic materials as everyone else. Tall or short, white or black—every one of us is a human being, and we are made of exactly the same ingredients. It is just how some of those ingredients are mixed around that makes us different.

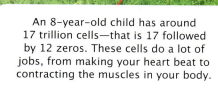

An 8-year-old child has around 17 trillion cells—that is 17 followed by 12 zeros. These cells do a lot of jobs, from making your heart beat to contracting the muscles in your body.

Bit by Bit

Your body's tiniest ingredients are atoms, which are the building blocks of every living thing, rock, or star in the Universe. Too small to be seen by the human eye, atoms join together in groups called molecules. In turn, molecules build cells: tiny powerhouses that carry out lots of different body jobs. Like bricks build a wall, similar cells join to form tissues, which come together to make the body's organs, such as the heart. Organs work with each other as organ systems.

Your body has 78 organs that work together in 10 organ systems. Together, your organ systems allow you to grow, think, and run.

DID YOU KNOW? Scientists estimate that an average-sized adult is made of around 7 octillion atoms—that is a 7 followed by 27 zeros.

Body Chemistry

Everything is made of atoms—including your body! There are 118 different types of atoms, including oxygen and iron. A chemical made of just one type of atom is called an element. Nearly half of the 118 known elements are found in your body.

Elementary Ingredients

Most elements in the body are "trace elements," which means we have only a tiny amount of them. They include metals such as magnesium (0.05 percent), iron (0.006 percent), zinc (0.0032 percent), and copper (0.0001 percent).

ELEMENTS AS A PERCENTAGE OF BODY WEIGHT

NITROGEN (3.2 %)
Nitrogen is found in proteins, used for nearly every process in a cell, and in the nucleic acids that make up DNA (see page 26).

TRACE ELEMENTS (3.8 %)
Trace elements include calcium (1.5 %), essential for healthy bones and teeth, and phosphorus (1 %), which provides energy in cells for chemical reactions.

HYDROGEN (9.5 %)
Hydrogen is found in water and many other materials made or needed by the body, such as lipids (including fats), proteins, carbohydrates, and nucleic acids.

OXYGEN (65 %)
Oxygen is mostly in the form of water. One oxygen atom (O) bonded to two hydrogen atoms (H_2) forms a molecule of water (H_2O).

CARBON (18.5 %)
Carbon is found in many groups of bonded atoms, known as molecules. A molecule that contains carbon is called an organic molecule.

An adult's weight is 55 to 60 percent water. Water is the base ingredient of blood, urine, and other liquids.

BODY BREAKTHROUGH

Scientist: John Dalton
Breakthrough: Theory of atoms
Date: 1803
The story: Dalton said that everything is made of atoms, that atoms are indivisible and indestructible, and that all atoms of a given element have the same properties. Dalton observed that a combination of two or more kinds of atom (such as oxygen and hydrogen) can form a compound (in that case, water).

10

This diagram shows one atom of carbon. A carbon atom's structure means that it easily forms bonds with other atoms. It has four tiny particles called electrons in its outer shell. It needs eight electrons in that shell to be stable, so it readily bonds with up to four other atoms, sharing one electron from each atom to fill its outer shell.

Basic Building Block

Many molecules in living things contain carbon. The structure of a carbon atom allows it to bond with lots of other elements to form stable molecules. It bonds with hydrogen and oxygen to form carbohydrates and lipids; with hydrogen, oxygen, and nitrogen to form proteins; and with hydrogen, oxygen, nitrogen, and phosphorus to form nucleic acids.

On Earth, life forms are carbon-based. Some scientists speculate that on other worlds there might be life based on silicon (imagined above), since it is chemically similar to carbon.

DID YOU KNOW? More than 96 percent of the body is made up of just four elements—oxygen, carbon, hydrogen, and nitrogen.

Cells

Scientists estimate that an average-sized adult has around 30 trillion cells! Cells are the smallest working parts of all living things.

Parts of the Cell

Most cells can only be seen through a microscope, but they are incredibly complex. They contain chemical machines called organelles that carry out different jobs.

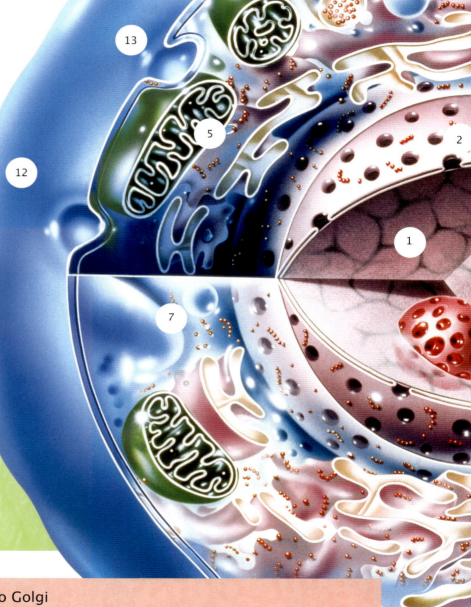

INSIDE A HUMAN CELL
1. Nucleus contains the body's DNA (see page 26).
2. Pore-pitted nuclear membrane
3. Nucleolus makes the substances that build ribosomes.
4. Endoplasmic reticulum makes and stores proteins.
5. Mitochondrion fuels the cell by releasing energy from food molecules.
6. Golgi apparatus stores substances or gets them ready to leave the cell.
7. Ribosomes build proteins (see pages 26-27).
8. Peroxisomes break down toxins, amino acids, and lipids.
9. Lysosomes break down waste.
10. Centrioles help the cell divide.
11. Cytoplasm is a jelly-like fluid in which organelles float.
12. Cell membrane protects the cell.
13. Pore, where some molecules can enter or leave the cell

BODY BREAKTHROUGH

Scientist: Camillo Golgi
Breakthrough: Identified the Golgi apparatus
Date: 1898
The story: Italian scientist Camillo Golgi invented a technique for staining cells black so that he could examine neurons under a microscope. The staining revealed a stack of "disks" inside the cell—the organelle we now call the Golgi apparatus. Golgi was later awarded a Nobel Prize for his work on the brain.

DID YOU KNOW? Animals, plants, and fungi are built from eukaryotic cells—cells that have a nucleus. In contrast, bacteria are living things made of one cell with no nucleus.

An average human cell is 0.025 mm (0.001 in) across. One of the largest, an ovum (egg cell), is about 0.12 mm (0.005 in) wide.

Specialist Jobs

We have more than 200 types of cell, each suited to a particular job. Epithelial cells, for example, line surfaces of the body, such as the skin, vessels, or organs. Depending on the job they do, they can be flat, cube-shaped, column-shaped, or column-shaped with hairs on top.

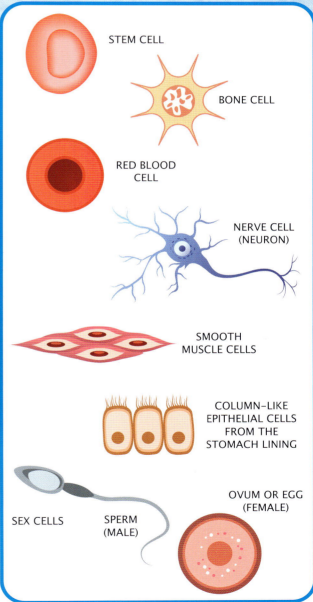

STEM CELL

BONE CELL

RED BLOOD CELL

NERVE CELL (NEURON)

SMOOTH MUSCLE CELLS

COLUMN-LIKE EPITHELIAL CELLS FROM THE STOMACH LINING

SEX CELLS — SPERM (MALE) — OVUM OR EGG (FEMALE)

13

Respiration

Cells are constantly at work, carrying out tasks from creating materials to making new cells. To do this work, cells need energy—which they get through a process called respiration.

This illustration shows a mitochondrion, which has the job of producing energy for its cell.

Aerobic Respiration

Most of the time, most cells rely on aerobic respiration (meaning "producing energy from oxygen") to get energy. In this type of respiration, cells use two ingredients: glucose and oxygen. Glucose is taken from the food we eat (see pages 98–99), while oxygen is taken from the air we breathe (see pages 72–73). Both ingredients are delivered to cells in the bloodstream. In aerobic respiration, glucose and oxygen react together to produce energy, as well as water and carbon dioxide. Carbon dioxide is a waste product, as cells do not need it.

Mitochondria float in a cell's jelly-like cytoplasm.

Inside a cell, aerobic respiration takes place in organelles called mitochondria.

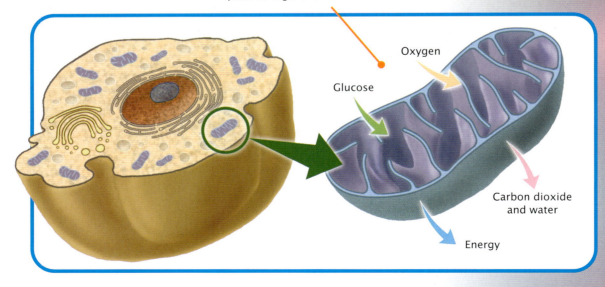

DID YOU KNOW? Muscle cells, which need lots of energy, may have more than 2,000 mitochondria.

When exercising hard, your body tries to take in extra oxygen by breathing faster. Even so, muscle cells may need to produce energy without oxygen.

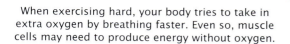

Anaerobic Respiration

During intense exercise, muscle cells may not get enough oxygen for all their hard work. In this case, muscle cells produce energy using anaerobic respiration (meaning "producing energy without oxygen"). This method, which can be used only for a short time, produces energy from glucose without using oxygen. It has a different waste product: lactic acid. This acid is responsible for the burning feeling in your muscles during extreme exercise, but the burning fades harmlessly within a few minutes if you rest.

Nearly all human cells contain mitochondria. Red blood cells—which have the job of carrying oxygen through the blood—do not have any mitochondria or other organelles, so they have more room for carrying oxygen.

BODY BREAKTHROUGH

Scientist: Albert von Kölliker
Breakthrough: Discovered mitochondria
Date: 1857
The story: Using a microscope, he was the first to notice mitochondria, in the muscle cells of insects. He was also the first to separate mitochondria from their cells and to spot that they are covered by a protective membrane.

15

Cell Membranes

Every cell is surrounded by a thin outer layer, called a membrane. The membrane is made from fatty chemicals that form a barrier for large molecules, while smaller ones can pass through. Larger molecules must enter and leave the cell through active transport.

Passive Transport

Molecules of water, oxygen, and carbon dioxide are small enough to enter and leave cells through the cell membrane, without the cell using up energy on transportation. These molecules pass to and fro between the cell and the blood or tissue fluid that surrounds cells. Small molecules travel through the cell membrane due to a physical process called diffusion, where substances naturally spread out from where they are common to where they are rare.

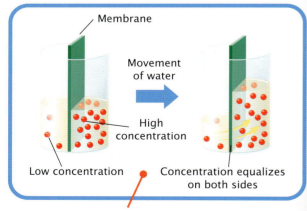

Cells rely on a special kind of diffusion called osmosis to move water in and out, keeping a balance of materials within the cell. When there is a high concentration of chemicals dissolved in a cell's cytoplasm, water will diffuse in from outside. If the cell is surrounded by water that has a higher concentration of chemicals, osmosis will push water out of the cell.

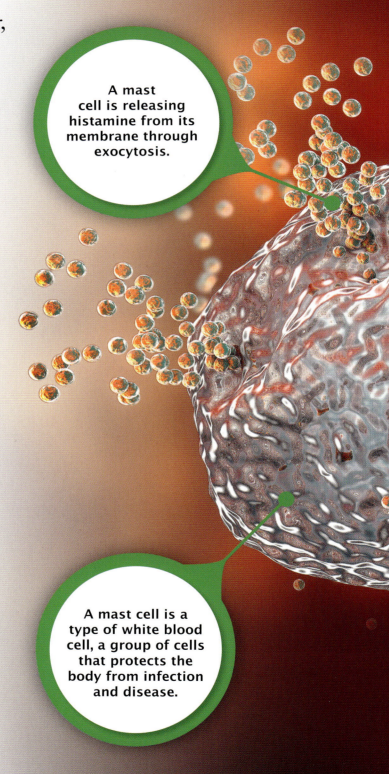

A mast cell is releasing histamine from its membrane through exocytosis.

A mast cell is a type of white blood cell, a group of cells that protects the body from infection and disease.

DID YOU KNOW? The body's goblet cells release slimy mucus to coat the inside of nose, lungs, and throat, making up to 6 cups every day between them!

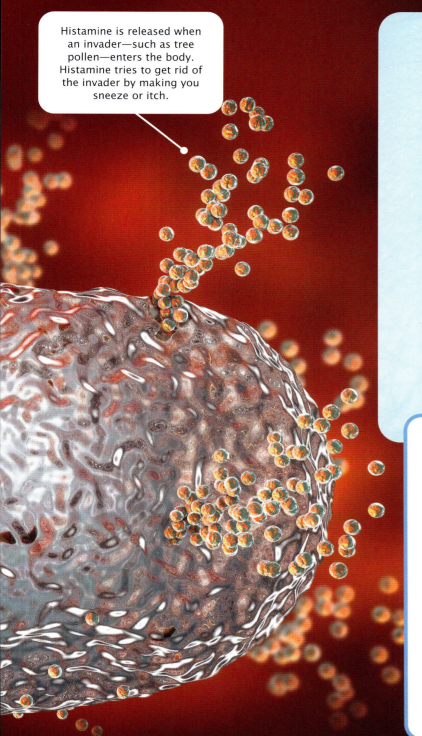

Histamine is released when an invader—such as tree pollen—enters the body. Histamine tries to get rid of the invader by making you sneeze or itch.

Active Transport

Large molecules, such as hormones, enzymes, and nutrients, are actively transported through the cell membrane. Exocytosis is a process that releases large molecules from a cell. Once a cell has made useful molecules, its Golgi apparatus packages the molecules into small bags, called vesicles. A vesicle merges with the cell membrane, then its contents are released outside the cell. Large molecules can enter a cell through endocytosis. Molecules are captured in a hollow section of the cell membrane, which then breaks off to form a vesicle inside the cell.

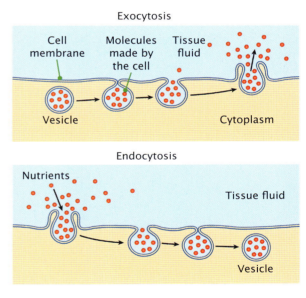

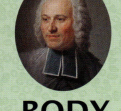

BODY BREAKTHROUGH

Scientist: Jean-Antoine Nollet
Breakthrough: Discovered osmosis
Date: 1748
The story: Nollet, a French priest, put pure alcohol in a sealed pig's bladder that had been immersed in water. Several hours later, the bladder was bulging with water under great pressure. Osmosis had pushed water inside to dilute the alcohol.

17

Mitosis

The body produces new cells so that we can grow, and also to replace cells that are damaged or dying. Cells have different lifespans. Some white blood cells survive for just a few days, while bone cells can last for 25 years. Most new body cells are made in a process called mitosis.

Copy That!

Mitosis produces an exact copy of the DNA in each cell. DNA contains the instructions for a cell's activities. Sex cells need to make "half" (not full) copies of their DNA, so they reproduce using a different method (see pages 30–31).

2
Each daughter cell will have its own membrane and be filled with jelly-like fluid called cytoplasm.

This artwork shows one cell dividing. Every minute, around 250 million cells in your body do this.

1
In cell division this is called the "mother." It will divide to form "daughter" cells.

MITOSIS

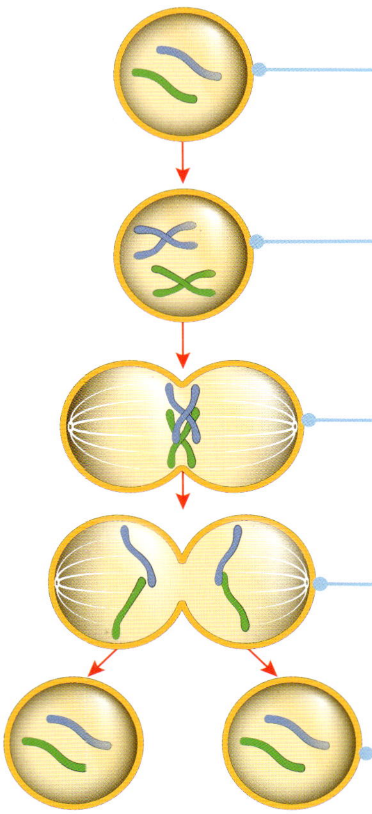

1. The cell contains DNA (see page 26) in the form of 46 "single" chromosomes. To keep things simple, only 2 of those chromosomes are shown here.

2. Before the cell can divide, it copies the DNA in its nucleus to create 46 "double" chromosomes.

3. The membrane around the nucleus breaks down, threads form across the cell, and the chromosomes line up on the threads.

4. The threads pull apart the duplicated chromosomes to opposite sides of the cell. A new membrane forms around each set of single chromosomes.

5. The cell splits to form two new cells. Each has a nucleus that contains an identical set of 46 chromosomes.

18

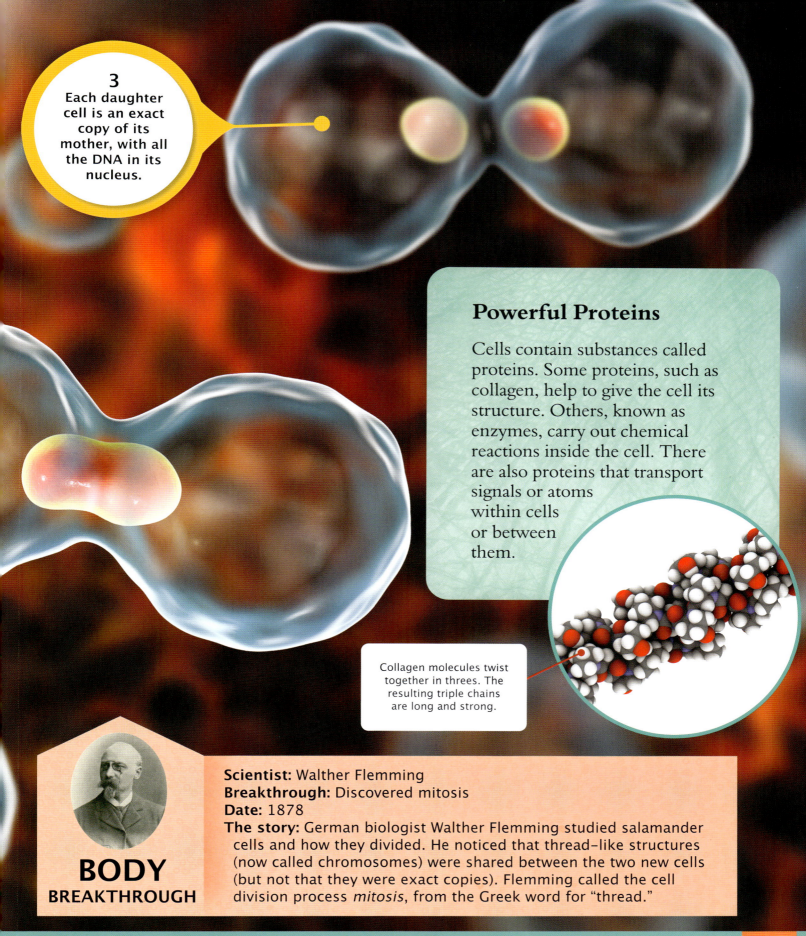

3 Each daughter cell is an exact copy of its mother, with all the DNA in its nucleus.

Powerful Proteins

Cells contain substances called proteins. Some proteins, such as collagen, help to give the cell its structure. Others, known as enzymes, carry out chemical reactions inside the cell. There are also proteins that transport signals or atoms within cells or between them.

Collagen molecules twist together in threes. The resulting triple chains are long and strong.

BODY BREAKTHROUGH

Scientist: Walther Flemming
Breakthrough: Discovered mitosis
Date: 1878
The story: German biologist Walther Flemming studied salamander cells and how they divided. He noticed that thread-like structures (now called chromosomes) were shared between the two new cells (but not that they were exact copies). Flemming called the cell division process *mitosis*, from the Greek word for "thread."

DID YOU KNOW? Every minute we lose around 1 million cells from the epidermis (surface of our skin) ... but we also produce around 1 million replacements.

Tissues

Cells join together to form tissue. The four main types of tissue are muscle, epithelial, connective, and nervous tissue. All tissues need a blood supply to deliver nutrients to them.

Tissue Functions

Muscle tissue lets us move or keep still. Epithelial tissue lines and protects our organs. Connective tissue, such as bone, cartilage, fat, and blood, holds other tissues together and protects them. Nervous tissue is made up of neurons, which carry messages between cells, and glial cells, which carry nutrients and oxygen to the neurons.

This SEM—an image from a scanning electron microscope—reveals the tissues that make up the lining of the jejunum (part of the small intestine).

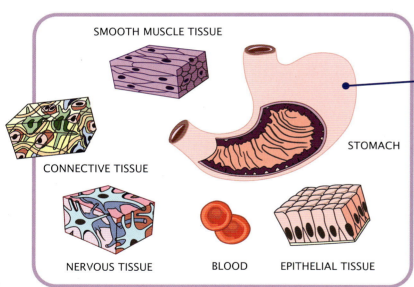

In an organ, several types of tissue work together. The stomach contains smooth muscle, epithelial, connective, nervous, and blood tissue.

The mucus membrane is formed from epithelial tissue. It houses glands and cells that secrete mucus.

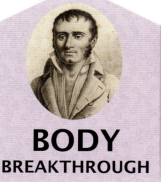

BODY BREAKTHROUGH

Scientist: Marie-François-Xavier Bichat
Breakthrough: Founded histology (the science of studying tissues)
Date: 1800
The story: French anatomist Marie-François-Xavier Bichat was one of the first to suggest that organs are formed from simple tissues that each has different functions. His *Treatise on Membranes* (1800) identified 21 types of tissue. However, Bichat did not use a microscope, so he didn't see that tissues are made up of cells.

DID YOU KNOW? Tissues also contain the intercellular matrix, which fills the spaces between the cells. It is made of fibers and proteins.

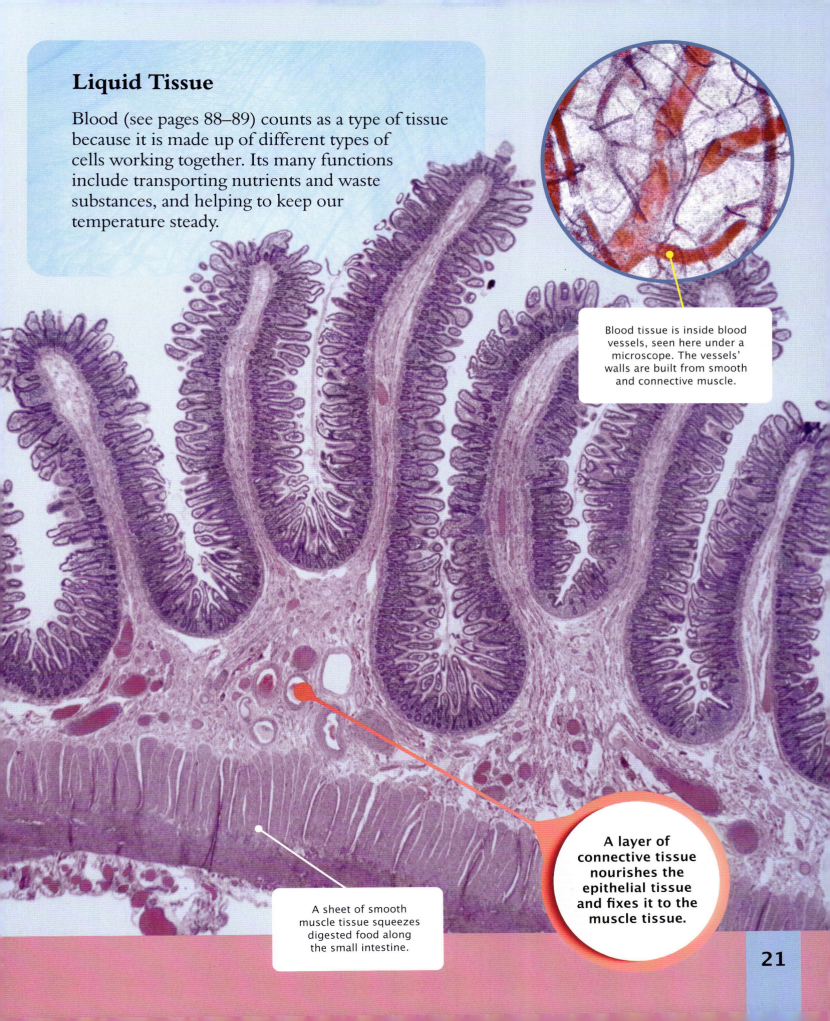

Liquid Tissue

Blood (see pages 88–89) counts as a type of tissue because it is made up of different types of cells working together. Its many functions include transporting nutrients and waste substances, and helping to keep our temperature steady.

Blood tissue is inside blood vessels, seen here under a microscope. The vessels' walls are built from smooth and connective muscle.

A sheet of smooth muscle tissue squeezes digested food along the small intestine.

A layer of connective tissue nourishes the epithelial tissue and fixes it to the muscle tissue.

21

Organs

Any working part of the body machine that is made from more than one type of tissue is an organ. We have 78 organs, ranging in size from the brain's pineal gland, just 5 mm (0.2 in) long, to the skin.

Work to Do

Each organ has a particular job or jobs to do. The brain controls the other organs. The heart pumps blood, carrying oxygen taken in by the lungs. The kidneys remove waste from blood, while the liver filters out harmful substances and produces bile, which helps to break down fats, and proteins that help our blood to clot.

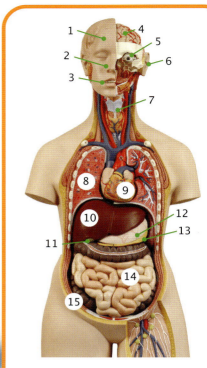

KEY TO ORGANS

1. Skin
2. Nose
3. Mouth
4. Brain
5. Eye
6. Ear
7. Larynx
8. Lungs
9. Heart
10. Liver
11. Gall bladder
12. Stomach
13. Pancreas
14. Small intestine
15. Large intestine

This torso, used to teach anatomy, shows some of the body's organs.

The brain is the most complex organ in the body. It controls everything else.

The nose is an organ used for breathing and smelling. It plays a part in both the respiratory and sensory systems.

DID YOU KNOW? The liver is the heaviest internal organ. The average weight of an adult's liver is 1.6 kg (3.5 lb).

BODY BREAKTHROUGH

Scientists: Ancient Egyptians
Breakthrough: First description of the body's organs
Date: c. 1600 BCE
The story: The Edwin Smith Papyrus, named after the American Egyptologist who bought it in 1862, is one of the four main medical works known from ancient Egypt. It gives treatments for 48 different injuries, which have been grouped together according to the organs they affect. It shows that the Egyptians studied the body scientifically.

The skin stops water and microbes entering the body. It is also a habitat for around 1,000 harmless bacteria species.

The brain controls the swimmer's muscles and movement. The lungs bring in oxygen, while the heart pumps blood.

The Biggest Organ

Weighing around 4.5 kg (10 lb) on an average adult, the skin is the body's biggest organ. It is one of the external organs, visible outside the body. Others include the eyes, tongue, and penis. Internal organs are inside the body.

On an average adult, the skin covers an area of about 1.8 sq m (22 sq ft).

Organ Systems

Like cells and tissues, organs do not work alone. They join up with other organs and tissues to form organ systems. Each system performs one function or set of functions, such as digestion or breathing.

Fully Functional

The body's systems need each other in order to work properly. They rely on the nervous and endocrine systems to control what they do, and when. They also need the circulatory system to bring oxygen that has been breathed in and energy from food that has been digested.

Muscles are organs made of muscle tissue, blood vessels, tendons, and nerves. They form the muscular system, which works with the skeletal system so we can move.

RESPIRATORY SYSTEM

ENDOCRINE AND EXOCRINE SYSTEM

DIGESTIVE SYSTEM

The thyroid gland secretes hormones that keep the body's temperature, metabolism, and heart rate steady.

Home of the Hormones

The endocrine system has glands that make chemical messengers called hormones. Each hormone triggers a different action—for example, adrenaline prepares the body for action, by increasing our heart rate and our rate of breathing.

The digestive system processes food. It includes the food pipe, stomach, and intestine.

24

BODY BREAKTHROUGH

Scientists: Rosalyn Sussman Yalow (left) and Solomon Berson
Breakthrough: Discovered radioimmunoassay (RIA)
Date: 1977
The story: Using forms of elements called isotopes, RIA makes it possible to measure substances in the body that were previously very hard to measure or even too small to detect. Yalow and Berson first used RIA to measure insulin levels and, later, many other hormones. Part of the endocrine system, insulin regulates the transport of sugar in the blood.

The lungs and airways take in oxygen and expel carbon dioxide.

Lymph vessels and nodes help to protect the body from disease.

The skeletal system is the bony framework that supports the body.

Skeletal, smooth, and cardiac muscles make up the muscular system.

REPRODUCTIVE SYSTEM

URINARY SYSTEM

NERVOUS SYSTEM

CARDIOVASCULAR SYSTEM

LYMPHATIC SYSTEM

SKELETAL SYSTEM

MUSCULAR SYSTEM

The female reproductive system includes the ovaries which release the eggs, and the uterus (or womb) which carries the baby.

The brain, spinal cord, and nerves make up the nervous system.

The circulatory system pumps blood around the body.

DID YOU KNOW? The pea-sized pituitary gland may be small, but it releases many hormones—which control our blood pressure and our growth, for example.

25

Genes and DNA

Genes are instructions for how cells look and what they do. Specifically, genes give instructions for building proteins—vitally important substances for life. Genes are stored in the nucleus of every cell on long, twisting molecules called DNA (deoxyribonucleic acid). Another type of molecule called RNA (ribonucleic acid) acts as a messenger, carrying the DNA's instructions out of the nucleus.

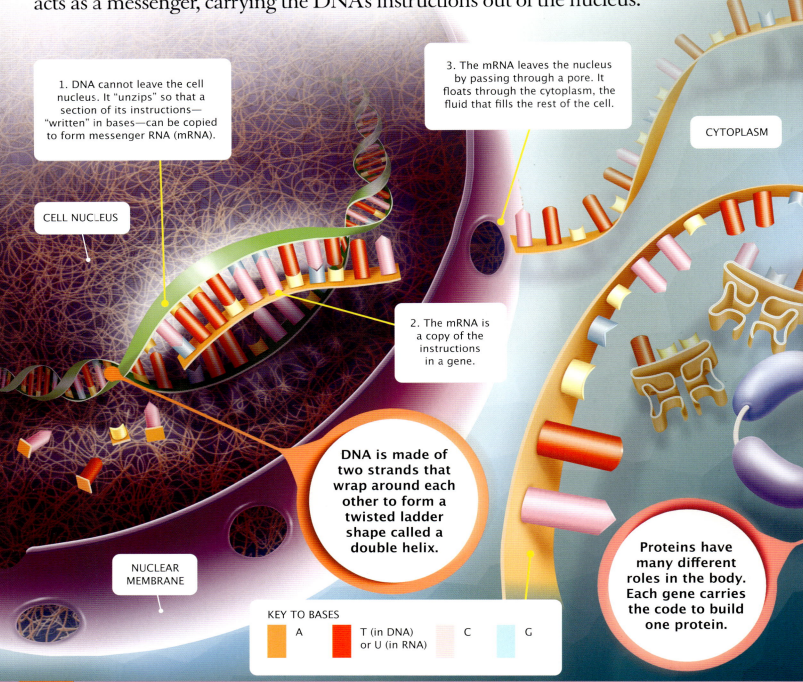

1. DNA cannot leave the cell nucleus. It "unzips" so that a section of its instructions—"written" in bases—can be copied to form messenger RNA (mRNA).

CELL NUCLEUS

3. The mRNA leaves the nucleus by passing through a pore. It floats through the cytoplasm, the fluid that fills the rest of the cell.

CYTOPLASM

2. The mRNA is a copy of the instructions in a gene.

DNA is made of two strands that wrap around each other to form a twisted ladder shape called a double helix.

NUCLEAR MEMBRANE

KEY TO BASES
A | T (in DNA) or U (in RNA) | C | G

Proteins have many different roles in the body. Each gene carries the code to build one protein.

DID YOU KNOW? The human body has 20,000–25,000 genes. Each gene is a section of DNA, made up of combinations of As, Cs, Gs, and Ts.

BODY
BREAKTHROUGH

Scientists: Francis Crick, James Watson, Rosalind Franklin, and Maurice Wilkins
Breakthrough: Discovering DNA's double helix structure
Date: 1953
The story: Francis Crick and James Watson used data gathered by fellow scientists Rosalind Franklin and Maurice Wilkins to work out the shape of the DNA molecule. They showed it formed a double helix, like a twisted ladder, with "rungs" of chemicals called bases.

4. The cytoplasm contains many different organelles, including ribosomes, the cell's protein–building "machines."

Bases

If you imagine DNA as a language, then its "letters" are bases. DNA has just four chemical bases: adenine (A), thymine (T), cytosine (C), and guanine (G). In double-stranded DNA, A always bonds with T, and C with G.

These bands show the bases in a DNA sequence.

tRNA

5. Ribosomes allow mRNA to connect to another molecule, tRNA. Each tRNA carries a simple compound called an amino acid.

AMINO ACID

Building from Bases

If bases are "letters" in the genetic code of DNA and RNA, then its "words" are codons, which are three bases long. Each codon is the key to build a particular amino acid—the building blocks of proteins. Only 20 amino acids are used to build the proteins in your body.

6. As mRNA and tRNA connect, chains of amino acids link together, forming proteins. Proteins play many different roles in the cell. They are sometimes called the cell's "workers."

This model shows a portion of a molecule of hemoglobin, the protein that makes red blood cells red and helps to carry oxygen around the body.

Chromosomes

A chromosome is a long, thread-like structure made of a coiled-up molecule of DNA and some proteins. All 46 of our chromosomes (23 pairs) are in every cell that has a nucleus.

This image of chromosome pair 3 was created by an electron microscope, which uses a beam of electrons to create images of objects too small to be seen under an ordinary microscope.

Keeping DNA Safe

DNA is quite a delicate substance. It is protected inside the cell's nucleus, where it is kept separate from other chemicals that might damage it and alter the genetic coding. To keep DNA even safer, the long strands are coiled up to make bundles called chromosomes. The DNA is only uncoiled when it is being copied and decoded. Before a cell divides (see page 18), each "single" chromosome is copied, forming a "double" chromosome made up of two identical strands of DNA (called chromatids) joined in an X shape.

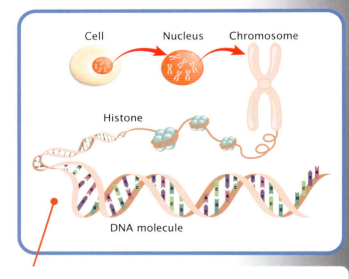

The DNA strands are coiled around support proteins called histones, and then these coils are coiled and coiled many times to make a compact "supercoil."

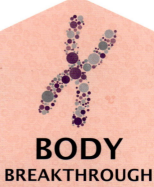

BODY BREAKTHROUGH

Scientists: Human Genome Project (HGP)
Breakthrough: Sequenced the human genome
Date: 2003
The story: Beginning in 1990, the HGP set out to map the human genome—to record the order of the 3.2 billion pairs of chemical bases (A, T, C, and G) that spell out the genetic code on our 46 chromosomes. The project took 13 years. Today, its findings are accessible to scientists all over the world.

Karyotype

A full set of chromosomes is called a karyotype. Each chromosome is part of a pair, with one coming from the mother and one from the father. Humans have 23 pairs. The last pair are often called the sex chromosomes. They usually determine the sex that a child is born with. Two large "X" chromosomes usually make a baby female, while a large "X" and small "Y" usually make a baby who is born male.

This image of the human karyotype shows a full set of "double" chromosomes, which have been copied ready for cell division.

Each of these "double" chromosomes is made up of two identical halves, called chromatids, which are joined at the middle in a region called the centromere.

Chromosome 3 contains 1,000 to 1,900 genes, including a cluster of genes that help to create the sense of smell.

DID YOU KNOW? If all the DNA in your body was uncoiled, it would stretch from the Earth to the Sun and back 20 times!

Meiosis

A special kind of cell division, called meiosis, is used to make sex cells, either male sperm cells or female egg cells. These cells have a half set of genes: 23 chromosomes. This means that a sperm and egg cell can merge to make a full set of genes—46 chromosomes—for a new individual. Meiosis makes sure that each child has a different set of genes from its brothers and sisters.

Dividing Twice

In meiosis, each cell divides twice, forming four daughter cells. The first division organizes the 46 chromosomes into pairs then draws one chromosome in each pair to opposite ends of the cell. The cell then divides in two, creating daughter cells with a half set of chromosomes. In the next division, the two half-set cells divide in two, creating four daughter cells, each with 23 "single" chromosomes.

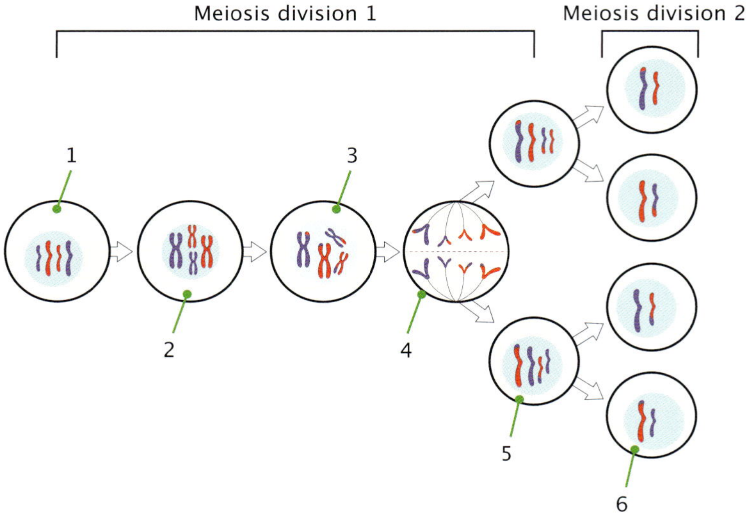

Meiosis division 1

Meiosis division 2

KEY
1. To keep things simple, this diagram shows meiosis using only 4 chromosomes rather than 23.
2. DNA is copied, turning "single" chromosomes into "double" chromosomes.
3. Recombination takes place (see below).
4. One half of each chromosome is pulled to opposite ends of the cell.
5. The cell divides.
6. The cell divides a second time, creating four daughter cells.

The chromosomes have an X shape because they have been copied ready for cell division. They have two identical copies of their DNA (called chromatids) connected in the middle.

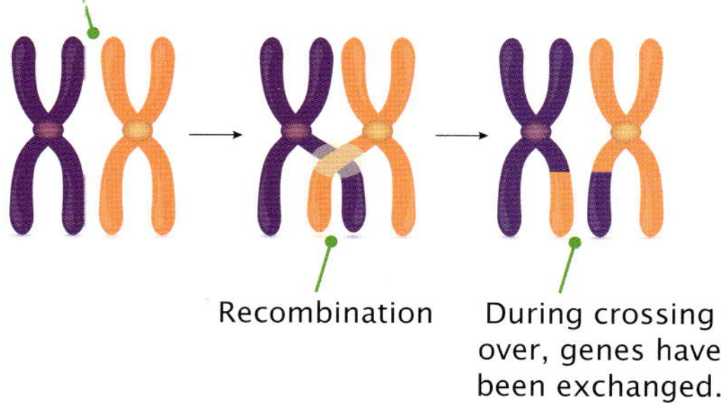

Recombination

During crossing over, genes have been exchanged.

Recombination

Unlike in mitosis (see pages 18–19), where the daughter cells always have identical genes, meiosis deliberately mixes chromosomes up to make four daughter cells that each have a unique set of DNA. One of the ways this is done is called recombination, also known as crossing over. During the first division in meiosis, the paired-up chromosomes are lined up next to each other. They are so close that they can tangle up and swap chunks of DNA.

30

Genotypes and Phenotypes

The genotype is a record of what chemical codes a person has in the DNA in their cells. The phenotype is a record of a body characteristic, such as hair shade, which is inherited from the parents. A big part of the study of genetics is figuring out how genotypes are linked to phenotypes.

> Family members look similar because children have inherited a set of genes from both parents. Often a grandchild has the same recessive phenotype as a grandparent—something not seen in either of their parents.

Breeding between a male pea plant (right) and female (below)

	B	b
B	BB	Bb
b	Bb	bb

When both parents have the dominant (B) and recessive (b) genes, three-quarters of the offspring will have the dominant phenotype, while a quarter will be recessive. If the dominant gene is for purple petals, three out of four "children" will be purple.

Dominance

A genotype always contains two copies of the same gene—one from each parent. In many cases, the phenotype created is controlled by which version of the gene is dominant. A dominant version will always create the phenotype if it is present. A nondominant, or recessive, version of the gene is only seen if the genotype contains two copies of this version.

Codominance

For some genes, the different versions are not dominant over each other. This means that, if the genotype has a mix of versions, their effects are merged together to make a phenotype that is halfway between the two characteristics. This system is called codominance.

The many different shades of cat fur are controlled by a few codominant genes.

BODY BREAKTHROUGH

Scientist: Gregor Mendel
Breakthrough: Made discoveries about dominance and codominance
Date: 1856-63
The story: This Austrian-Czech monk spent several years studying how different characteristics (what we now call phenotypes) of pea plants were passed on generation after generation. Mendel knew nothing about DNA (it had not been discovered), but his discoveries about dominance and codominance became the foundations of the science of genetics.

Black is the dominant version of the hair shade gene. If people inherit that version of the gene, they will always have black hair.

A child shares half of its genes with each of its parents and a quarter of its genes with each grandparent.

DID YOU KNOW? About 98 percent of the DNA in a cell carries no genes, but it is not "junk": It contains regulatory sequences that determine when and where genes are turned on and off.

33

Unique You

Around 99.9 percent of your genes are the same as every other human's, which is why humans have a great deal in common. It is the remaining 0.1 percent that makes you different.

Same and Different

There are nearly 8 billion people in the world, but—unless you are an identical twin—not one of them has exactly the same DNA. Identical twins have the same genes because they grew from the same egg, fertilized by the same sperm. Non-identical twins (who grew from two eggs) and other brothers and sisters, share more genes than people who are not related: On average, they share 50 percent of the 0.1 percent of genes that differ between humans. Parents and children also share around 50 percent of those different genes, while grandparents and grandchildren share around 25 percent.

> Genes do not only affect how we look. They contribute to our mental state and how we behave.

An identical twin (pictured) has the same version of each gene as their twin. However, a non-identical twin has a 50 percent chance of getting the same version as their twin, because each parent could pass down one of their two versions (one from their mother; one from their father) of each gene.

BODY BREAKTHROUGH

Scientists: Emmanuelle Charpentier (left) and Jennifer Doudna
Breakthrough: Developed CRISPR-Cas9
Date: 2012
The story: Charpentier and Doudna made a huge leap forward in gene-editing when they figured out how to make use of a section of genes from the immune system of bacteria. These genes can cut DNA. In 2020, the scientists became the first women to win a Nobel Prize jointly.

DID YOU KNOW? Identical twins may have different heights, weights, and interests because of their different experiences, diets, and lifestyles.

CRISPR–Cas9 can both recognize and open up specific strands of DNA so they can be edited.

Cas9

Guide RNA finds the required section of DNA.

Target DNA

Curing Disease

Scientists study the 0.1 percent of genes that are different between humans, as some of these differences hold clues about the causes of disease. For example, most cases of inherited breast cancer are linked to differences in two genes, BRCA1 and BRCA2. In the future, scientists hope to wipe out inherited diseases by "editing" genes: adding, taking away, or altering faulty bits.

Characteristics such as what we eat and how much we sleep are determined by a mix of our genes and non-genetic factors.

In the Family

As a human, you are a type of animal … and that means that you are related to other animals. You may not be covered in fur or scales, but you and your genes have a lot in common with many other creatures.

Mammals

The more closely related an animal is to you, the more similar its DNA. Humans belong to a group of animals called mammals, along with cats, elephants, and mice. All mammals share some characteristics, such as growing hair and feeding babies on milk. Mammals also share an ancestor that lived around 180 million years ago. This means that all mammals have genes passed down from that ancestor.

Along with their cousins the bonobos, common chimpanzees are humans' closest relatives: They share 96 percent of our genes.

Around 90 percent of your genes are the same as a cat's.

Humans share around 50 percent of their genes with banana plants. Banana plants and humans share an ancestor that lived 1.6 billion years ago.

Distant Relatives

All animals and plants developed from tiny, simple living things that appeared in the ocean more than 3.7 billion years ago. Living things changed over millions of years to look and behave differently, becoming humans, banana plants, and fruit flies. Over time, tiny changes to DNA, called mutations, take place. Many mutations happen randomly when DNA is being copied before cell division. However, when a mutation is helpful—such as giving a giraffe a longer neck, which helps with feeding from tall trees—it spreads through the population, as giraffes with a longer neck are more likely to survive, and then pass on their mutation to their children.

Chimpanzees and humans share an ancestor that lived 7–10 million years ago.

Differences in the genes that code for skeletons make it easy for humans to stand up, while chimps are on all fours a lot of the time.

DID YOU KNOW? You share around 60 percent of your genes with a small, winged insect called a fruit fly.

Chapter 2
Body Structure

Without your skeleton, you would be a slug-like blob. It is bones that give your body structure, while also protecting your organs. Working with your muscles, bones allow you to move. Wrapping the whole human-body package is the skin, which protects you, stops you from drying out, and helps you to feel your surroundings.

Brilliant Bones and Muscles

Your bones provide your body with support, linking up in a framework called your skeleton. Bones need to be strong enough to carry your weight, but light enough to help you stay active. Your muscles hold your bones together and guide them. You call on them every time you need to move. Behind the scenes are other muscles that work day and night—automatically—to keep your body functioning, with your heart beating and your lungs breathing.

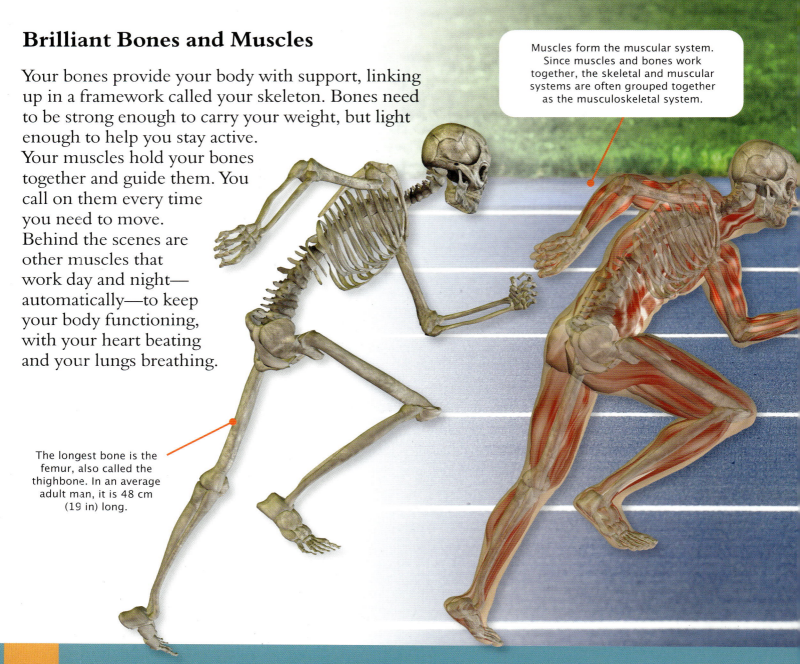

Muscles form the muscular system. Since muscles and bones work together, the skeletal and muscular systems are often grouped together as the musculoskeletal system.

The longest bone is the femur, also called the thighbone. In an average adult man, it is 48 cm (19 in) long.

Super Skin

Your skin does more than just cover your body like a huge sheet of wrapping paper. It keeps you warm or cools you down, and it acts like a cushion to protect what is inside. It is also waterproof and it protects you from the sun's most harmful rays.

Skin, hair, and nails make up the integumentary system. The name for this system comes from the Latin word *integumentum*, which means "covering."

DID YOU KNOW? An average adult's skeleton weighs around 10 kg (22 lb), while their muscles weigh more than 25 kg (55 lb).

The Skeleton

Like animals from dogs to eagles, humans are vertebrates, which means we have a backbone, or spine, made up of linked bones called vertebrae. Together, all the bones in the body—from tiny ear bones to the lengthy femur (thighbone)—form the skeleton.

Jobs for the Bones

The skeleton gives the body shape and support. The bones that make up the central (axial) skeleton—skull bones, spine, ribs, and breastbone (sternum)—protect our vital organs. The attached (appendicular) skeleton—arms, hands, legs, feet, shoulder blades, and pelvis—allow us to move.

The upper arm bone is called the humerus. It runs from the shoulder to the elbow.

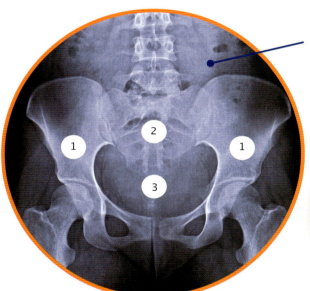

This X-ray shows the pelvis, which supports the upper body; links the legs to the spine; and shields the bladder, reproductive organs, and bowel. It is made up of the hip bones (1), sacrum (2), and coccyx (3).

The "funny bone" is not a bone—it is a nerve! If we bump it at the elbow, it really hurts.

BODY BREAKTHROUGH

Scientist: Wilhelm Röntgen
Breakthrough: First X-rays of the human skeleton
Date: 1895
The story: German physicist Wilhelm Röntgen discovered X-rays by accident. These rays could pass through certain solids. Röntgen realized X-rays allowed doctors to view bones without cutting open the body. The first X-ray was of his wife's hand. Röntgen won the Nobel Prize for his discovery.

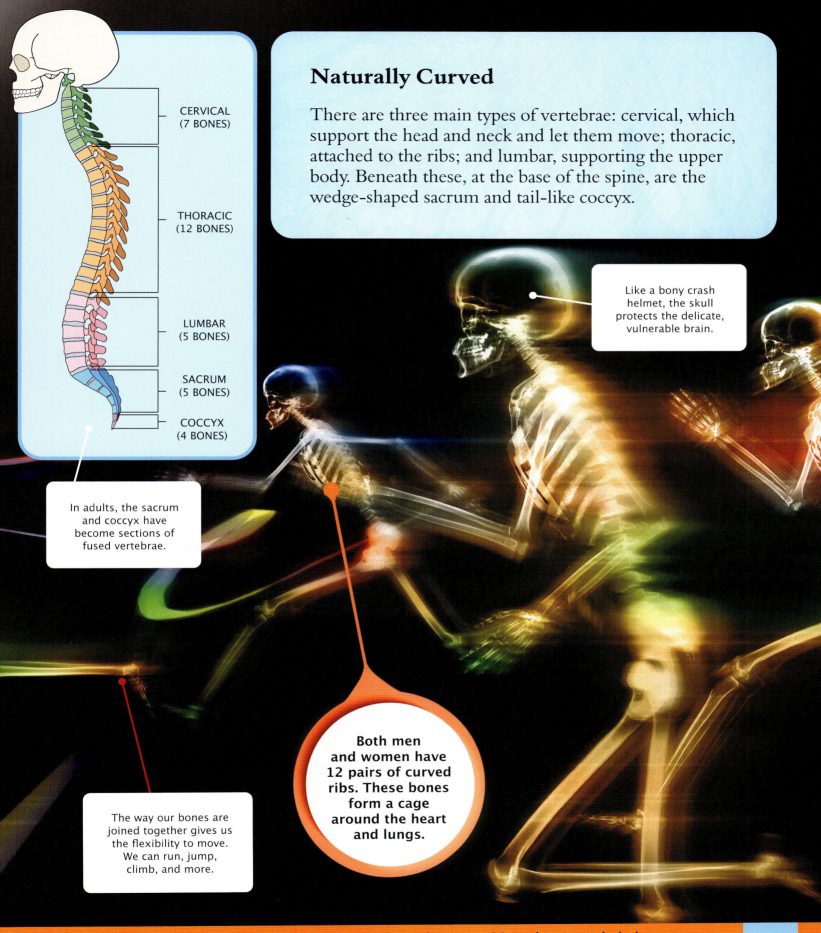

CERVICAL (7 BONES)
THORACIC (12 BONES)
LUMBAR (5 BONES)
SACRUM (5 BONES)
COCCYX (4 BONES)

Naturally Curved

There are three main types of vertebrae: cervical, which support the head and neck and let them move; thoracic, attached to the ribs; and lumbar, supporting the upper body. Beneath these, at the base of the spine, are the wedge-shaped sacrum and tail-like coccyx.

Like a bony crash helmet, the skull protects the delicate, vulnerable brain.

In adults, the sacrum and coccyx have become sections of fused vertebrae.

The way our bones are joined together gives us the flexibility to move. We can run, jump, climb, and more.

Both men and women have 12 pairs of curved ribs. These bones form a cage around the heart and lungs.

DID YOU KNOW? An adult has 206 individual bones. There are 80 in the central skeleton; the other 126 make up the attached skeleton.

41

Our Bones

Bones look solid, but only the outer layer is hard and compact. Their core is light and spongy. This structure means that bones are strong, difficult to break, and incredibly lightweight.

Types of Bone

The five bone types are short, long, flat, sesamoid, and irregular. Short bones, such as the carpals in the wrist, are as wide as they are long. Long bones, such as the leg bones, are longer than they are wide. Flat bones are plate-like and include the breastbone (sternum) and bones of the pelvis. The kneecap is one of the sesamoid bones—small, round bones usually found in joints. Irregular bones, such as the hyoid bone in the neck, do not fit any of the other groups.

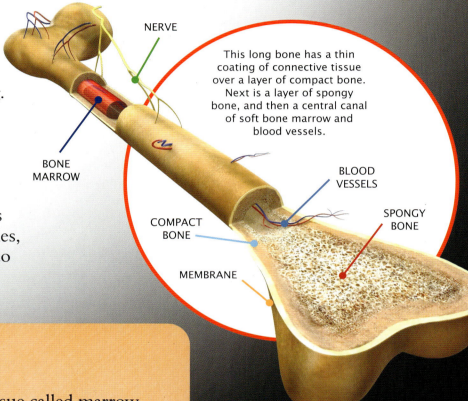

This long bone has a thin coating of connective tissue over a layer of compact bone. Next is a layer of spongy bone, and then a central canal of soft bone marrow and blood vessels.

Bone Marrow

Bones contain soft, jelly-like tissue called marrow. Red bone marrow produces blood cells. At birth, all bone marrow is red, but as people age, this marrow is gradually replaced by yellow bone marrow, which makes fat, cartilage, and bone. However, adults keep red marrow in the skull, spine, sternum, ribs, shoulder, hip bones, and ends of long bones.

This SEM scan shows the honeycomb structure of spongy bone. Its bone marrow (shown in blue) is making blood cells (pink).

The top teeth are held by two bones called the maxillae, which are fused to the cheek bones.

BODY BREAKTHROUGH

Scientist: Mansur ibn Ilyas
Breakthrough: Created the first illustrated atlas of the human body
Date: c. 1390
The story: Persian scholar Mansur ibn Ilyas divided his atlas of the human body into five chapters: bones, nerves, muscles, veins, and arteries. The section on bones included small diagrams of the joints where (in adults) the skull bones have fused together.

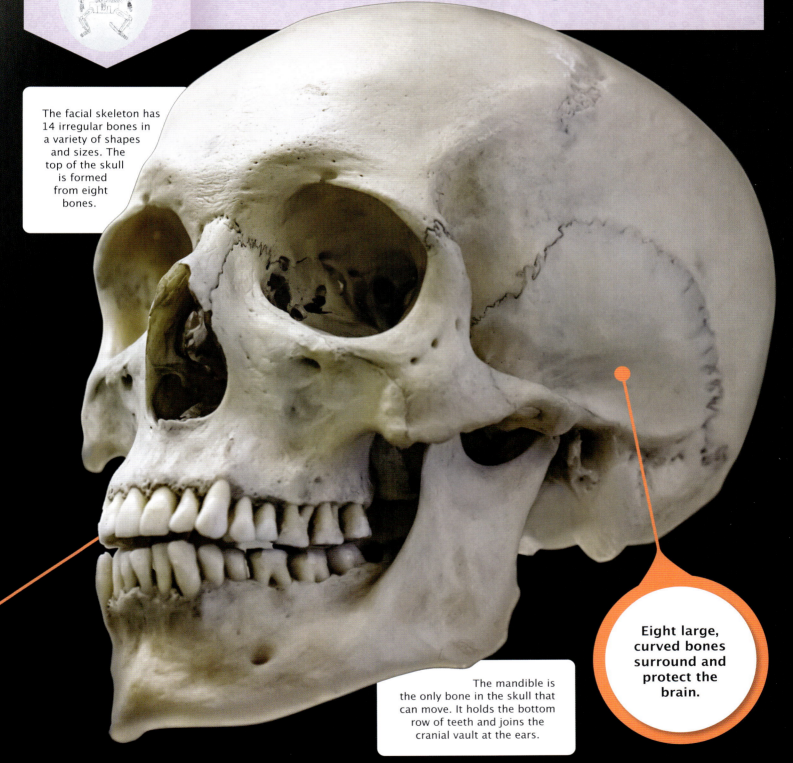

The facial skeleton has 14 irregular bones in a variety of shapes and sizes. The top of the skull is formed from eight bones.

The mandible is the only bone in the skull that can move. It holds the bottom row of teeth and joins the cranial vault at the ears.

Eight large, curved bones surround and protect the brain.

DID YOU KNOW? The face is symmetrical because all its bones, apart from the mandible and vomer (the bone between the nostrils), are in pairs.

43

How Bones Grow

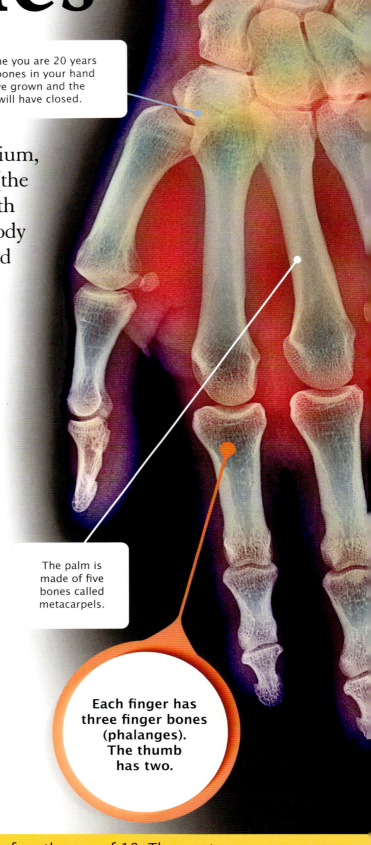

By the time you are 20 years old, the bones in your hand will have grown and the joints will have closed.

Bones are made up of calcium, phosphorus, sodium, and other minerals. They also contain collagen (the protein that gives tissues in the body their strength and stretchiness). Using these ingredients, the body can build bones so that we grow into fully formed adults and mend bones that fracture (break).

Lengthy Process

Bone grows from a soft, rubbery substance called cartilage. Inside the cartilage, small lumps of bone develop. These are called ossification centers—*ossification* means "hardening of a soft tissue into bone." As these areas spread, our cartilage becomes bone, and our bones grow longer.

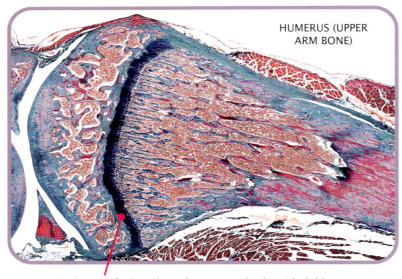

HUMERUS (UPPER ARM BONE)

Each end of a long bone has a growth plate (dark blue in this SEM scan), where new cartilage cells form.

The palm is made of five bones called metacarpels.

Each finger has three finger bones (phalanges). The thumb has two.

DID YOU KNOW? Over half of us break a bone before the age of 18. The most common childhood fractures are to the wrist, elbow, fingers, or collarbone.

Bone Repair

Some fractures break the bone completely, while others just make a crack in the bone. However serious the break, blood seeps into the space to form a clot. Then a thick patch of cartilage called a callus forms around the clot. Over time, this cartilage turns to bone (ossifies).

At three years old, only a few of the eight carpels (wrist bones) have formed.

The joints between the finger bones have cartilage where bone will form and grow.

This X-ray shows bone as greeny-yellow and cartilage and flesh as red and purple.

The doctor lines up the broken limbs so that they will mend in the right positions. Supports called casts hold the bones in place while they are healing.

BODY BREAKTHROUGH

Scientists: Professors Matthew Dalby and Stuart Reid, and their team at the University of Glasgow, Scotland
Breakthrough: Used nanotechnology to make artificial bone
Date: 2017
The story: Matthew Dalby, Stuart Reid, and their team used a technique called nanokicking—hitting cells with very precise, faint vibrations—to grow human bone. Nanokicking stem cells in collagen turned the collagen into synthetic bone or "bone putty."

45

Joints

Our body has about 400 joints, which are places where bones meet. Some joints are fixed; others are semi-movable (for example, the tough pads of cartilage between the vertebrae do not allow much movement). However, most joints move freely. The shapes of the bone ends decide how much mobility each movable joint has.

Types of Movable Joint

At pivot joints, one bone rotates in a collar formed by another bone. In saddle joints, one bone "sits" on the other, like a rider on a horse. Hinge joints simply bend and straighten. At plane joints, flat bones slide over each other, back and forth or sideways. Ellipsoidal joints are where a rounded bone fits into a cavity. Ball-and-socket joints, where a round bone end fits a "cup," are the most mobile.

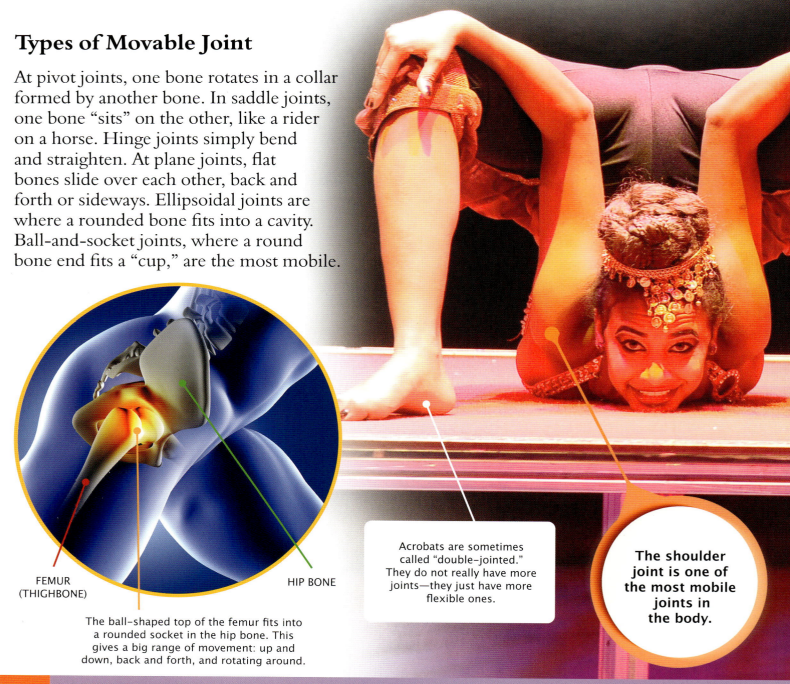

FEMUR (THIGHBONE)

HIP BONE

The ball-shaped top of the femur fits into a rounded socket in the hip bone. This gives a big range of movement: up and down, back and forth, and rotating around.

Acrobats are sometimes called "double-jointed." They do not really have more joints—they just have more flexible ones.

The shoulder joint is one of the most mobile joints in the body.

DID YOU KNOW? In adults, the skull bones have fixed joints. Connective tissue called sutures has knitted them together so they cannot move.

BODY BREAKTHROUGH

Scientist: John Charnley
Breakthrough: Developed total hip replacement surgery
Date: 1962
The story: Early hip replacements were painful, did not allow much movement, and sometimes even squeaked! British orthopedic surgeon John Charnley designed an artificial hip joint with a low-friction coating on the socket so that the femur could move freely. Its design, and Charnley's surgical technique, are still used today.

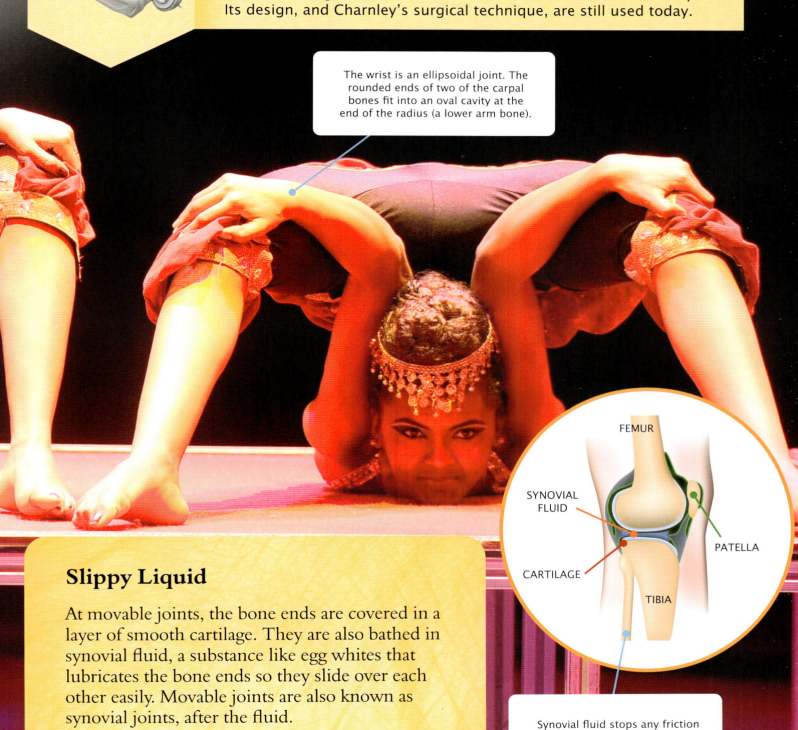

The wrist is an ellipsoidal joint. The rounded ends of two of the carpal bones fit into an oval cavity at the end of the radius (a lower arm bone).

Slippy Liquid

At movable joints, the bone ends are covered in a layer of smooth cartilage. They are also bathed in synovial fluid, a substance like egg whites that lubricates the bone ends so they slide over each other easily. Movable joints are also known as synovial joints, after the fluid.

Synovial fluid stops any friction (rubbing) between the bones that meet at the knee joint: the femur (thighbone), patella (kneecap), and tibia (shin).

47

Muscles

Muscle is the stretchy tissue that lets us move or keep still. We have around 650 skeletal muscles that pull the bones to which they are attached. The other types of muscle move our body organs. They are cardiac (heart) muscle and smooth muscle, which forms the walls of organs such as the stomach.

Fibrous Features

Skeletal muscle is made of long, strong fibers (strands) that can contract quickly and powerfully, but not for long. Cardiac muscle has short, crisscrossed fibers that keep moving rhythmically. The short fibers that make up smooth muscle form flat "sheets" that can contract for long periods.

The latissimus dorsi, or "lats," are the biggest muscles in the trunk (upper body). They stretch across the back from below the armpit.

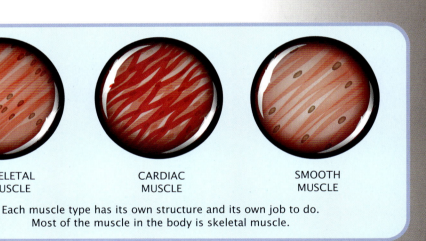

SKELETAL MUSCLE   CARDIAC MUSCLE   SMOOTH MUSCLE

Each muscle type has its own structure and its own job to do. Most of the muscle in the body is skeletal muscle.

BODY BREAKTHROUGH

Scientist: Andreas Vesalius
Breakthrough: Described human muscles
Date: 1543
The story: Flemish anatomist Andreas Vesalius's *On the Fabric of the Human Body* was a groundbreaking book on human anatomy. Vesalius dissected (cut open) dead bodies so he could study the muscles and other body systems at first hand. As a result, the illustrations in his book were incredibly detailed and accurate.

DID YOU KNOW? According to researchers at the University of Chicago, a frown uses 11 important facial muscles and a smile uses 12.

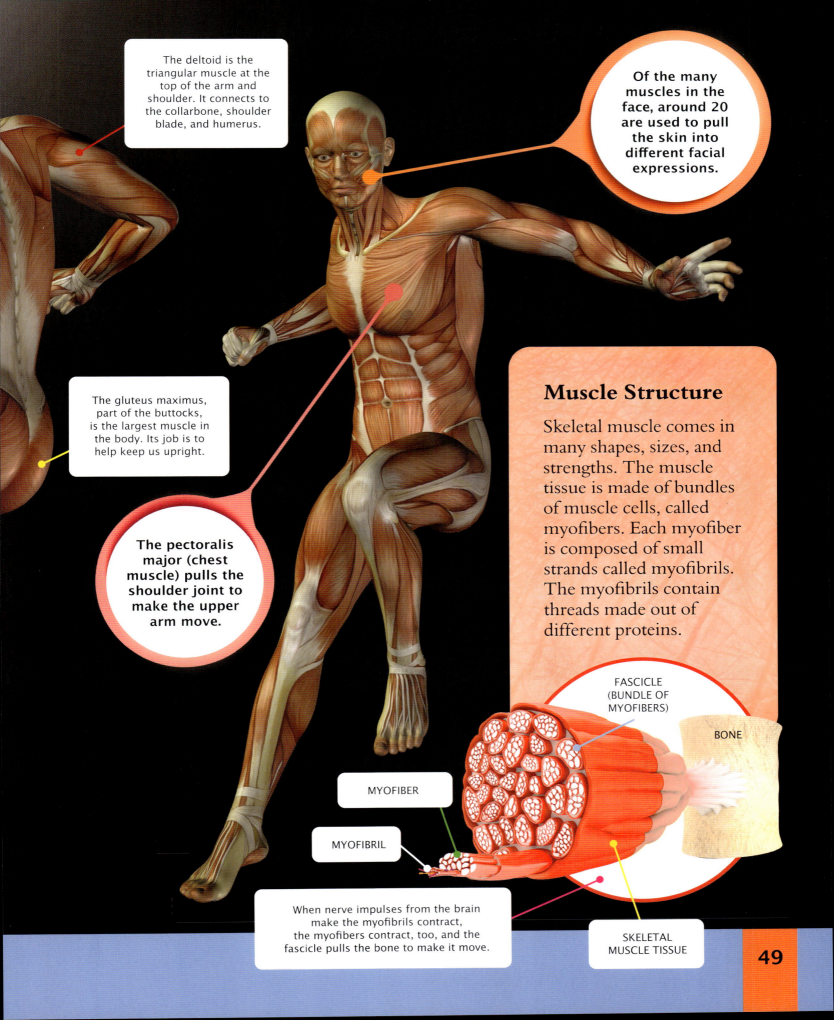

Movement

Running, jumping, throwing … every single move we make depends on our muscles and how they act on our bones. Skeletal muscles are attached to bones by tendons. When muscles contract, tendons pull on the bone and make it move. Because our muscles can only pull, not push, many of them work in pairs.

Opposing Pairs

Muscle pairs work together by performing opposite actions. When one muscle contracts, the other relaxes. The biceps and triceps muscles in the upper arm work together to let the arm bend or straighten.

Tendons and Ligaments

Strong cords of a protein called collagen attach bones and muscles. The ones that link bone to bone are called ligaments, and the ones that connect bone to muscle are tendons. Their fibers attach to the bone's outer membrane.

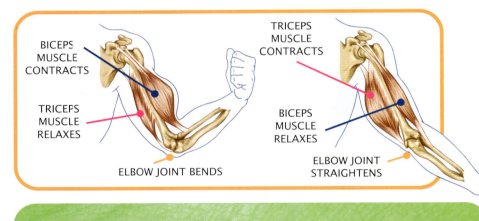

The 15-cm (6-in) Achilles tendon is the thickest, strongest tendon in the body. It stretches from the heel bone to the calf muscles.

When we jump, our Achilles tendons withstand loads of up to ten times our body weight.

The triceps straightens the arm. Now the player can shoot the ball at the hoop with great force.

Nerve endings in the muscles contain sensors called proprioceptors. These gather information about the position of the body in space.

To work hard, muscles need lots of oxygen from the blood. If we are short of oxygen, we may get muscle cramps.

BODY BREAKTHROUGH

Scientists: Team at the Technical University of Munich (TUM)
Breakthrough: Microstructure of the Achilles tendon
Date: 2017
The story: Using a microscope that lit up different proteins, the team saw that where the Achilles tendon meets the heel bone, it splits into super-thin fibers. The cells of these fibers do not exactly match those of tendons—their proteins also share characteristics with cartilage, making the bond especially strong.

DID YOU KNOW? In Greek myths, Achilles was a hero who died of an arrow wound in his heel. Today the phrase Achilles heel means "weak spot."

Brain to Muscles

Most of the time, it is your brain that tells your skeletal muscles to make a move. The brain sends electrical signals that tell your fingers to twitch or your leg to kick! These signals travel at 70–120 m (230–393 ft) per second.

Making a Move

To create a movement, such as a kick of your leg, an electrical signal travels from the brain and down your spinal cord. The spinal cord is a bundle of nerves that is enclosed in the spine. From the spinal cord, the signal travels along a particular type of nerve, called a motor neuron. The signal passes from a motor neuron to myofibers, which contract—making you kick.

As you prepare to kick a soccer ball, your hamstring muscle (at the back of the thigh) gets a signal to contract, which bends the knee.

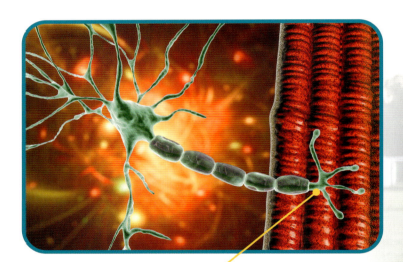

A neuromuscular junction is where a motor neuron connects with the myofibers of a muscle.

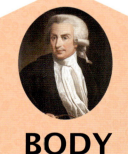

BODY BREAKTHROUGH

Scientist: Luigi Galvani
Breakthrough: Studied "animal electricity"
Date: 1780
The story: He discovered that a dead frog's muscles could be made to twitch by striking them with an electric spark. Gradually, this work led to our current understanding of how electrical signals, carried by motor neurons, make muscles move.

DID YOU KNOW? For an average young adult, muscles make up nearly 40 percent of bodyweight, but that percentage usually drops as the body ages.

To make contact with the ball, the quadriceps muscle (at the front of the thigh) gets the signal to contract to extend the knee.

Reflexes

In addition to your conscious movements, the skeletal muscles can also make reflex movements. These are automatic movements that are in response to a trigger, such as touching a sharp or hot object. They bypass the brain so they can happen even faster, protecting you from being hurt.

When a cactus spine pricks your skin, the pain signal travels along a sensory neuron.

The pain signal is received by your brain while the reflex action is already being carried out.

In the spinal cord, a relay neuron passes the signal directly to a motor neuron.

SPINAL CORD

The motor neuron passes the signal to myofibers, which contract to lift your hand from the cactus.

53

Exercising Muscles

Regularly exercising your muscles makes them grow stronger. Stronger muscles need less energy to do the same work, which means they need less oxygen—and you can run faster without getting breathless!

Stronger Muscles

Muscles use oxygen from your blood supply to get energy. Normal blood flow allows you to perform daily activities, such as walking. But if your activities are more vigorous, your muscle cells need more oxygen, which makes you breathe harder. However, regular exercise can make your skeletal muscles grow stronger (and need less oxygen), by increasing the size of the myofibers. Repeatedly performing a muscle contraction, such as lifting a weight, makes harmless tears in the myofibers. The body mends them and grows new myofilaments, bulking up the muscle.

A body builder's big muscles are caused by the body mending tears in myofibers. This process is called muscle hypertrophy (meaning "extra growth").

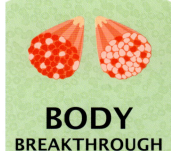

BODY BREAKTHROUGH

Scientist: Stefano Lorenzini
Breakthrough: Identified two types of myofiber
Date: 1678
The story: Lorenzini noticed "red" and "white" muscle fibers. We now know that slow-twitch myofibers are redder because they contain a lot of myoglobin, a red pigment that helps deliver oxygen to cells. Fast-twitch fibers rely on anaerobic respiration (without using oxygen; see page 15), which is why they are ideal for quick contractions over a short period.

Record-breaking sprinter Usain Bolt has many fast-twitch myofibers.

Unlike exercising the skeletal muscles, exercising the heart's muscles with regular physical activity does not grow more heart muscle. Yet it does make the heart muscle grow stronger.

Fast and Slow Twitch

There are two types of myofibers: slow twitch and fast twitch. Most muscles contain a mixture of both. Slow-twitch myofibers contract slowly but are slow to tire. People who are natural long-distance runners have more slow-twitch fibers. Fast-twitch myofibers contract quickly but tire more quickly. Sprinters have more of these fibers. Most scientists think that neither type of myofiber can be turned into the other, but both types will perform better with regular exercise.

Muscle hypertrophy is more common in fast-twitch than slow-twitch muscles, so the legs of a sprinter have greater muscle mass than those of a long-distance runner.

Champion long-distance runner Elvan Abeylegesse has many slow-twitch myofibers.

DID YOU KNOW? If all the muscles in your body pulled in one direction, you would be able to lift 23 tonnes (25 US tons), which is the weight of a humpback whale.

Involuntary Muscles

Most skeletal muscles rest when you rest, but there are other muscles in your body that are constantly working. They are your involuntary muscles, which work without you consciously thinking about their activity! Cardiac muscles keep your heart beating, and smooth muscles are busy in the walls of many of your organs.

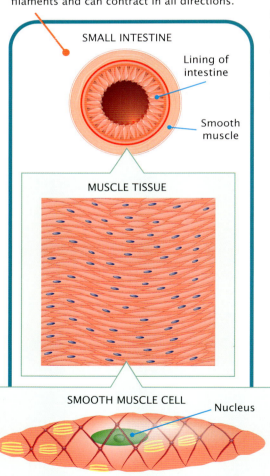

Skeletal muscle cells and filaments are parallel to each other, which means they can contract in only one direction. In contrast, smooth muscle tissue has crisscrossing filaments and can contract in all directions.

SMALL INTESTINE — Lining of intestine — Smooth muscle

MUSCLE TISSUE

SMOOTH MUSCLE CELL — Nucleus

Abdominal Muscles

Smooth muscles are constantly hard at work so you can digest food. Smooth muscles have shorter cells than skeletal muscle cells. Smooth muscle cells make slow, wavelike movements that enable them to work for long periods without getting tired—so they can squeeze food through the tubes of the digestive system.

Eye Muscles

A smooth muscle called the ciliary muscle contracts and relaxes to change the shape of the lens in your eye. This allows the lens to focus light, creating a clear image on the retina at the back of the eye. Smooth muscles also encircle the iris to control the amount of light entering the eye, so you are not dazzled in sunlight or unable to see in low light.

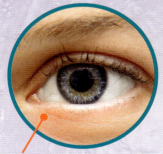

The cells of the iris dilator muscle contract to widen the pupil and allow more light into the eye.

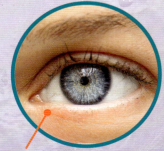

The cells of the iris sphincter muscle contract to narrow the pupil.

BODY BREAKTHROUGH

Scientist: César Julien Jean Legallois
Breakthrough: Identified the function of the medulla oblongata
Date: 1812
The story: A French physician, Legallois showed that breathing is controlled by the medula oblongata, which is in the brainstem. It oversees the work of many involuntary muscles, keeping your heart beating and your lungs breathing.

Smooth muscles keep the airways to your lungs open.

Smooth muscles in your bladder's walls relax as it fills with urine.

Smooth muscles react to the pressure in the walls of blood vessels to control the flow of blood.

DID YOU KNOW? The diaphragm is a skeletal muscle in the abdomen that contracts and relaxes so you can breathe, making it one of the few involuntary skeletal muscles.

Hair

How we do or do not style our hair determines our appearance and becomes part of our identity. But hair is not only about how we look. Made of a tough protein called keratin, hair helps to protect the body from the sun, cold, and dust.

Keratin Strands

Hairs are strands of tough, dead keratin-making cells called keratinocytes. These push up from dips in the skin called hair follicles. Living cells at the base of the hair shaft divide to make the hair grow longer. Longer hairs protect the scalp and keep it warm. Eyelashes protect the eyes from dust and dirt.

In this SEM scan, scalp hairs are magnified 1,320 times. Each hair has a flower-like cuticle at its base. Made of overlapping dead cells, the cuticle protects and strengthens the rest of the hair shaft.

Women of the Himba people of northwest Namibia are known for their elaborate hairstyles.

Himba hairstyles show a person's life stage. This style is for girls going through puberty.

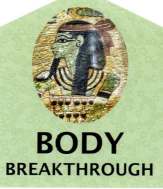

BODY BREAKTHROUGH

Pioneers: Ancient Egyptians
Breakthrough: Use of henna as hair dye
Date: 1574 BCE
The story: Henna is a reddish-brown pigment made from the crushed, dried leaves of the henna plant. Indian body artists have used it to decorate the skin for more than 5,000 years. The first evidence of it as hair dye comes from the Egyptians. The mummy of Queen Ahmose-Henuttamehu (1574 BCE) has hennaed hair.

DID YOU KNOW? Xie Qiuping of China has the record for the longest head hair. When her hair was measured in 2004, it was 5.6 m (18.5 ft) long.

Falling Out

Each hair on your scalp grows for up to six years before falling out. Hairs on the body grow for a few weeks, which is why they are much shorter.

A hair falls out because its follicle shrinks, pushing the hair away from blood vessels that deliver oxygen and nutrients.

A new hair grows, pushing out the old.

The braids have been reddened with a mix of goat hair, butter, and ocher (a pigment from ground red rock).

Nails

Like human skin and hair—and the claws, scales, feathers, and beaks of animals—nails contain tough keratin. Nails protect the ends of the fingers and toes, as well as helping us to pick things up.

Growing Tough

Nails are harder and less flexible than hair because they contain more keratin. Nail growth takes place in the root, at the base of the nail, beneath the skin of the finger or toe. Here, keratin-making cells, called keratinocytes, divide continually, creating new cells that push out the older ones, creating growth. The older cells thicken and die, so the nail you can see is made of dead cells.

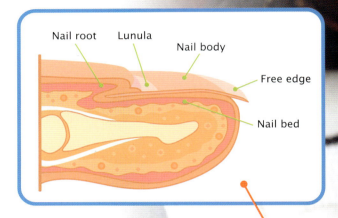

There are no nerves in nails, so you cannot feel them being cut. However, if a nail is ripped, the nerves in the skin below are exposed, which can feel sensitive or even painful.

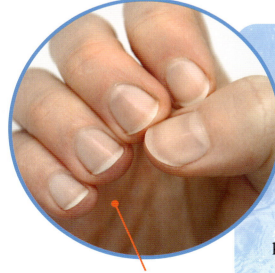

The word lunula comes from the Latin for "little moon."

Little Moons

At the base of each nail is a whiter, half-moon-shaped area called the lunula. The lunula appears whiter than the rest of the nail because of a thicker layer of skin beneath, blocking out our view of the blood vessels below. The lunula is sometimes wholly or partly hidden by the cuticle, a thickened layer of skin that grows over the junction between the nail and skin to protect it from bacteria.

DID YOU KNOW? Nails grow around 0.5 cm (0.2 in) a month, with fingernails growing a little faster than toenails, probably because they face more wear and tear.

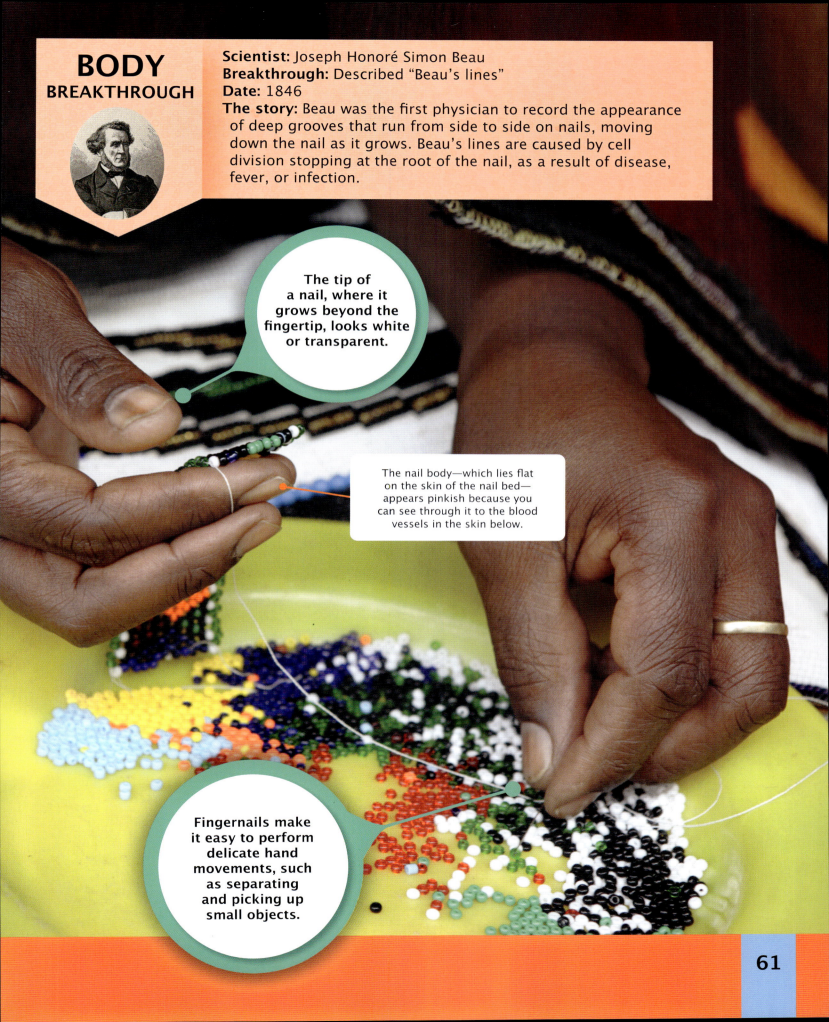

Skin

The skin is the body's largest organ. It helps to stop harmful tiny organisms entering the body. Its hairs and sweat glands keep our temperature steady. Its nerve endings let us feel touch.

Protective Layers

Up to 1.5 mm (0.06 in) thick, the outer layer of skin (the epidermis) is kept waterproof by a fatty substance called sebum. The epidermis is where we shed old, dead skin cells—as many as 1 million every minute! Below the epidermis, the dermis has a rich blood supply, sensitive nerve endings, and glands. The bottom layer is the hypodermis, an insulating store of fat that lies over muscles, bones, and organs.

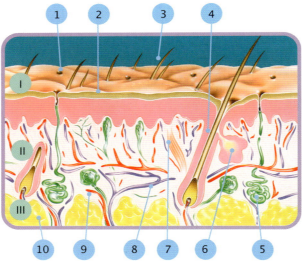

LAYERS OF THE SKIN

I EPIDERMIS
1. Pore
2. Surface layer of dead skin cells
3. Hair shaft

II DERMIS
4. Hair follicle
5. Coiled sweat gland
6. Sebum gland
7. Hair-raising muscle
8. Sensory nerve

III HYPODERMIS
9. Blood vessel
10. Fat

> The thickness of the epidermis (outer layer of skin) depends on where it is on the body. The thinnest layer is on the eyelids.

BODY BREAKTHROUGH

Scientists: William Herschel and Henry Faulds
Breakthrough: Fingerprinting
Date: 1858 and 1880
The story: William Herschel, a civil servant in India (and grandson of the famous astronomer), used fingerprints to identify people on legal documents from 1858. However, Scottish physician Henry Faulds was the first to use them to solve a crime. In 1880, Faulds created a system for organizing types of fingerprint into groups.

DID YOU KNOW? Ridges on the skin of the fingertips form patterns that are unique to each person. Even identical twins have different fingerprints.

Magnificent Melanin

Melanin is a pigment found in the epidermis. It protects skin cells from the harmful effects of ultraviolet radiation, which is found in sunlight. It also darkens our skin and hair. People with darker skin are less likely to develop skin cancer.

Freckles are groups of skin cells that overproduce melanin. They are most visible on fair skin.

A pigment called melanin decides how dark or light the skin is.

Young skin is smooth and tight. Over time, the epidermis will lose its elasticity.

63

Caring for Skin

Your skin has such an important job to do—and comes under so much attack—that it is worth taking care of! Challenges to your skin come from sunlight, bumps, dehydration, and aging.

Sun Damage

To reduce the chance of sunburn, always use sunscreen with an SPF (sun protection factor) of at least 30, which blocks out much of the harmful radiation from the sun.

If your skin is exposed to too much sunlight, the living cells in the epidermis can be damaged. Your immune system responds by opening up blood vessels to send in healing white blood cells. This increased blood flow makes your skin feel warm and look red, which is known as sunburn. In the longer term, exposing skin—particularly pale skin—to too much sunlight can increase the risk of skin cancer. The cells that make melanin—called melanocytes—can become cancerous, causing a growth called melanoma that usually affects pigmented patches called moles.

Bruises

If you bump yourself, you may get a bruise. This forms when the injury breaks tiny blood vessels, called capillaries, which leak into the tissue nearby. The blood gets trapped under the skin, forming a mark that is tender when touched. Bruises usually fade in about 2 weeks, as the body breaks down and absorbs the blood. The shade of a bruise on white skin can tell us how old it is: It often begins as red, turning bluish or black in 1–2 days, and green or yellow in 5–10 days.

Minor bruises will fade on their own, but talk to a doctor if a bruise is swollen, very painful, or does not fade.

BODY BREAKTHROUGH

Scientists: Dr. Heather Shaw and the team at University College London
Breakthrough: Personalized anti-melanoma vaccination
Date: 2024
The story: Cancer specialists developed the first vaccination against melanoma that is personalized to fight each person's particular cancerous cells. The vaccine is given to patients with melanoma, after surgery to remove the diseased cells. Developed from those cells, the vaccine tells the person's immune system to hunt down any matching cells if they reappear.

Drink plenty of water to keep your skin cells hydrated, preventing the epidermis getting dry and flaky. Well-hydrated skin may age more slowly.

Eat foods containing plenty of vitamin C—such as oranges, blackberries, and broccoli—to help your skin build collagen, a tough protein found in the dermis that keeps skin elastic and strong.

Avoid being in the summer sun when it is hottest, which is usually between midday and 3 pm. Cover skin with clothing and a hat, and reapply sunscreen frequently.

DID YOU KNOW? The Scottish surgeon John Hunter performed the first operation to remove a melanoma, in 1787.

Homeostasis

All living bodies use a system called homeostasis, which means "stay the same." The human body is constantly working to keep internal conditions just right for its processes to function as well as possible. The system is mainly focused on keeping its temperature, water content, and chemical balance more or less constant.

Keeping Warm

A normal human body temperature is around 37 °C (98 °F), which is generally warmer than the surrounding air. That means the body is always losing heat, and must find ways of slowing that process and staying warm. When the body temperature falls too low, the main muscles will start to twitch. This process is called shivering. These moving muscles give out warmth, which helps to keep the body temperature from falling dangerously low.

Wearing thick clothes on a cold day helps by trapping a layer of air against the body. Heat moves slowly through this layer of air, so the body stays warm.

Goose Bumps

The human body is covered in hairs—just as many as our close relatives, chimps and gorillas, have. However, the body hairs are generally much shorter and harder to see. In cold conditions, each hair stands upright, making "goose bump" lumps on the skin. The upright hairs trap a layer of still air against the skin, reducing heat loss.

A goose bump is created by a tiny muscle just below the surface of the skin. The muscle pulls on the hair shaft to make it erect, and that pushes up a bump on the surface.

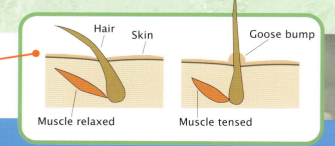

66

BODY BREAKTHROUGH

Scientist: Walter Bradford Cannon
Breakthrough: Developed the theory of homeostasis
Date: 1932
The story: In his book *The Wisdom of the Body*, Cannon wrote that any tendency toward change in the body is automatically met with factors that resist the change. For example, an increase in blood sugar causes thirst as the body tries to reduce the concentration of sugar.

Osmoregulation is the area of homeostasis involved in keeping the right amount of water in the body. We become thirsty when we need more water. Excess water is removed in urine.

On warm days, the body must get rid of the heat created by life processes. Sweating is the main cooling system. Water spreads over the skin and takes away the heat as it evaporates.

The blood vessels in the skin are involved in thermoregulation, or the control of body temperature. On cold days, they shrink in width so less blood flows through them, and the skin goes pale. On warmer days, the vessels expand, letting more blood through (so it can release its heat) and making the skin look redder.

DID YOU KNOW? While it is possible for the human body to go without eating for three weeks before becoming seriously ill, it cannot survive for longer than three days without water.

Spare Parts

If you think of your body as a machine, it has some spare parts that do not get used very often—even if they once served a real purpose. In some cases, that is because, over millions of years, human beings have evolved.

Blasts from the Past

Some body parts, such as your coccyx, appendix (see pages 124–125), and wisdom teeth, are reminders of how we lived millions of years ago. The coccyx is the remains of a tailbone from our ancestors, who used tails for climbing and swinging from trees more than 20–25 million years ago. Our ancestors needed wisdom teeth to chew tough roots and raw meat. Yet our changing diet has made us evolve to have smaller jaws than our ancestors. This means our wisdom teeth may become painfully stuck against other teeth when they break through the gums.

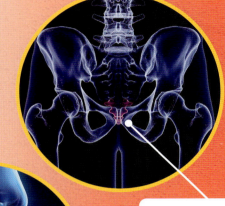

The coccyx is the lowest part of your backbone.

Wisdom teeth are back teeth that might emerge in your late teens or early twenties.

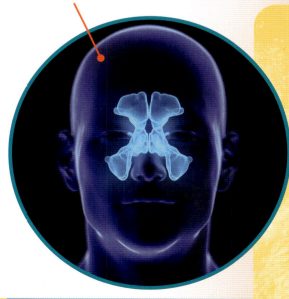

Some scientists think the sinuses allow your voice to resonate, in the same way that the strumming of a guitar's strings echoes inside the guitar's hollow body, becoming richer and louder.

One Big Headache

Some bits of your body remain a mystery, with no one sure what they were ever meant to do. For example, your sinuses are hollow areas in the skull, behind your nose and cheeks. They can give you a bad headache if they become infected during a bout of cold or flu, but no one is certain why we have them. One theory is that sinuses stop your head from being too heavy, because air weighs less than bone.

Eyebrows may once have been useful for preventing sweat flowing into the eyes while hunting.

Muscles around the ears, called the auricular muscles, were once able to pivot the outer ear (auricle) toward a particular sound, but today most people cannot even use these weakened muscles to wiggle their ears.

Mothers use their nipples for feeding babies with milk, but nipples have no use in men. However, nipples develop in all babies in the first few weeks in the uterus.

BODY BREAKTHROUGH

Scientists: Doctors in the Indian subcontinent
Breakthrough: First tonsillectomy
Date: 1000 BCE
The story: The tonsils are two glands in your throat that produce antibodies to counter various diseases. However, since tonsils themselves often become infected and it is possible to live without them, the first operation to remove them, called a tonsillectomy, took place more than 3,000 years ago.

DID YOU KNOW? Although their original function may no longer be very useful, eyebrows are now highly useful for communicating emotions.

Chapter 3
Lungs and Heart

Your lungs and heart work together to carry life-sustaining oxygen to every part of the body. The lungs are responsible for breathing, which gives oxygen to your blood. The heart pumps blood through a network of tubes called blood vessels.

Respiratory System

Your respiratory system is made up of your lungs and airways, which are all the tubes that carry air. This body system's key role is gas exchange. This is when a gas called oxygen is passed to the blood; and a gas called carbon dioxide is taken from the blood. Oxygen is needed as fuel by the body's cells so they can break up the sugar glucose (from the food you eat) to make energy. As a cell carries out this process, it also makes carbon dioxide as a waste product. This waste is passed to the blood, which carries it to the lungs, so it can be breathed out.

The total length of the airways running through an adult's lungs is 2,400 km (1,500 miles).

DID YOU KNOW? The average 11-year-old has around 2.6 liters (0.7 US gallons) of blood—which would fill 11 cups.

When resting, an adult's heart can pump 5 liters (1.3 US gallons) of blood per minute. When an adult is exercising, making their muscles thirst for oxygen, this can rise to 35 liters (9.2 US gallons) per minute—enough to fill two builder's buckets.

Cardiovascular System

The heart, blood vessels, and blood form the cardiovascular system. As your heart beats, it pumps blood through blood vessels that range in size from the aorta, around 2 cm (0.8 in) wide, to tiny capillaries, which have one-cell-thick walls that allow oxygen and carbon dioxide to pass through to tissues and organs. Blood also carries other important materials around the body, including nutrients from food; messengers called hormones; proteins needed around the body; and waste products from the body's processes.

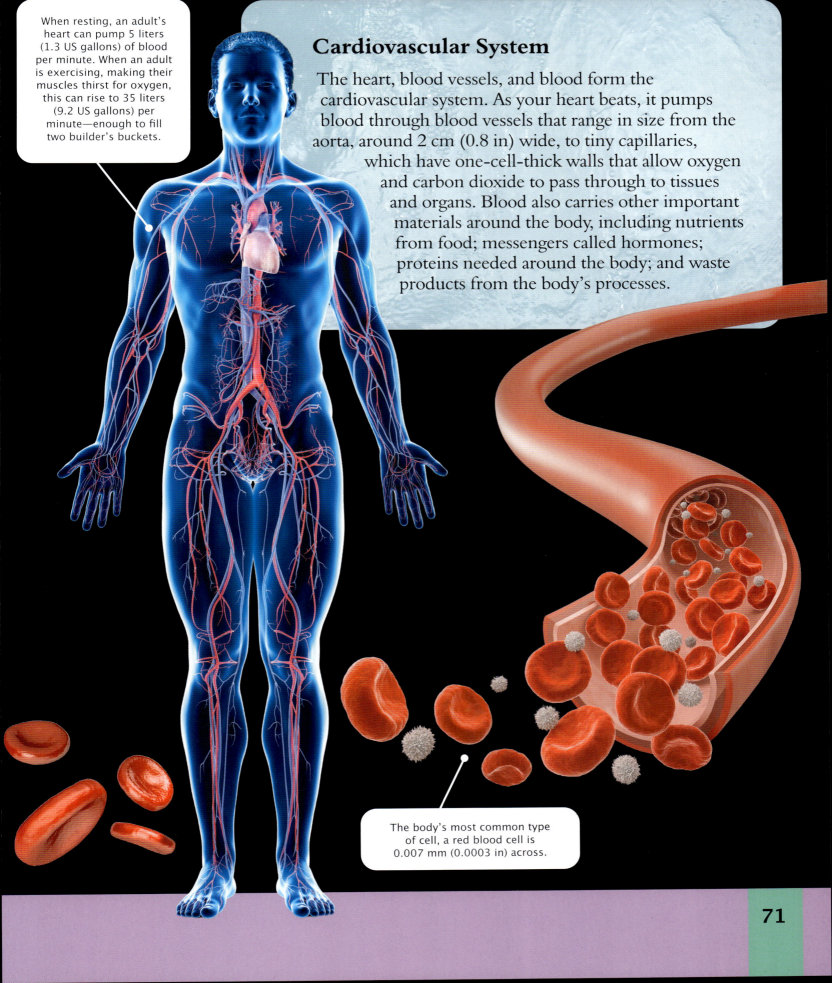

The body's most common type of cell, a red blood cell is 0.007 mm (0.0003 in) across.

Oxygen for Life

Every minute that we are alive, our body is working to its own rhythms: the beat of our heart, and the rise and fall of our lungs. These two vital organs work together. They deliver the oxygen that we need for life and take away waste carbon dioxide.

The Basics

When we breathe, we draw oxygen down into our lungs. Blood flowing through the lungs transports the oxygen around the body. The blood keeps moving because of the actions of our very own pump: the heart.

Seen from below in a CT scan, this heart has been partly dissected to show the left atrium and ventricle. On either side are the branching blood vessels (red) and air passages (blue) in the lungs.

LEFT ATRIUM

LEFT VENTRICLE

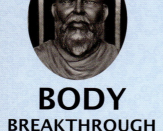

BODY BREAKTHROUGH

Scientist: Ibn al-Nafis
Breakthrough: Described the pulmonary circulation of the blood
Date: 1242
The story: Syrian anatomist Ibn al-Nafis was the first to describe the way that blood vessels carry blood from the right side of the heart to the lungs (where we now know it picks up oxygen) and then return that blood to the left side of the heart. From there, we now know it travels around the body, releasing oxygen, before returning to the heart.

Where this Sherpa mountaineer lives, at high altitudes, there is a low concentration of oxygen in the air.

The Sherpas are a people who live in the Himalaya Mountains. Over the centuries, they have evolved to cope with less oxygen.

Oxygen Cycle

The lungs and airways form the respiratory system, while our heart and blood vessels are the cardio-vascular system. Oxygen and carbon dioxide enter and leave our lungs through small blood vessels called capillaries by gas exchange—the swapping of one gas for another. They are carried around the body by the cardiovascular system.

OXYGEN (O_2)
CARBON DIOXIDE (CO_2)
LUNGS
RED BLOOD CELLS
ORGANS

Sherpas have thinner blood that flows easily at high altitude. They also have more capillaries and can carry oxygen more efficiently to muscles, tissues, and organs.

When we are resting, we must breathe about 15 times a minute to provide our organs with enough oxygen.

Sherpas' cells are different from most people's. Their mitochondria produce more energy from less oxygen.

DID YOU KNOW? The thin atmosphere on top of the Himalayas' Mount Everest means that every breath contains one-third less oxygen than at sea level.

Breathing

During a day we take more than 20,000 breaths—but most of the time, we do not even notice! Our lungs inflate and deflate automatically, controlled by the brain, which alters how deeply we breathe, and how fast, in response to what we are doing.

Breathing is essential to life, but we can also have fun with it. To blow bubbles, we take a deeper breath and control how we exhale it.

Journey to the Lungs

From the mouth or nostrils, air passes through the throat (pharynx). A flap called the epiglottis stops food or drink entering the windpipe (trachea). As it reaches the lungs, the windpipe branches into two airways called the main bronchi.

A bubble is a mixture of water and soap that is filled with air we have breathed out.

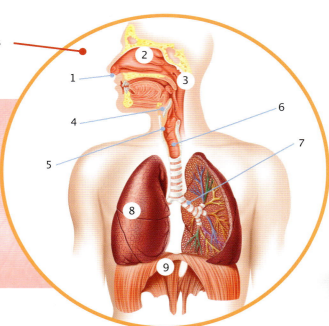

The trachea is the largest airway in the respiratory system. In most adults it is about 11 cm (4.3 in) long and 2 cm (0.8 in) across.

RESPIRATORY SYSTEM
1. Nostril
2. Nasal cavity
3. Pharynx (throat)
4. Epiglottis
5. Larynx (voicebox)
6. Trachea (windpipe)
7. Bronchus
8. Lung
9. Diaphragm

We can breathe through the nose or mouth. Nasal breathing allows the lungs to take in more oxygen, and the nasal cavity filters and warms the air.

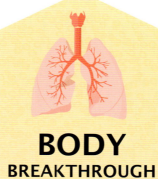

BODY BREAKTHROUGH

Scientists: Wei Zuo and team, Tongji University, China
Breakthrough: First lung stem cell transplant
Date: 2023
The story: In 2015 Professor Wei Zuo's team found stem cells in mice that regrew damaged bronchioles (see page 76) and other lung structures. Since then, he has found stem cells to do this in humans. Zuo has transplanted patients' own lung stem cells to a damaged part of their lung and seen it recover.

DID YOU KNOW? Every minute, about 5,500 cu cm (1.5 US gallons) of air pass into and out of the lungs of an average adult.

74

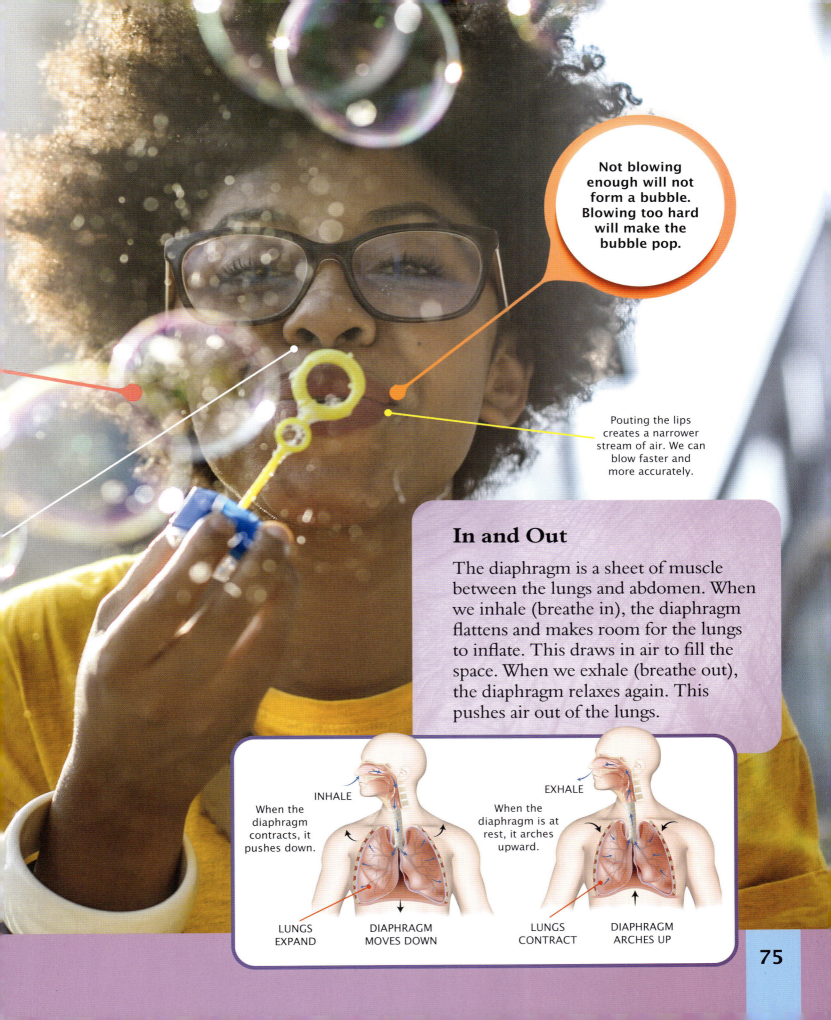

Not blowing enough will not form a bubble. Blowing too hard will make the bubble pop.

Pouting the lips creates a narrower stream of air. We can blow faster and more accurately.

In and Out

The diaphragm is a sheet of muscle between the lungs and abdomen. When we inhale (breathe in), the diaphragm flattens and makes room for the lungs to inflate. This draws in air to fill the space. When we exhale (breathe out), the diaphragm relaxes again. This pushes air out of the lungs.

INHALE — When the diaphragm contracts, it pushes down. LUNGS EXPAND. DIAPHRAGM MOVES DOWN.

EXHALE — When the diaphragm is at rest, it arches upward. LUNGS CONTRACT. DIAPHRAGM ARCHES UP.

Inside the Lungs

To breathe, we inflate and deflate our lungs. The lungs feel like soft sponges, because of the hundreds of millions of tiny airways and air sacs inside them. This structure means that the lungs are easy to damage.

Branching Out

Inside the lungs, the two main bronchi split into smaller and smaller branches called bronchioles. Each bronchiole ends in a tiny air sac called an alveolus.

Alveoli look like miniature bunches of grapes. Each one is covered in a mesh of tiny blood vessels that take away oxygen in exchange for carbon dioxide.

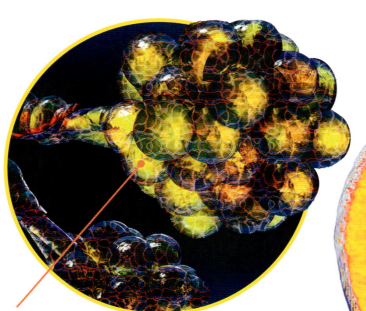

The left lung is smaller than the right because of the space taken up by the heart.

Having a Clearout

Coughing or sneezing clears our airways and forces out dust, pollen, mucus, or other irritating particles. Viral infections, such as the common cold, can cause coughs and sneezes. Lung damage from smoking can also cause a dry cough and shortness of breath.

A single sneeze can produce 40,000 droplets of germ-laden mucus, most too tiny to see with the naked eye.

This CT scan shows a normal, healthy heart and lungs, seen from below.

BODY BREAKTHROUGH

Scientist: John Mudge
Breakthrough: Invented the inhaler
Date: 1778
The story: English doctor John Mudge invented the Mudge Inhaler to treat people with coughs. It was a tankard with a lid and flexible breathing tube. Hot water was poured in, along with herbs or a painkiller such as opium or ether, and the patient breathed it all in as steam through the tube.

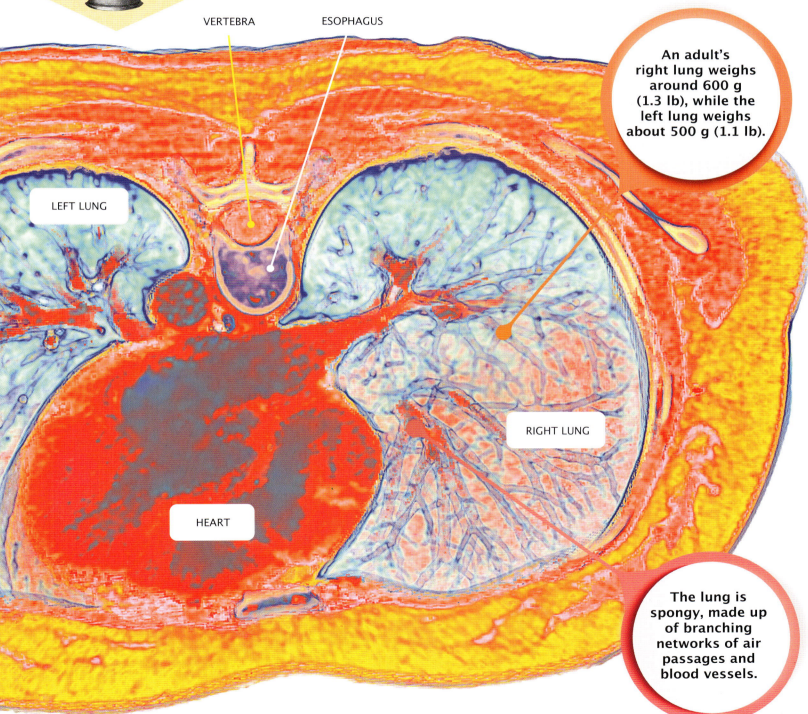

VERTEBRA
ESOPHAGUS
LEFT LUNG
RIGHT LUNG
HEART

An adult's right lung weighs around 600 g (1.3 lb), while the left lung weighs about 500 g (1.1 lb).

The lung is spongy, made up of branching networks of air passages and blood vessels.

DID YOU KNOW? The heart takes up more space in the left lung because its left ventricle (which pumps blood around the body) is larger than its right (which pumps only to the lungs).

77

Alveoli

Alveoli are where gas exchange happens: Oxygen passes from the lungs into the blood, and carbon dioxide passes from the blood to the lungs. You have around 500 million alveoli in each lung, each one around 0.2 mm (0.008 in) across.

> The air we breathe in is a mixture of gases, including nitrogen (78 percent) and oxygen (21 percent), as well as argon, carbon dioxide, and others.

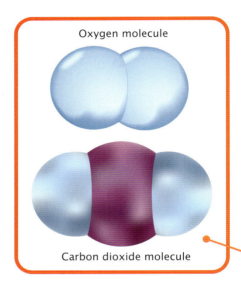

In and Out

Air containing oxygen enters the nose or mouth, travels through the windpipe (trachea), bronchi, and bronchioles—into tiny bags called alveoli. Here, oxygen passes into the dense network of tiny, thin-walled blood vessels, called capillaries, that surrounds them. Oxygen hitches a ride on red blood cells (see page 90) for distribution around the body. At the same time, alveoli are soaking up unwanted carbon dioxide from the blood.

The oxygen molecules you breathe in, are made of two, joined oxygen atoms. A carbon dioxide molecule is made of one carbon and two oxygen atoms.

Gas Exchange

Gas exchange can take place in the alveoli because they have very thin walls, just one cell thick. Oxygen and carbon dioxide can pass through this barrier easily. The gases travel between the alveoli and capillaries through a process called diffusion (see page 16), which causes molecules to spread out from where they are common to where they are rare. Oxygen diffuses from the lungs, where it is common, to the blood, where it is uncommon. Exactly the opposite is true for carbon dioxide.

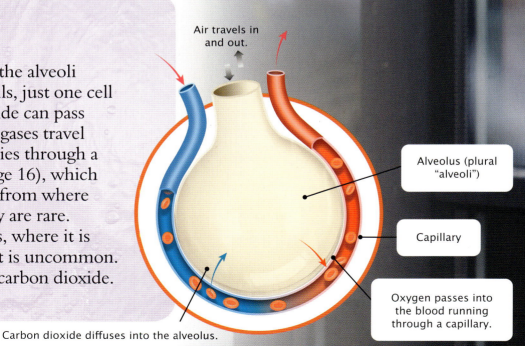

Carbon dioxide diffuses into the alveolus.

78 **DID YOU KNOW?** Alveoli have a combined surface area of around 70 sq m (753 sq ft)—about the area of five parking spaces—across which gas exchange can take place.

When we breathe out, the body's waste carbon dioxide flows up through the windpipe and out of the nose or mouth.

Breath also contains nitrogen and some unused oxygen, as well as moisture from the mouth and lungs in the form of water vapor, the gaseous form of water. Water vapor condenses into water droplets when it touches a cold surface.

BODY BREAKTHROUGH

Scientist: Marcello Malpighi
Breakthrough: Discovered alveoli
Date: 1661
The story: While studying frog lungs under a microscope, Italian physician Malpighi was the first to discover alveoli and the network of capillaries that surrounds them. He also noticed that frogs and dogs have similar lungs to humans, but insects do not.

Blood Vessels

The main types of blood vessel are arteries, veins, and capillaries. Arteries carry blood *away from* the heart, and veins transport blood *to* it. Capillaries, the smallest blood vessels, connect the arteries and veins. Their thin walls allow oxygen and nutrients *out* into nearby cells, and take any waste *in*.

Arteries and Veins

Arteries have thick, muscular walls that contract to help pump the blood. Veins transport blood at lower pressures, so they have thinner walls. One-way valves in the veins make sure that the "used" blood flows toward the heart.

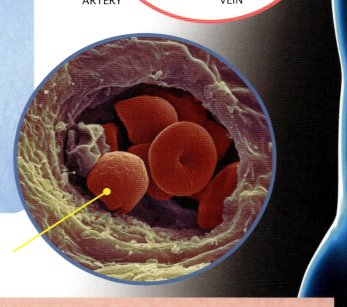

Capillary Beds

Oxygen, nutrients, and waste are exchanged in the capillary beds—the meshes of capillaries that crisscross the body's tissues and organs. Capillary walls are just one cell thick, so gases and other substances easily pass through them.

This SEM scan shows red blood cells in a capillary in the liver. They are bringing oxygen from the lungs.

BODY BREAKTHROUGH

Scientist: Moses Maimonides
Breakthrough: Described arteries, veins, and capillaries
Date: 1190s
The story: In *The Medical Aphorisms of Moses*, the 12th-century Jewish physician Moses Maimonides explained the difference between "pulsating" arteries and "non-pulsating" veins. He also described narrow vessels, too small to see, which connected arteries and veins.

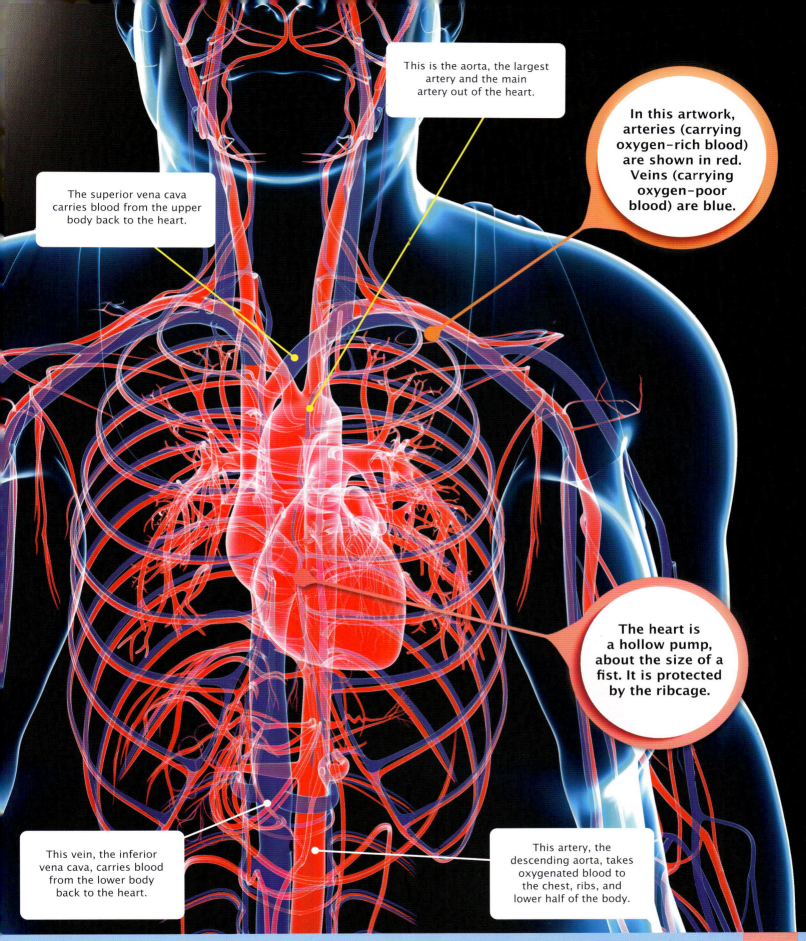

DID YOU KNOW? Placed in a line, an adult's blood vessels would measure around 100,000 km (60,000 miles)—enough to circle the Earth twice.

Circulation

We need good circulation (movement of blood around the body) for the body to function. The force with which blood circulates is called blood pressure. If it is too low, not enough oxygen and nutrients reach the organs. If it is too high, it puts stress on the organs, especially the heart.

Double Circuit

Blood circulates in two circuits. One circuit is the pulmonary circulation. It connects the heart and lungs, carrying oxygen-poor blood from the heart to the lungs to be oxygenated, then oxygenated blood from the lungs to the heart. The second circuit is the systemic circulation. It carries oxygenated blood and nutrients from the heart to the rest of the body, and then returns deoxygenated blood to the heart.

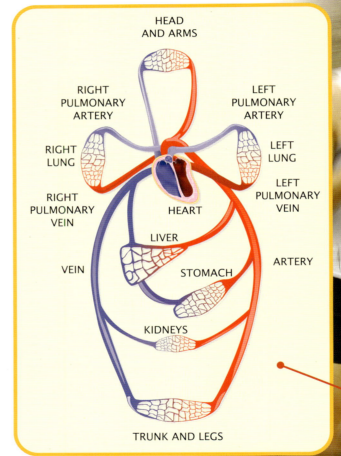

Heart rate is the number of times your heart beats per minute, while blood pressure is the force of blood flowing against the walls of your arteries.

This diagram shows the pulmonary circulation connecting the heart with the right and left lungs. The systemic circulation connects the heart with the rest of the body.

BODY BREAKTHROUGH

Scientist: Scipione Riva-Rocci
Breakthrough: Invented the cuff-based blood pressure monitor
Date: 1896
The story: Austrian doctor Samuel von Basch invented the first sphygmomanometer (*sfig-moh-ma-NOH-mee-tuh*) in 1881, but it was fragile and awkward to use. Fifteen years later, Italian doctor Scipione Riva-Rocci came up with a much handier version that had an inflatable cuff for the arm—a simple design that is still used today.

DID YOU KNOW? During its 120-day lifespan, a red blood cell travels about 485 km (300 miles) around the body.

Taking the Pressure

Blood pressure is a measure of the force that your heart uses to pump blood around the body (see pages 86–87). Pressure is highest as the heart pumps blood out (systolic pressure) and lowest while the heart fills with blood (diastolic pressure).

Ideally, systolic blood pressure is 90–120 mmHg (millimeters of mercury), and diastolic pressure 60–80 mmHg.

A marathon runner's blood pressure is lower than average. At rest, their systolic pressure is around 105 mmHg and their diastolic 65 mmHg. We say this as "105/65."

Heart rate and blood pressure may both rise during exercise. During a marathon, the average runner's heart rate is 160 beats per minute. Systolic blood pressure may rise to between 160 and 220 mmHg during exercise. However, if blood pressure is high when a person is resting, this may indicate that their cardiovascular system needs attention.

The Heart

PARTS OF THE HEART
1. Superior vena cava
2. Inferior vena cava
3. Right atrium
4. Right ventricle
5. Pulmonary artery
6. Pulmonary veins
7. Left atrium
8. Left ventricle
9. Aorta (main artery)

In an average lifetime, the heart beats more than 3 billion times. This muscular organ never stops. Every minute, it pumps about 5 liters (1.3 US gallons) of blood through the lungs and round the body.

Blood Flow

The heart has four chambers, in two linked pairs—a right atrium and ventricle, and a left atrium and ventricle. The right atrium and right ventricle receive oxygen-poor blood and pass it on to the lungs. The left atrium and ventricle receive oxygen-rich blood from the lungs and pass it on to the body.

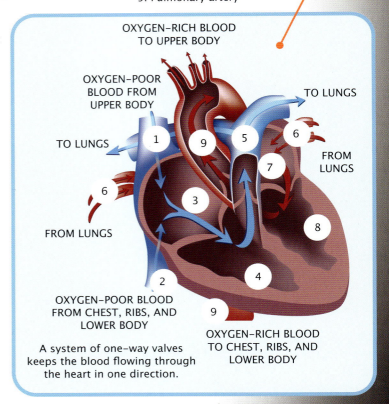

A system of one-way valves keeps the blood flowing through the heart in one direction.

Seat of the Soul

The heart has been a powerful symbol in many cultures, used to represent affection and love. It can be stylized (♥) or look like an anatomical heart. In Mexico, Roman Catholics wear the heart as a symbol of Jesus's love for humankind.

At a parade for the Mexican Day of the Dead (October 31), this woman's fancy dress includes a "heart" with dummy blood vessels.

BODY BREAKTHROUGH

Scientist: Nina Starr Braunwald
Breakthrough: Implanted the first artificial heart valve
Date: 1960
The story: The USA's first female cardiac surgeon, Nina Starr Braunwald, used a prosthetic heart valve that she had designed to perform the first successful valve replacement. She also designed the Braunwald-Cutter valve (left), which was the first to have cloth-covered struts to make patients less uncomfortable.

Scan of the heart

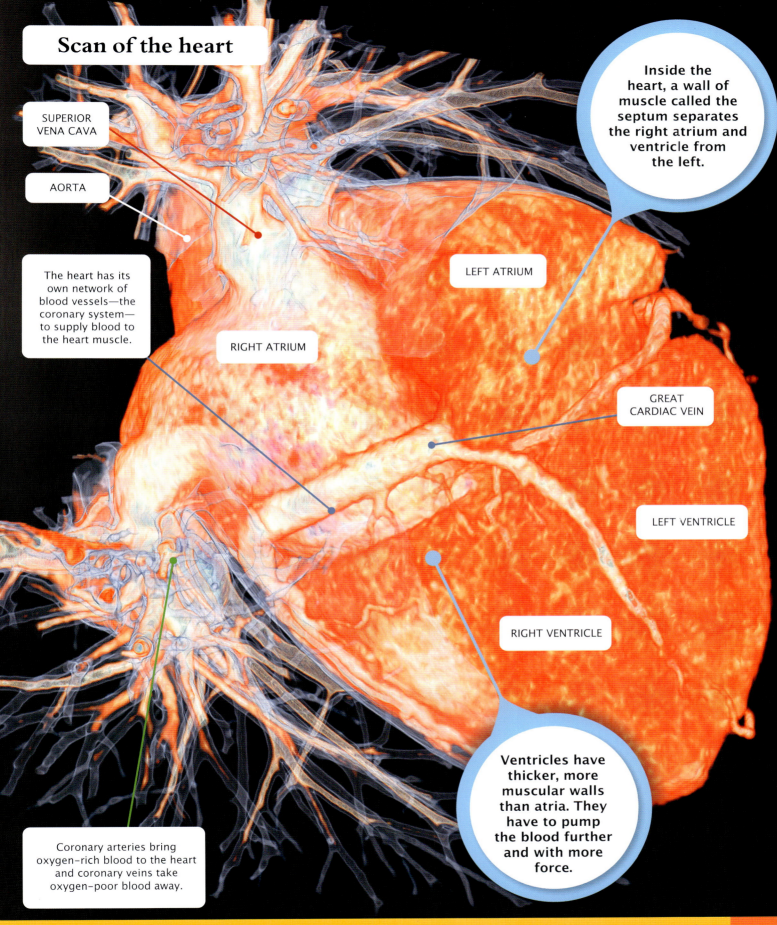

Inside the heart, a wall of muscle called the septum separates the right atrium and ventricle from the left.

SUPERIOR VENA CAVA

AORTA

LEFT ATRIUM

The heart has its own network of blood vessels—the coronary system—to supply blood to the heart muscle.

RIGHT ATRIUM

GREAT CARDIAC VEIN

LEFT VENTRICLE

RIGHT VENTRICLE

Ventricles have thicker, more muscular walls than atria. They have to pump the blood further and with more force.

Coronary arteries bring oxygen-rich blood to the heart and coronary veins take oxygen-poor blood away.

DID YOU KNOW? The ancient Egyptians tucked amulets shaped like real hearts into mummies' bandages to protect the dead.

Heart Cycle

At rest, an adult's heart beats 60 to 100 times a minute. Each cycle has a pause or rest, followed by a "duh-dum." The "duh" is valves closing as blood leaves the atria; the "dum" is valves closing as blood leaves the ventricles.

One Direction

One-way valves control the flow of blood through the heart, so that it enters the atria and the ventricles at alternate times. The heart muscle squeezes (contracts) and then relaxes, which opens and shuts the valves.

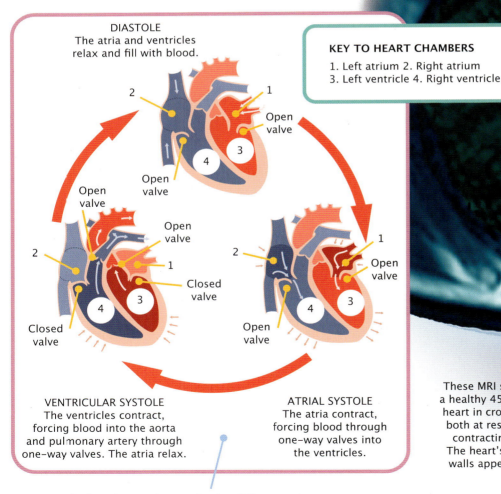

KEY TO HEART CHAMBERS
1. Left atrium 2. Right atrium
3. Left ventricle 4. Right ventricle

DIASTOLE The atria and ventricles relax and fill with blood.

ATRIAL SYSTOLE The atria contract, forcing blood through one-way valves into the ventricles.

VENTRICULAR SYSTOLE The ventricles contract, forcing blood into the aorta and pulmonary artery through one-way valves. The atria relax.

The heart's pumping mechanism follows a constant cycle of rest (diastole) and contraction (systole).

These MRI scans show a healthy 45-year-old's heart in cross-section, both at rest (left) and contracting (right). The heart's muscular walls appear purple.

When the heart is relaxed, blood fills both upper chambers, or atria.

Steady Beat

Most of us have a regular heartbeat—the chambers of the heart contract and relax at a steady rate. The contractions are triggered by regular electrical pulses, sent from special cells in the walls of the right atrium.

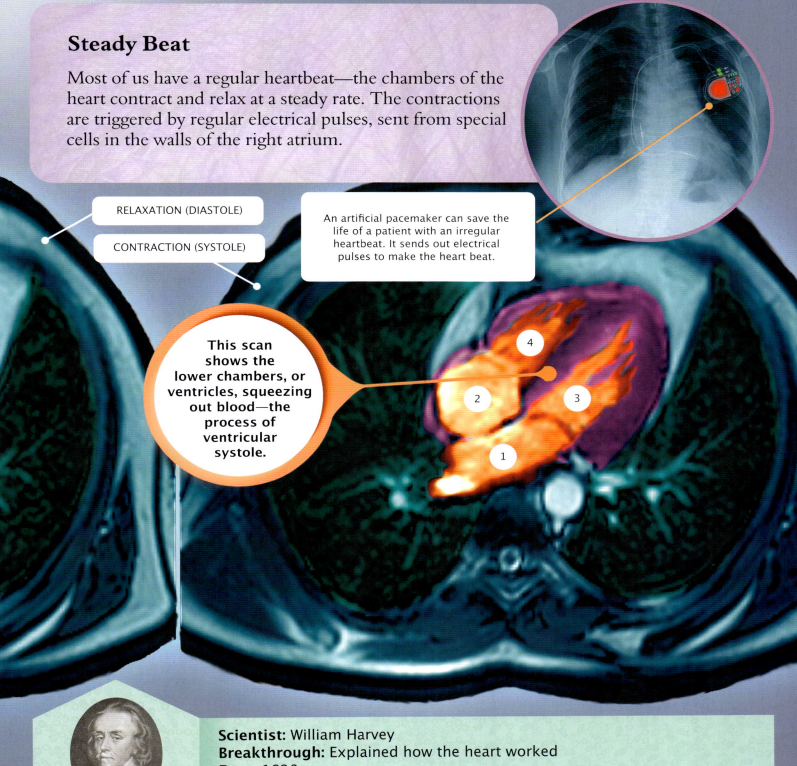

RELAXATION (DIASTOLE)

CONTRACTION (SYSTOLE)

An artificial pacemaker can save the life of a patient with an irregular heartbeat. It sends out electrical pulses to make the heart beat.

This scan shows the lower chambers, or ventricles, squeezing out blood—the process of ventricular systole.

BODY BREAKTHROUGH

Scientist: William Harvey
Breakthrough: Explained how the heart worked
Date: 1628
The story: Personal doctor to two English kings, William Harvey was the first scientist to accurately and fully describe the function of the heart and one-way circulation of the blood, and be able to back up his theory with evidence. He presented his ideas to the Royal College of Physicians in 1616, and published them 12 years later.

DID YOU KNOW? The implantable pacemaker was invented in Sweden by Rune Elmqvist and Åke Senning in 1958, then improved on by an American, Wilson Greatbatch. It was fitted in 1960.

Blood

Blood—the remarkable red liquid that flows through our arteries and veins—is made up of three types of blood cell floating in a yellowy fluid called plasma. As well as transporting oxygen, waste, and nutrients, blood helps us fight off infection and is an important part of our immune system.

Blood Cell Types

Most of our blood cells are the red ones that give blood its hue. They make up 40–45 percent of the blood's volume. The other types of blood cell are white blood cells (see page 142) and platelets.

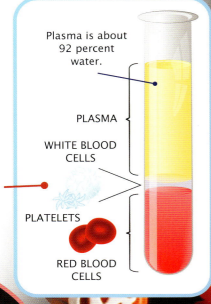

Plasma is about 92 percent water.

PLASMA
WHITE BLOOD CELLS
PLATELETS
RED BLOOD CELLS

Around 55 percent of blood is plasma. Many useful substances are dissolved in plasma, including proteins, electrolytes, sugars, hormones, and vitamins.

Blood Clots

Platelets are shapeshifters. Usually plate-shaped, they turn spiky if a blood vessel is damaged. This shape helps the platelets to cling together and form a clot to plug the damage. Clots are a healthy response to injury—they help us heal.

Helped by platelets, these red blood cells have formed a clot called a thrombus. It can be dangerous if it blocks the flow of blood.

BODY BREAKTHROUGH

Scientist: Jan Swammerdam
Breakthrough: First to see red blood cells
Date: 1658
The story: Dutch biologist Jan Swammerdam was the first to describe red blood cells—he had studied the blood of a frog through an early microscope. Sixteen years later another Dutch scientist, Antoine van Leeuwenhoek, made his own observations of red blood cells. He named them "corpuscles."

DID YOU KNOW? In a typical day, an adult makes 200 billion new red blood cells, 10 billion white ones, and 100 billion platelets.

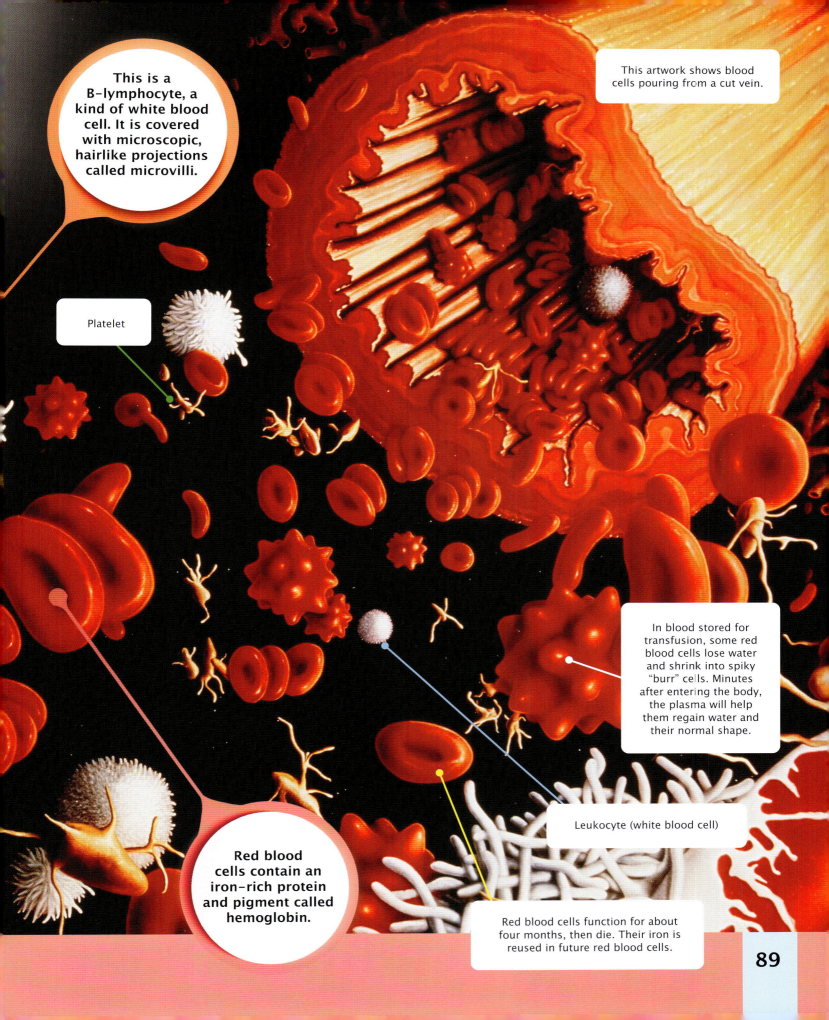

Red Blood Cells

There are 20 to 30 trillion red blood cells in the average adult's blood. A red blood cell is disk-shaped, with a dip on each side, which increases its surface area so it can exchange as much gas as possible.

This scanning electron micrograph (SEM) image shows a red blood cell in a capillary.

Carrying Oxygen

Each red blood cell is packed with around 270 million molecules of a substance called hemoglobin. Hemoglobin is red, which is why blood looks red. Hemoglobin contains iron, which binds to oxygen. This is how red blood cells can transport oxygen from the lungs to wherever it is needed. When a red blood cell reaches tissue in need of oxygen, the hemoglobin releases its oxygen.

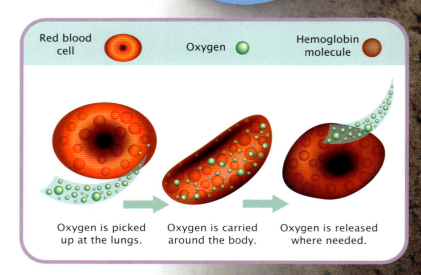

Carrying Carbon Dioxide

Most of the waste carbon dioxide made by cells is carried away by red blood cells, which take it to the lungs. The rest (around 10 percent) of the waste carbon dioxide travels to the lungs in plasma.

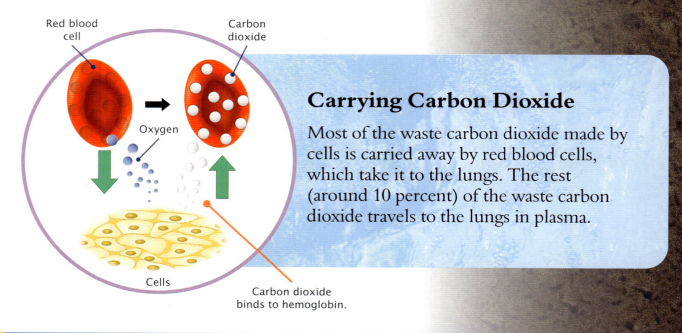

DID YOU KNOW? Made in bone marrow, red blood cells make up about 70 percent of all the cells in the body.

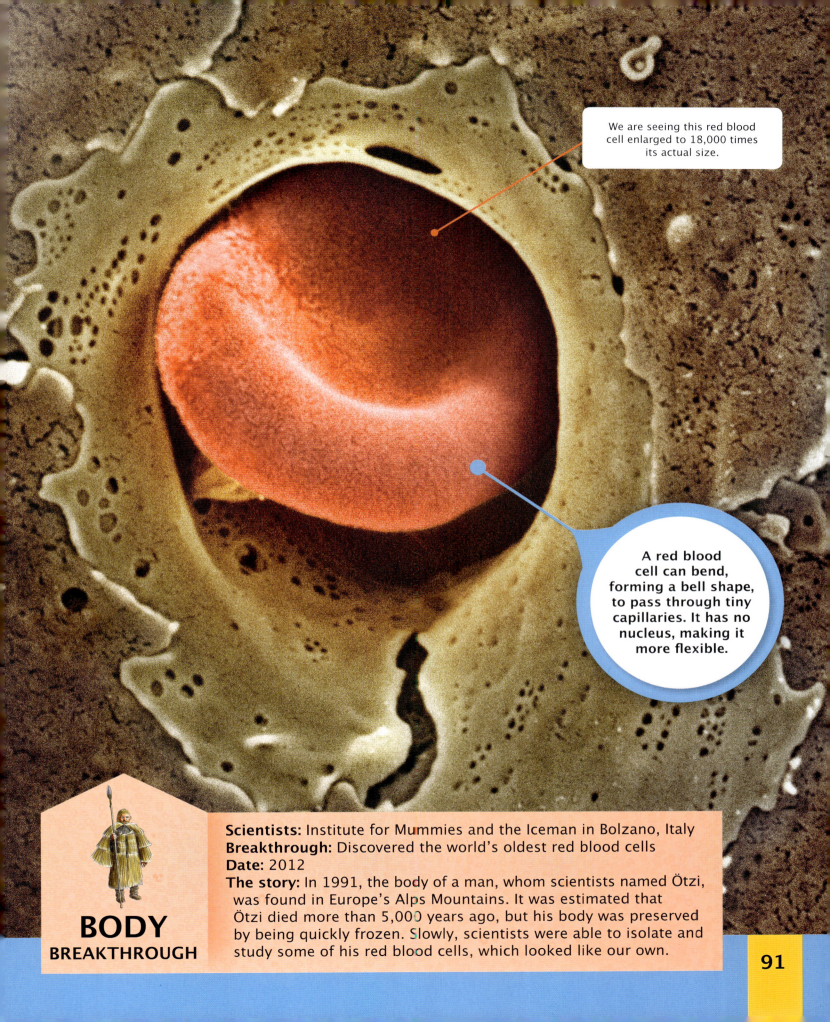

We are seeing this red blood cell enlarged to 18,000 times its actual size.

A red blood cell can bend, forming a bell shape, to pass through tiny capillaries. It has no nucleus, making it more flexible.

BODY BREAKTHROUGH

Scientists: Institute for Mummies and the Iceman in Bolzano, Italy
Breakthrough: Discovered the world's oldest red blood cells
Date: 2012
The story: In 1991, the body of a man, whom scientists named Ötzi, was found in Europe's Alps Mountains. It was estimated that Ötzi died more than 5,000 years ago, but his body was preserved by being quickly frozen. Slowly, scientists were able to isolate and study some of his red blood cells, which looked like our own.

91

Exercising

When you run, dance, or play a sport, your busy muscles need more oxygen to fuel their work. The lungs and heart have to work harder, so you take more breaths per minute and your heart beats more frequently. Exercising regularly makes the heart and lungs stronger.

> If you run frequently, you will become less breathless over time.

Breathing and Beating Faster

To meet your muscles' extra need for oxygen, your breathing has to increase from about 15–30 times per minute when resting, up to about 40–60 times per minute during exercise. When not exercising, an adult's heart beats 60 to 100 times per minute. When exercising, the average adult's heart can beat 180 times per minute or more.

The average 11-year-old's heart beats around 130 times per minute during exercise.

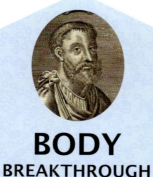

BODY BREAKTHROUGH

Scientist: Galen
Breakthrough: First practitioner of sports science
Date: 2nd century
The story: This Greek and Roman physician wrote 87 essays about strengthening health, fitness, and muscles through exercise. This was the beginning of the field of sports science, which studies how sports can improve health—and better health can improve sporting success.

DID YOU KNOW? The maximum healthy heart rate for someone exercising exceptionally hard is roughly estimated as 220 beats per minute, minus the person's age.

It is a good idea to take regular exercise that makes you breathe faster and makes your heart beat faster. Exercise such as running, bicycling, and fast-paced team sports will make the heart and lungs more efficient at getting oxygen into the blood and transporting it to the muscles.

Taking Your Pulse

Your number of heart beats per minute, known as heart rate, can be checked by taking the pulse on your wrist. The beats can be felt as blood surges through the wrist's radial artery.

Hold out one of your hands, with your palm facing upward.

Using a stopwatch or timer, count the number of pulses in one minute.

Gently press the first finger and middle finger of your other hand on the inside of your wrist, at the base of your thumb.

Regular exercise makes the muscles stronger and more efficient, so they need less oxygen to do their work.

Heart Health

Your heart may work automatically, but keeping a healthy heart is mostly up to you. As well as exercising regularly, you can keep your heart in top condition by trying to eat well and by avoiding substances that damage the cardiovascular system.

Eat Heart-Healthy Food

Eating fresh vegetables and fruit in a balanced diet is good for you, as your body gets the nutrients it needs to operate smoothly. In addition, fresh foods do not contain added ingredients that can cause trouble with your heart and blood vessels. For example, fresh foods (rather than ready-made meals, sauces, and snacks) do not usually contain too much salt. Eating too many salty snacks causes your body to hold on to more water. The extra liquid in your blood puts more pressure on the walls of the blood vessels and also on your heart.

A cardiologist is a doctor who specializes in the health of the heart and cardiovascular system.

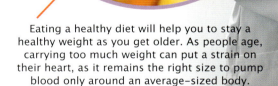

Eating a healthy diet will help you to stay a healthy weight as you get older. As people age, carrying too much weight can put a strain on their heart, as it remains the right size to pump blood only around an average-sized body.

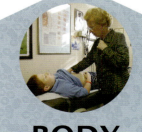

BODY BREAKTHROUGH

Scientist: Jacqueline Noonan
Breakthrough: Described Noonan syndrome
Date: 1963
The story: This cardiologist was the first to describe the genetic disorder that now takes her name. Caused by a genetic mutation (see page 36), Noonan syndrome causes problems with the heart's pulmonary valve, leading to a disruption of blood flow to the lungs. In turn, this can cause shortness of breath and dizziness.

No Smoking!

The chemicals in cigarettes make the walls of arteries sticky. This can make fatty waste materials in the blood stick to the artery walls. Over many years, the fatty material can begin to clog arteries and reduce the space for blood to flow properly. This can lead to heart disease, heart attacks (when the flow of blood to the heart is blocked), and even heart failure.

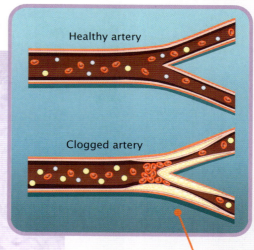

If someone develops clogged arteries, they can be treated with medications, surgery, and improvements to their diet and lifestyle.

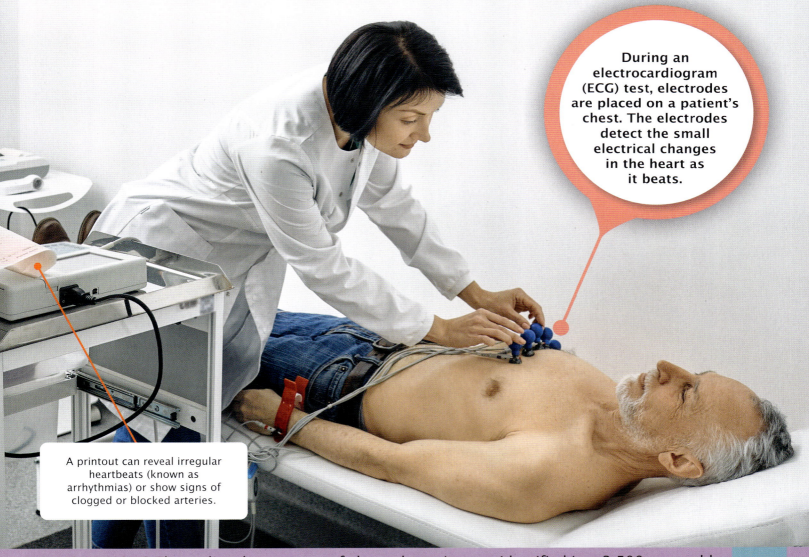

During an electrocardiogram (ECG) test, electrodes are placed on a patient's chest. The electrodes detect the small electrical changes in the heart as it beats.

A printout can reveal irregular heartbeats (known as arrhythmias) or show signs of clogged or blocked arteries.

DID YOU KNOW? The earliest known case of clogged arteries was identified in a 3,500-year-old Egyptian mummy.

Chapter 4
Digestive System

Your body has to break down the food you eat to get nutrients, which are the substances you need to keep healthy. This process is called digestion. Along the way from your mouth to your backside, your digestive system churns, pushes, squeezes, and breaks down food until all of the nutrients are released into your body.

Digestive Tract

The digestive tract is the route that food takes through the body. The tract starts in the mouth and continues through the esophagus (foodpipe), stomach, and intestines. Along the way, the body strips food of its nutrients, which pass into the bloodstream. The journey ends in the rectum, from which smelly waste is expelled from the body as feces (poop).

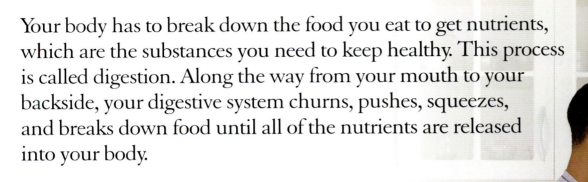

Bananas contain a mineral called potassium. The body needs potassium to keep a balance of fluids, to send nerve signals, and to regulate the contractions of muscles, including those of your heart.

A Long Process

The process of digestion usually takes many hours or even days, although your body can process some foods and drinks more quickly. Your digestive system has many tools to get the job done efficiently—powerful chemicals, strong acids, expanding organs, and muscles that work continuously without you even realizing it!

Apples are a good source of fiber, a material made by plants that cannot be fully digested by the body. Fiber travels all the way through the digestive system, keeping your poop moving!

DID YOU KNOW? In an average adult, the digestive tract—from the mouth to the rectum—is about 9 m (30 ft) long.

Eating for Energy

Everything we do uses energy: breathing or keeping warm; running a race or reading a book. The digestive system breaks down food so it can be used as energy—or as materials for building and maintaining the body.

Organs in the System

The main organs in the digestive system are the mouth, esophagus (foodpipe), stomach, and intestines. Yet several other organs help with the digestive process, including the pancreas, which makes digestive enzymes (chemicals that bring about change); and the liver, which makes a liquid called bile to digest fats. Bile is stored in a small pouchlike organ called the gallbladder.

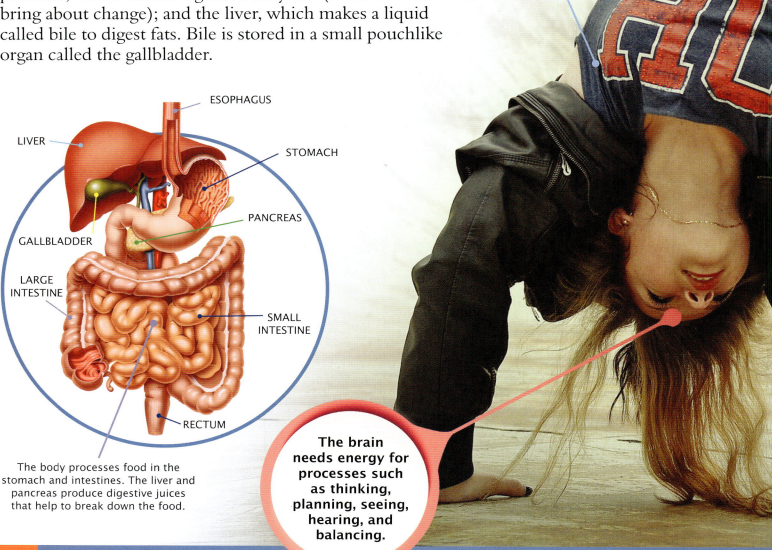

Breakdancing takes strength, timing, and energy. The toughest moves are freezes, where the body stops and holds a balance.

The body processes food in the stomach and intestines. The liver and pancreas produce digestive juices that help to break down the food.

The brain needs energy for processes such as thinking, planning, seeing, hearing, and balancing.

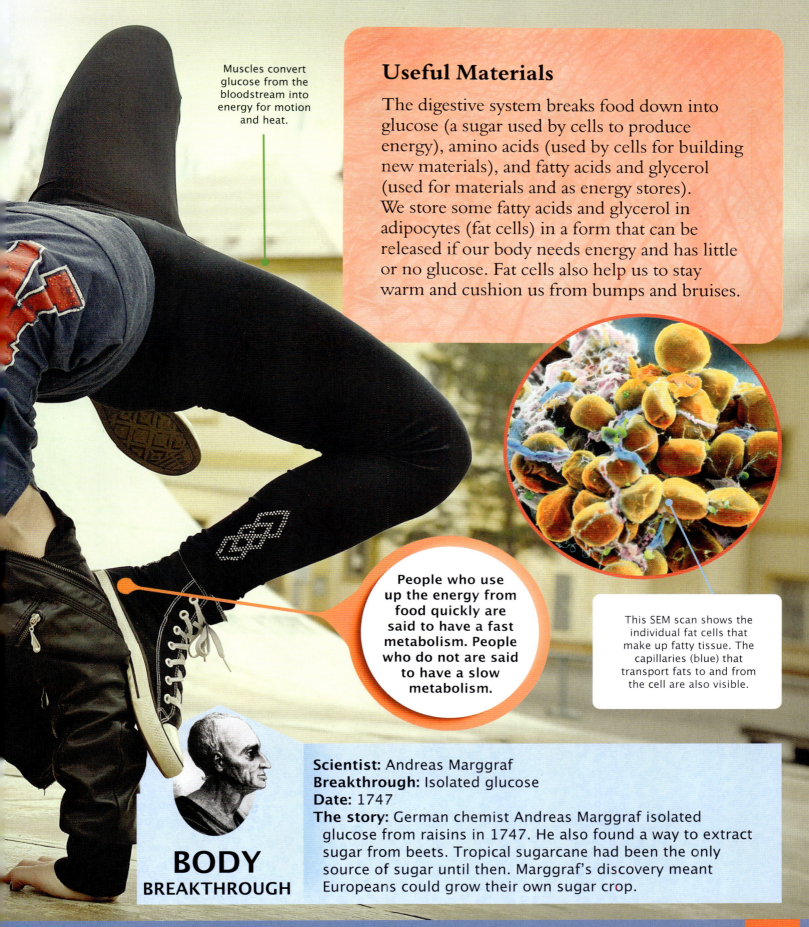

Muscles convert glucose from the bloodstream into energy for motion and heat.

Useful Materials

The digestive system breaks food down into glucose (a sugar used by cells to produce energy), amino acids (used by cells for building new materials), and fatty acids and glycerol (used for materials and as energy stores). We store some fatty acids and glycerol in adipocytes (fat cells) in a form that can be released if our body needs energy and has little or no glucose. Fat cells also help us to stay warm and cushion us from bumps and bruises.

People who use up the energy from food quickly are said to have a fast metabolism. People who do not are said to have a slow metabolism.

This SEM scan shows the individual fat cells that make up fatty tissue. The capillaries (blue) that transport fats to and from the cell are also visible.

BODY BREAKTHROUGH

Scientist: Andreas Marggraf
Breakthrough: Isolated glucose
Date: 1747
The story: German chemist Andreas Marggraf isolated glucose from raisins in 1747. He also found a way to extract sugar from beets. Tropical sugarcane had been the only source of sugar until then. Marggraf's discovery meant Europeans could grow their own sugar crop.

DID YOU KNOW? Around 10 percent of the world's population goes hungry some or all of the time, while 35 percent cannot afford to eat a healthy diet.

The Digestive Process

The aroma of delicious food can start off the digestive process before food has even passed our lips. Cooking smells make our mouth water—glands in our mouth produce saliva that will play a part in the first stage of breaking food down.

Physical and Chemical Digestion

On its twisty path through the digestive system, food breaks down in two ways. Being chewed in the mouth and churned in the stomach tears it into smaller pieces. This is a physical change. Then substances called enzymes set off chemical reactions that break food molecules into smaller molecules that can be absorbed by the blood.

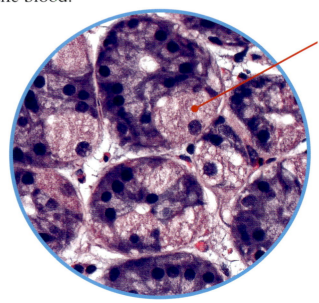

When we see appealing food, our brain sends messages to the digestive system, preparing it for action.

Parietal cells (shown here in pink) in the stomach wall make hydrochloric acid, a substance strong enough to dissolve metal! The acid helps break down food and also kills some bacteria that enter the stomach on food. Other stomach cells produce mucus that prevents the acid from damaging the wall of the stomach.

As we bring food to the mouth, we produce saliva. This will moisten the food so it is easy to swallow.

DID YOU KNOW? The time from food entering the mouth to its waste leaving the body as feces (poop) can sometimes be as long as 72 hours.

BODY BREAKTHROUGH

Scientist: William Beaumont
Breakthrough: Discovered chemical digestion
Date: 1820s
The story: In 1822, American doctor William Beaumont treated fur trader Alex St. Martin for a gun shot in the stomach. He saved the man's life, but the fistula (hole) never fully healed. Beaumont employed St. Martin and, over the next decade, used his open stomach to conduct experiments and study the stages of digestion. He published his findings in 1833.

Indigestion

Stress, overeating, gobbling food too fast, and eating junk food can all result in indigestion. Ulcers (open sores) in the stomach or small intestine can cause it, too. The symptoms include stomach pain, gas, and feeling bloated.

Indigestion can create an uncomfortable burning sensation.

Food can have meaning. These *tangyuan* (round rice dumplings) symbolize family togetherness.

As well as keeping us alive, food contributes to our mental well-being. Eating with family or friends keeps us connected.

101

A Balanced Diet

Like all animals, humans survive by eating food. Food is made from the bodies of other living things, mostly plants, animals, and fungi. Whatever the source, food is composed of the same kinds of chemicals that are useful to the body.

Food Groups

There are three main types of food. Carbohydrates include sugars and starches. They are used as the main source of energy for the body. Fats and oils belong to a food group called lipids. These are used by the body as an energy store. The brain is also 60 percent fat. Proteins are complex chemicals used inside every cell and in muscles. The proteins in foods can be broken up into smaller building blocks, which can be rebuilt into whatever type of protein the body needs.

These foods contain starch, which is a kind of complex carbohydrate. Simple carbohydrates are sweet sugars, and the sugars combine into larger forms to make starchy foods like bread and pasta.

PROTEIN
The meat of animals is a good source of protein and fats, although these food groups can be found in plants and mushrooms as well.

BODY BREAKTHROUGH

Scientist: James Lind
Breakthrough: Realized that limes prevent scurvy
Date: 1747
The story: British sailors were dying from a disease called scurvy after eating poor diets on long voyages. This Scottish naval doctor tried to discover which fresh fruits made them healthy and found that limes helped. It was later discovered that limes and other citrus fruits contain a lot of vitamin C, which prevents scurvy.

FRUIT AND VEGETABLES
Plant foods contain fiber. This is a special complex carbohydrate called cellulose, which humans cannot digest. Instead the fiber passes right through, helping to keep the gut strong and healthy.

Varied Diet

The body is able to make most of the chemicals it needs from the main food groups. However, it also needs a small but frequent supply of vitamins and minerals. These are essential chemicals needed for the body to work properly but some of which cannot be made by the body. It is important to eat a wide range of fresh foods to get the vitamins and minerals you need.

A baby's first food is milk. Some people keep drinking milk from cows, sheep, and goats for their whole lives, and they eat other dairy products made from this milk, such as cheese and yogurt.

Many meals make use of grains, such as rice, corn, and wheat. They can be made into breads, noodles, and pasta or eaten as they are.

SUGARS
Simple sugars taste sweet. The sugar can coat the teeth, where bacteria produce acids that damage the tooth's hard coating. Always brush your teeth 30 minutes after eating sugars.

DID YOU KNOW? At least 1,900 species of insects are safe for humans to eat. Around 2 billion people worldwide regularly eat insects, such as locusts and crickets.

103

Special Diets

Eating depends on our personal taste, family traditions, and local culture, as well as the actions of the digestive system. Local foods and farming have even changed our bodies over time—we have evolved to cope with different diets and process the ingredients that suit the local climate.

Intolerances and Allergies

If we have a food intolerance, we cannot digest that food without pain, bloating, wind, diarrhea, vomiting, rashes, or itching. With a food allergy, the immune system treats the food as a threat. The most severe allergic reaction, anaphylaxis, can cause a drop in blood pressure, difficulty breathing, and even death. Common food allergens are milk, eggs, nuts, seafood, soy, and wheat.

An autoinjector pen can stop the effects of anaphylaxis. It injects a chemical that reopens the airways.

BODY BREAKTHROUGH

Scientist: Aretaeus of Cappadocia
Breakthrough: Described celiac (or ceoliac) disease
Date: c. 150 CE
The story: Writing in Roman times, Greek doctor Aretaeus was the first to describe celiac disease. He called it *koiliakos*, meaning "disease of the abdomen." Celiac disease is an allergic reaction to gluten, a protein found in wheat and other grains. It stops the small intestine from being able to absorb nutrients.

DID YOU KNOW? A genetic mutation that stopped adults being lactose intolerant spread through Europe 7,500 years ago. Now some adults could drink milk without feeling ill.

Only about a quarter of all adults worldwide produce lactase—the enzyme we need to digest the lactose in milk.

Fasting

Going without food or drink for a period of time is called fasting. Some illnesses can be treated by fasting. A few doctors say that fasts can have health benefits for everyone. Fasting is also an important ritual in many faiths.

Blowing a horn called the shofar marks the end of Yom Kippur, the holiest day in the Jewish calendar. People mark the day with a 25-hour fast.

In people with a dairy allergy, drinking milk can cause hives (itchy bumps on the skin), vomiting, diarrhea, or even anaphylaxis.

There is less lactose in goat's milk than cow's milk. It can be a good alternative for people with lactose intolerance—but not good for people with a lactose allergy.

105

Carbohydrate

Along with proteins and fats, carbohydrates are macronutrients (meaning "large feeders"), which your body needs in big quantities. Carbohydrates provide your body with glucose, which your cells convert to energy. Try to eat three to five portions of carbohydrates on most days.

Breaking It Down

Digestive enzymes break large, complex molecules (groups of joined atoms) into small, simple molecules that can be absorbed and used by cells. Carbohydrates are broken down by carbohydrase enzymes, becoming glucose. This process starts in the mouth with amylase, a carbohydrase enzyme found in your saliva.

> Starch is found in whole grains, vegetables, fruits, beans, and legumes. Starch is broken down slowly, supplying your body with energy over several hours.

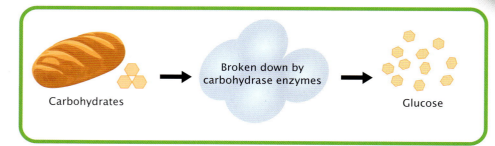

Carbohydrates → Broken down by carbohydrase enzymes → Glucose

Different Carbohydrates

There are three main types of carbohydrates: sugars, fibers, and starches. The healthiest sources of carbohydrates are whole grains, vegetables, fruits, and beans, which contain plenty of fibers and starches. Less healthy carbohydrates include white bread, cakes, and sweetened drinks, because they contain more sugars and less fibers and starches. Aim to cover about a third of your mealtime plate with healthy carbohydrates.

> Whole grain foods are made with entire seeds. They include whole grain bread, brown rice, wholewheat pasta, and whole grain breakfast cereals. Refined grains, such as white rice, white bread, and white pasta, have been ground into flour or meal in a way that removes the fiber-rich outer layer and many of the vitamins of the seeds.

Fiber is found in whole grains, vegetables, fruits, nuts, seeds, beans, and legumes. Fiber cannot be broken down by the body, so it bulks out your poop, making it travel easily through your intestines—and out!

Sugar is found in healthy amounts in fruit, vegetables, and milk. Sugar (usually taken from sugar cane or sugar beet plants) is added in less healthy quantities to sodas, candies, baked goods, and desserts. Sugar is broken down quickly by the body, giving a large but fast-fading burst of energy.

BODY BREAKTHROUGH

Scientist: Carl Schmidt
Breakthrough: Named carbohydrates
Date: 1844
The story: This German chemist suggested the name "carbohydrates" because these molecules contain carbon ("carbo-") as well as hydrogen and oxygen (which are found in water; "-hydrate") atoms. Carbohydrates are molecules made by living things, usually by plants.

DID YOU KNOW? All foods can have their place in a healthy diet, as long as we try to limit less healthy options and choose the healthy ones when we can.

107

Protein

The body turns proteins into amino acids, which it uses as building materials for growing, mending, and maintaining everything from muscles to bones. Try to eat two to three portions of protein on most days.

First made in Egypt, falafel is eaten throughout the Middle East.

Building a Body

Proteins are broken down into amino acids by protease enzymes, which are made by the stomach, small intestine, and pancreas. The body uses amino acids as building materials for producing proteins in cells, tissues, enzymes, and hormones.

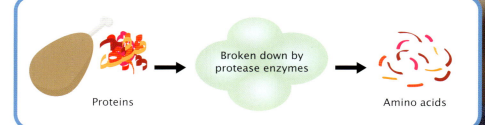

Proteins → Broken down by protease enzymes → Amino acids

BODY BREAKTHROUGH

Scientist: Marie Maynard Daly
Breakthrough: Discovered the effects of saturated fats
Date: 1950s
The story: An American biochemist, Daly discovered the effects of eating saturated fats, which are found in red meats such as beef, pork, and lamb. Saturated fats can raise the levels of a fatty substance called cholesterol in the blood. The body needs some cholesterol to build healthy cells, but in large amounts it can clog arteries, causing heart problems in older people.

Falafel is made with ground fava beans or chickpeas, as well as onions, garlic, and spices such as cumin or coriander. The mixture is shaped into balls that are fried or baked.

Picking Protein

You can find protein in fish, meat, beans, nuts, seeds, legumes, eggs, and dairy foods, such as milk, cheese, and yogurt. Although meat is a great source of protein, try to choose unfatty, unprocessed meats such as chicken and turkey, which do not contain too much saturated fat (see "Body Breakthrough") and salt (see page 94). Protein should cover around a quarter of your mealtime plate.

Legumes such as fava beans and chickpeas are a healthy source of protein and fiber.

Children and teens can enjoy a glass of low-fat milk a day, alongside other dairy foods such as yogurt or cheese.

DID YOU KNOW? Lack of protein can cause hair to break easily, skin to become dry and flaky, and nails to develop deep ridges.

109

Fat

Fats and oils are essential to your body's health, so try to eat some healthy fats every day. Your digestive system breaks them down until they can be used as essential materials or as stores of energy.

Building and Storing

Your digestive system breaks down fats and oils using lipase enzymes, with help from bile, which is made in the liver. Lipase enzymes are produced in the mouth, stomach, pancreas, and small intestine. Fats and oils are broken into fatty acids and glycerol, which are used for making structures such as cell membranes (see page 16). Some are stored in fat cells, which release them into the blood if you are short of energy. Fat cells are most common in the skin and around your organs.

> Oily fish, such as salmon and sardines, are excellent sources of healthy fats.

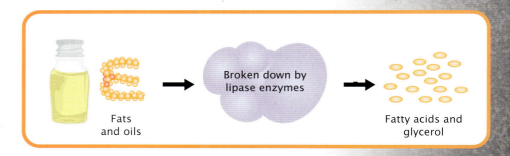

Fats and oils → Broken down by lipase enzymes → Fatty acids and glycerol

Less healthy fats are found in meat, such as beef or pork, and full-fat dairy products, such as butter. Yet any form of fat is fine if it is part of a balanced diet. Worrying about food and fat does not help us be healthy!

More or Less Healthy

Fats—such as butter and margarine—are solid at room temperature. Oils—such as olive or sunflower oil—are liquid. Just as with carbohydrates and proteins, there are more healthy and less healthy sources of fats and oils. The healthiest sources include vegetable oils, nuts, seeds, and fish.

BODY BREAKTHROUGH

Scientist: Florence Nightingale
Breakthrough: Introduced nutrition concerns into army and hospital planning
Date: 1854 onward
The story: This English nurse realized the importance of nutrition (eating the food necessary for health) for improving the health of soldiers injured during the Crimean War (1853-1856). Nightingale's concerns about the suitability and quality of food remain central to hospital cooking and nursing care to this day.

Vegetables, nuts, and seeds that are high in healthy fats include avocados, flaxseeds, almonds, and peanuts.

Vegetable oils, including olive, rapeseed, sesame, safflower, and sunflower oils, can be used for frying foods or for making dressings.

DID YOU KNOW? Body fat is an essential store of energy and vitamins, protects organs from injury, keeps us warm, and makes hormones.

Vitamins and Minerals

As well as the macronutrients—carbohydrate, protein, and fat—which your body needs in large quantities, the body also needs micronutrients ("small feeders") in littler quantities. Micronutrients are the vitamins and minerals your body needs to stay healthy. If you eat a varied diet, you are getting all the essential vitamins and minerals.

Vitamin or Mineral?

Vitamins and minerals are natural materials. Vitamins are made by animals and plants, so they can be gained by eating a range of animals or a variety of plants and their parts. Minerals are not made by living things, but those we need for health are found in soil. You can get the minerals you need by eating plants that soaked them up from soil or the animals that ate those plants.

Vitamin C is made by many fruits, including citrus fruits (such as oranges, lemons, and grapefruits), strawberries, blueberries, and kiwis, as well as vegetables such as bell peppers and broccoli. Your body needs vitamin C for growth and repair.

Red cabbage is high in vitamin C, potassium (which helps maintain healthy blood pressure), and magnesium (which keeps bones strong).

Vital Vitamins and Mighty Minerals

Vitamins have been identified with letters of the alphabet. Your body needs 13 vitamins: A, C, D, E, K, and eight B vitamins. Your body also needs around 21 minerals, including calcium, potassium, phosphorus, magnesium, and iron.

The mineral calcium, found in cheese, milk, and green leafy vegetables, is needed to maintain strong bones and teeth.

DID YOU KNOW? A head of broccoli contains twice as much vitamin C as an orange and almost as much calcium as a glass of whole milk.

Green leafy vegetables contain lots of vitamin K (which helps blood to clot if you are injured) and iron (which helps the body transport oxygen).

Carrots are a great source of vitamin A (which helps maintain good eyesight) and B_6 (which helps brain cells send messages).

BODY BREAKTHROUGH

Scientist: Casimir Funk
Breakthrough: Discovered vitamins
Date: 1912
The story: Polish chemist Casimir Funk discovered vitamin B_3, the substance in brown rice that prevents the disease beriberi. He predicted the existence of more protective nutrients (vitamins B_1, B_2, C, and D). Funk thought they would be amines (nitrogen-based compounds) like B_3, so he called them "vitamines" (vital amines).

113

Inside the Mouth

Digestion begins in the mouth. The teeth (see page 116) slice and chew food. Saliva—which contains mucus, antibodies, and enzymes, but is mostly water—prepares the chewed-up food for its journey.

Super Saliva

Mucus in saliva makes food slimy so that it will slide down the throat (esophagus). Antibodies help to kill off bacteria in food before they enter the body. Enzymes in saliva start to break down food chemically.

How We Swallow

Our tongue shapes the chewed-up, moistened food into a ball (bolus) and pushes it to the back of the mouth. As the top of the foodpipe (esophagus) opens, the airways are briefly blocked by the epiglottis, tongue, and palate. This reflex action stops our breathing for a split second, and prevents us from choking.

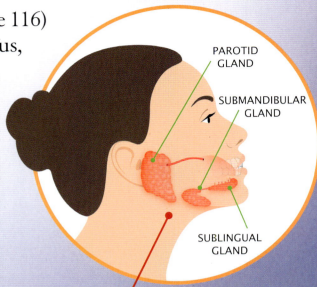

PAROTID GLAND
SUBMANDIBULAR GLAND
SUBLINGUAL GLAND

The glands that make saliva are called salivary glands. You have two parotid glands (in front of each ear), two submandibular glands (beneath the floor of your mouth), and two sublingual glands (beneath your tongue).

When the bolus is at the back of the mouth (1), the airways automatically close (2). Once it is in the esophagus (3), they reopen.

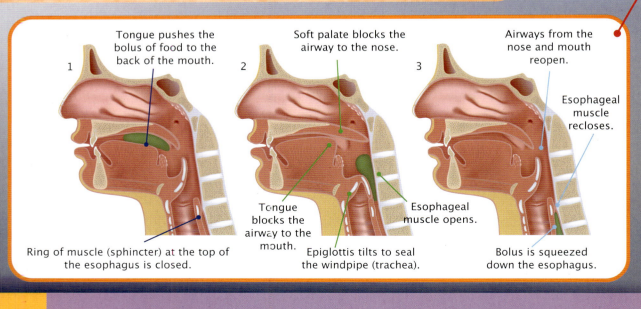

1. Tongue pushes the bolus of food to the back of the mouth. Ring of muscle (sphincter) at the top of the esophagus is closed.

2. Soft palate blocks the airway to the nose. Tongue blocks the airway to the mouth. Epiglottis tilts to seal the windpipe (trachea).

3. Airways from the nose and mouth reopen. Esophageal muscle recloses. Esophageal muscle opens. Bolus is squeezed down the esophagus.

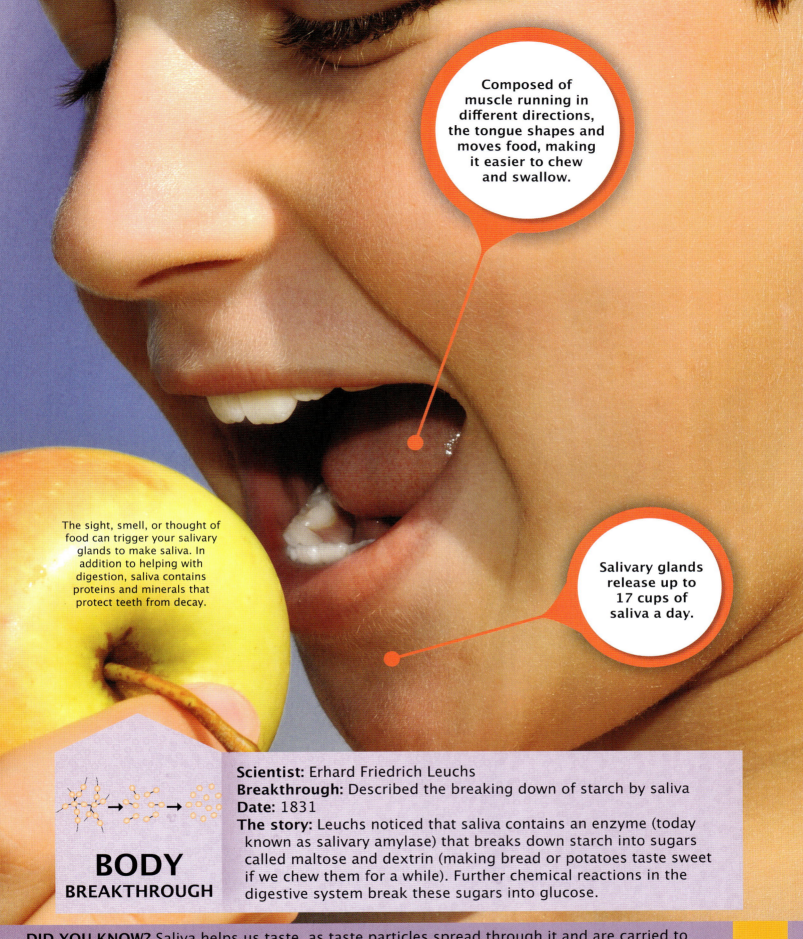

Composed of muscle running in different directions, the tongue shapes and moves food, making it easier to chew and swallow.

The sight, smell, or thought of food can trigger your salivary glands to make saliva. In addition to helping with digestion, saliva contains proteins and minerals that protect teeth from decay.

Salivary glands release up to 17 cups of saliva a day.

BODY BREAKTHROUGH

Scientist: Erhard Friedrich Leuchs
Breakthrough: Described the breaking down of starch by saliva
Date: 1831
The story: Leuchs noticed that saliva contains an enzyme (today known as salivary amylase) that breaks down starch into sugars called maltose and dextrin (making bread or potatoes taste sweet if we chew them for a while). Further chemical reactions in the digestive system break these sugars into glucose.

DID YOU KNOW? Saliva helps us taste, as taste particles spread through it and are carried to taste-sensitive receptors on the tongue and around the mouth.

Teeth

Teeth have the job of slicing and grinding food so it is in small enough pieces to be swallowed safely. Working with movements of your tongue and lips, teeth also help you make different sounds to form words.

> Dentists advise on keeping teeth healthy, but can also do work such as fillings (replacing decayed tooth structure), crowns (completely capping a damaged tooth), and bridges (replacing a missing tooth with an artificial one, joined to nearby teeth).

Different Teeth

Adults have 32 secondary teeth, also called permanent teeth. Some adults have only 28 teeth, as they do not have the back teeth on each jaw, called wisdom teeth. Children have 20 primary teeth, also called baby teeth, which fall out between the ages of 5 and 12 as the adult teeth push on them.

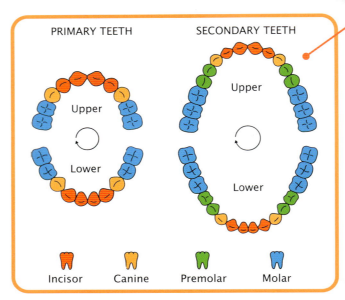

Sharp-edged incisor teeth are used for biting food. The four sharp-tipped canine teeth are for tearing food. An adult's eight premolars, which are wider and have bumps called cusps, are used for both cutting and chewing. The bigger, bumpier molars give food a final grind before it is swallowed.

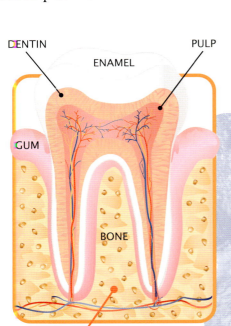

A tooth is surrounded by gum, which is tightly bound to underlying bone.

Inside a Tooth

The outer coating of a tooth, called enamel, is the body's hardest material, containing tough minerals such as calcium. Below the enamel is dentin, the body's second-hardest tissue, containing minerals, strong collagen, and water. Dentin's softer texture helps it absorb the pressure from eating, preventing teeth from cracking. However, enamel and dentin can be broken down by acids, which are made by mouth bacteria that thrive on sugar. The core of a tooth, called pulp, contains blood vessels and nerves, which enable us to feel pain when tooth decay has reached the pulp.

BODY BREAKTHROUGH

Scientist: Frederick McKay
Breakthrough: Discovered that the mineral fluoride protects teeth
Date: 1931
The story: In 1909, Colorado Springs dentist Frederick McKay noticed that his patients had awful-looking, mottled teeth—but no tooth decay! By 1930 he had proved that something in the water supply was staining but also strengthening their teeth. Tests the following year showed that the water had high levels of fluoride.

A dentist uses a mirror to get a better look at the health of teeth, gums, and mouth.

Children and teenagers should visit the dentist at least once every 6 to 12 months to stop any tooth decay in its tracks.

DID YOU KNOW? As early as the 7th century BCE, the ancient Etruscans made false teeth from human or other animal teeth joined together with gold bands.

Mouth to Stomach

This illustration is based on a CT scan of the neck.

From the throat, the bolus is squeezed along the esophagus (foodpipe) in rhythmic, rippling waves, called peristalsis. It is pushed to the stomach, a stretchy bag that makes highly acidic gastric juices. Rings of muscle (sphincters) at the stomach's entrance and exit stop the juices escaping.

Inside the Stomach

The muscular walls of the stomach squash and churn the food. They mix it with gastric juices, which are packed with enzymes that start off chemical reactions. The mashed-up food turns into a partly digested, bitter "soup" called chyme.

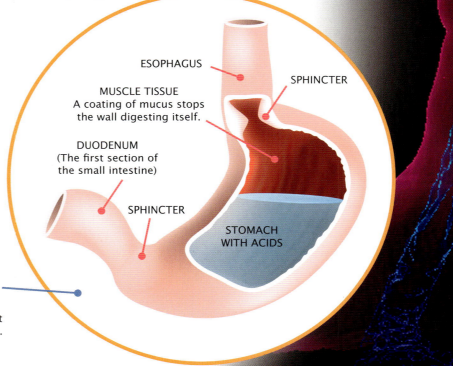

ESOPHAGUS

SPHINCTER

MUSCLE TISSUE
A coating of mucus stops the wall digesting itself.

DUODENUM
(The first section of the small intestine)

SPHINCTER

STOMACH WITH ACIDS

As well as digesting food, the stomach can store it until there is room in the intestines. In most adults, it can hold around 1 l (1.8 pt).

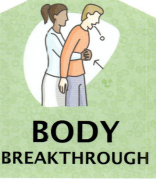

BODY BREAKTHROUGH

Scientist: Henry Heimlich
Breakthrough: Invented the Heimlich maneuver
Date: 1974
The story: The traditional first aid response to choking was a slap on the back. US surgeon Henry Heimlich believed his maneuver was more likely to dislodge the object blocking the airway and make it shoot out. It involved standing behind the patient and applying strong abdominal thrusts—pushing hard on the bottom of the diaphragm.

DID YOU KNOW? The stomach makes hydrochloric acid, a substance strong enough to dissolve a thin metal bar!

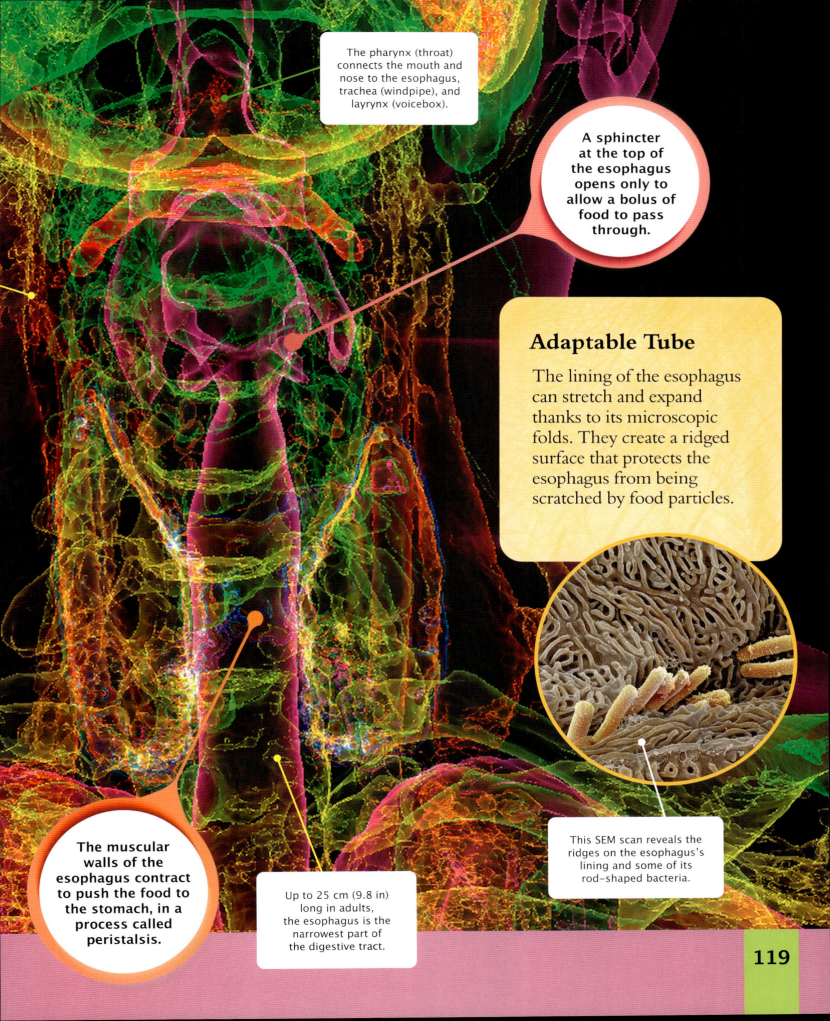

The pharynx (throat) connects the mouth and nose to the esophagus, trachea (windpipe), and layrynx (voicebox).

A sphincter at the top of the esophagus opens only to allow a bolus of food to pass through.

Adaptable Tube

The lining of the esophagus can stretch and expand thanks to its microscopic folds. They create a ridged surface that protects the esophagus from being scratched by food particles.

This SEM scan reveals the ridges on the esophagus's lining and some of its rod-shaped bacteria.

The muscular walls of the esophagus contract to push the food to the stomach, in a process called peristalsis.

Up to 25 cm (9.8 in) long in adults, the esophagus is the narrowest part of the digestive tract.

119

The Intestines

From the stomach, chyme is pushed through the coiled tubes that make up the small intestine, followed by the large intestine. Food's nutrients pass through the intestine walls (see pages 122–123). Whatever is left over, forms feces (poop) and passes out of the anus.

Recipe for Poop

The small intestine absorbs about 90 percent of the water we take in. The large intestine absorbs most of the rest, leaving a little to keep poop soft. Poop is made of undigested food, digested substances that were not absorbed, millions of bacteria, old cells from the intestine lining, and undigestible salts.

Ridged folds in the middle section of a healthy duodenum make the chyme spiral and slow down. This allows time for the nutrients to be fully absorbed.

"Friendly" Bacteria

Living in our intestines is a community of tens of trillions of microbes, including up to 1,000 species of bacteria. Some are probiotics, or "friendly" bacteria, that help to break down our food and also fight the pathogens (germs) that cause sickness.

Fermented foods such as sauerkraut contain probiotics that improve our gut health.

BODY BREAKTHROUGH

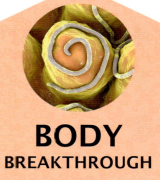

Scientists: Hippocrates and his followers
Breakthrough: Described parasitic intestinal worms (left)
Date: c. 500s BCE
The story: The *Hippocratic Corpus*, a set of medical writings from about 2,500 years ago, describes the symptoms of patients with parasitic worms. In 2017, archeologists were able to confirm worms were present in Hippocrates' time. They found whipworm and roundworm eggs in ancient, decomposed poop!

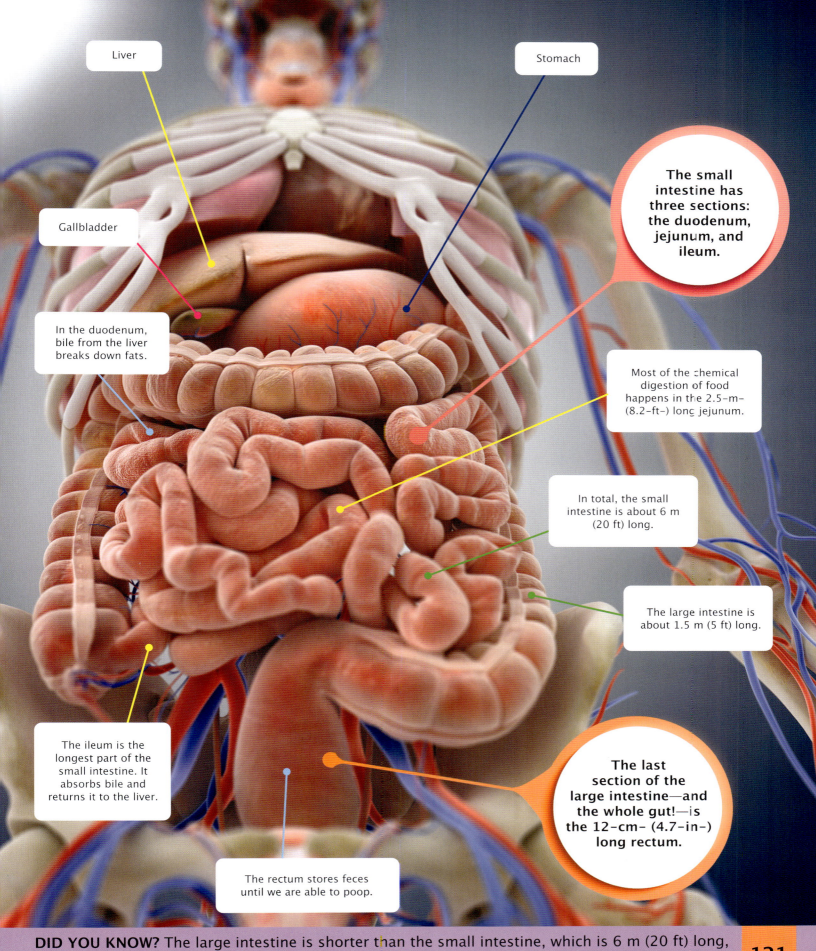

DID YOU KNOW? The large intestine is shorter than the small intestine, which is 6 m (20 ft) long, but got its name for being wider: 8 cm (3 in) compared to the small intestine's 2.5 cm (1 in).

Absorbing Nutrients

This innermost layer of the small intestine's wall, the mucosa, is where nutrients are absorbed.

In the small intestine, enzymes produced by the pancreas and bile released from the gall bladder finish extracting nutrients from the food. They change proteins, fats, and carbohydrates into simple molecules that can pass through the intestine's thin lining.

All About Area

The small intestine is a narrow, folded tube about 6 m (20 ft) in length. Its surface area is made even bigger by finger-like structures called villi on the inner walls. Even smaller projections, called microvilli, stick out from the villi. Having a surface area the size of a tennis court enables the small intestine to absorb nutrients quickly—and in large quantities.

The submucosa has blood vessels and nerves.

This layer of muscle tissue squeezes the food along.

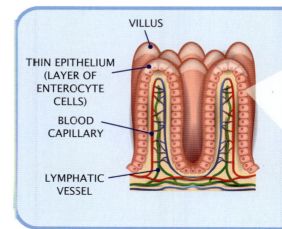

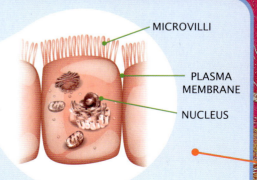

Microvilli cover the surface cells on the villi. Together, they increase the small intestine's surface area for absorption by around 600 times.

DID YOU KNOW? There are up to 24,000 microvilli in every 1 sq mm (0.0016 sq in) of small intestine.

BODY BREAKTHROUGH

Scientist: Ludwig Brieger
Breakthrough: Discovered skatole
Date: 1877
The story: This German doctor discovered the chemical skatole. Largely responsible for the strong smell of feces, skatole is produced by helpful bacteria that live in the large intestine and break down amino acids.

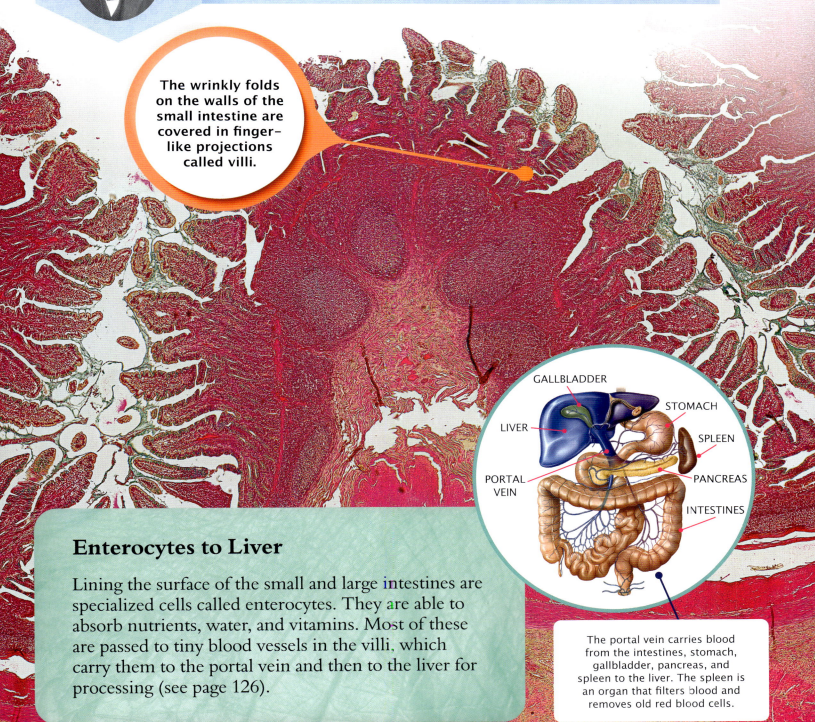

The wrinkly folds on the walls of the small intestine are covered in finger-like projections called villi.

Enterocytes to Liver

Lining the surface of the small and large intestines are specialized cells called enterocytes. They are able to absorb nutrients, water, and vitamins. Most of these are passed to tiny blood vessels in the villi, which carry them to the portal vein and then to the liver for processing (see page 126).

The portal vein carries blood from the intestines, stomach, gallbladder, pancreas, and spleen to the liver. The spleen is an organ that filters blood and removes old red blood cells.

123

Appendix

The appendix is a narrow pouch that connects with the large intestine, on the lower right side of the abdomen. It is sometimes called a vestigial organ, which means it was useful in our ancestors but useless today. However, doctors now believe that it does have a job: housing bacteria that help with digestion.

This scanning electron micrograph (SEM) scan shows *Lactobacillus* bacteria, which are common in the intestines.

Actually Useful

Scientists think that long ago, when our ancestors ate a more plant-based diet, the appendix was part of a structure that helped to digest tough vegetation. It was not until 2007 that doctors realized the appendix acts as a safe haven for useful bacteria when illness has flushed them from the rest of the intestines. The surviving bacteria then repopulate the intestines.

Useful bacteria, such as *Bacteroides* species (shown in blue), digest materials that the body finds hard to break down, such as carbohydrates. This generates energy for themselves and releases nutrients that are absorbed into the blood.

Appendicitis

Sometimes, the appendix becomes inflamed, causing a painful condition known as appendicitis. Usually, surgeons carry out an operation to remove the appendix, called an appendectomy. People who have had their appendix removed do not suffer from ill effects.

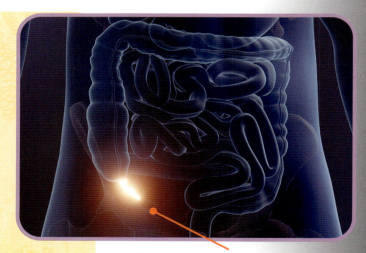

The appendix can become infected and inflamed if something—such as mucus or feces—blocks the opening where it connects with the intestine.

DID YOU KNOW? The appendix also houses white blood cells that fight harmful invaders that make it as far as the large intestine.

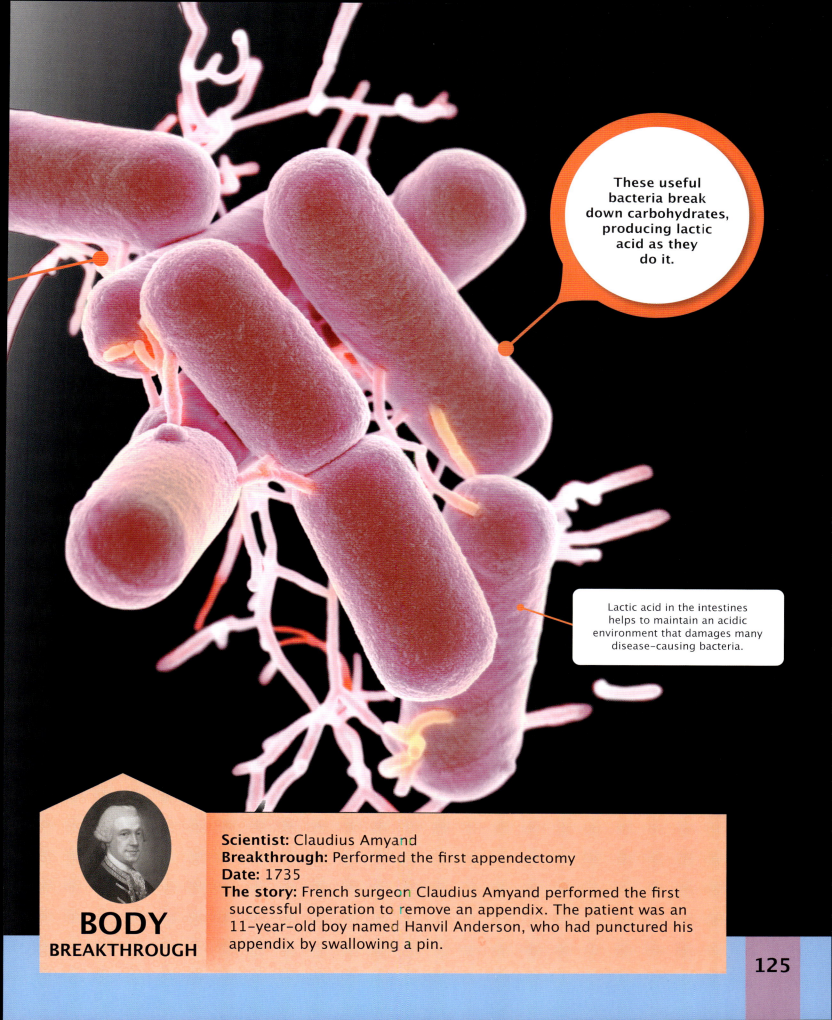

These useful bacteria break down carbohydrates, producing lactic acid as they do it.

Lactic acid in the intestines helps to maintain an acidic environment that damages many disease-causing bacteria.

BODY BREAKTHROUGH

Scientist: Claudius Amyand
Breakthrough: Performed the first appendectomy
Date: 1735
The story: French surgeon Claudius Amyand performed the first successful operation to remove an appendix. The patient was an 11-year-old boy named Hanvil Anderson, who had punctured his appendix by swallowing a pin.

125

Liver

One of the liver's many jobs is to filter the nutrient-rich blood arriving from the stomach and intestines along the portal vein. The liver separates harmful toxins from nutrients. It stores some nutrients and sends the rest to the heart for pumping round the body.

This computed tomography (CT) scan shows the liver (in red-brown), spleen (in pink), and large blood vessels.

Sending and Storing

The liver contains millions of cells called hepatocytes. It is the job of these cells to sort through the blood arriving from the stomach and intestines. Nutrients the body needs immediately are sent along the hepatic vein to the heart. The liver stores some nutrients in case food is in short supply in the future: Glucose is packaged and stored as a substance called glycogen.

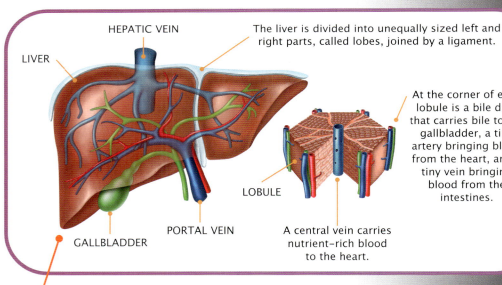

HEPATIC VEIN — The liver is divided into unequally sized left and right parts, called lobes, joined by a ligament.

LIVER

At the corner of each lobule is a bile duct that carries bile to the gallbladder, a tiny artery bringing blood from the heart, and a tiny vein bringing blood from the intestines.

LOBULE

GALLBLADDER

PORTAL VEIN

A central vein carries nutrient-rich blood to the heart.

The liver contains thousands of hexagonal lobules, each of which contains thousands of hepatocytes.

DID YOU KNOW? The liver is the second heaviest organ in the body (after the skin), weighing around 1.4 kg (3.1 lb) in an adult.

Getting Rid of Waste

When the hepatocytes come across waste from the body's processes—or toxins such as waste from medications—they convert them into more harmless waste products and send them to the kidneys. One waste product is called urea, which is a result of the process of breaking down proteins.

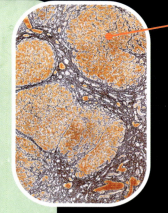

The liver can be scarred by constant attack from toxins such as alcohol. Scarring of the liver is called cirrhosis. Under a microscope, you can see scar tissue (dark areas) growing between the liver lobules (orange areas).

The liver's hepatocytes store some vitamins and minerals, such as iron and copper, which may be useful to the immune system.

The liver also makes bile to digest fats in the small intestine; makes hormones that aid cell growth and platelet production; and makes proteins that help the blood to clot.

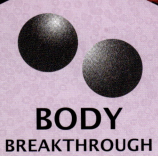

BODY BREAKTHROUGH

Scientist: Team at University College, London
Breakthrough: Developed a possible new treatment for cirrhosis
Date: 2021
The story: A team of scientists at the UK's University College, London developed tiny, swallowable carbon beads. These are designed to absorb harmful bacteria and toxins from the digestive system. It is hoped this will prevent further scarring of the liver, reducing the risk of liver failure.

Pancreas

About the size of your hand, the pancreas is located at the back of your abdomen, behind your stomach and next to your small intestine. It is part of both your digestive system and your endocrine system, which is the body system that makes hormones.

Helping Digestion

When food arrives in the small intestine, the pancreas releases a powerful, enzyme-packed juice. This enters the duodenum (the first part of the small intestine, located between the stomach and the small intestine's jejunum) through the pancreatic duct.

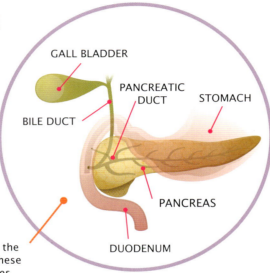

Tucked into the curve of the duodenum, the pancreas produces digestive enzymes. These enter the duodenum, which also receives bile from the gallbladder.

Diabetes is a disease caused by the pancreas either not making insulin or the body's cells not responding to insulin properly.

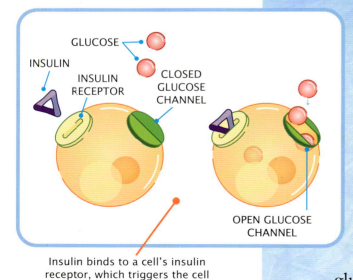

Insulin binds to a cell's insulin receptor, which triggers the cell to take in glucose.

Making Hormones

The pancreas makes hormones that regulate the levels of glucose sugar in your blood. When your blood sugar is too high, the pancreas makes insulin, releasing it into the blood. Insulin lowers blood sugar by triggering the body's muscle, fat, and liver cells to take in glucose from the blood. This glucose is used as energy by the cells, or converted into fat. When your blood sugar is too low, the pancreas makes glucagon, which tells the liver to release stored glucose into the blood. The glucose is then delivered to cells for energy.

BODY BREAKTHROUGH

Scientist: Paul Langerhans
Breakthrough: Found the cells that make insulin
Date: 1869
The story: German biologist Paul Langerhans identified "islands" of clear cells in the pancreas—but their function remained a mystery for more than 50 years. In 1923, Canadian doctor Frederick Banting and Scottish biochemist John Macleod won the Nobel Prize for the discovery of insulin.

This paler area of pancreatic tissue is called an islet of Langerhans. It makes insulin, a hormone which controls the amount of glucose in the blood.

Diabetes can cause hyperglycemia (high blood sugar), which—if left untreated—can damage nerves, blood vessels, tissues, and organs.

Someone with diabetes can manage the condition by injecting manufactured insulin using a pen (pictured), pump, or needle, or by inhaling insulin.

DID YOU KNOW? Every day, your pancreas makes around 8 cups of enzyme-rich juice to help you digest food.

Kidneys

The kidneys, bladder, and connecting tubes form the urinary system. This system's role is to filter the blood, removing waste from the body as a liquid called urine—otherwise known as wee or pee.

Filtering Blood

The abdominal aorta carries blood to the kidneys for filtering. The two kidneys filter the blood to make sure the amount of water and salts remains constant, while also removing waste products such as urea from the liver (see page 127) and creatinine from the muscles (produced when muscle tissue breaks down). The inferior vena cava carries filtered blood away from the kidneys. The filtered-out material, called urine, flows into tubes called ureters.

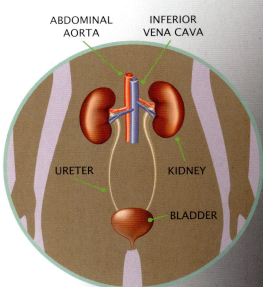

Nephrons

Each kidney contains at least 1 million filtering structures called nephrons. Each tiny nephron filters blood and produces urine.

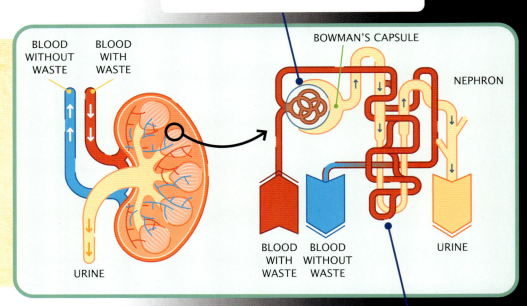

Pressure builds in this knot of capillaries, forcing water and waste through the thin walls and out of the blood.

As the thin-walled capillaries twist around the nephron's looping tubes, some water and nutrients can pass back from the urine into the blood to ensure the balance is right.

130

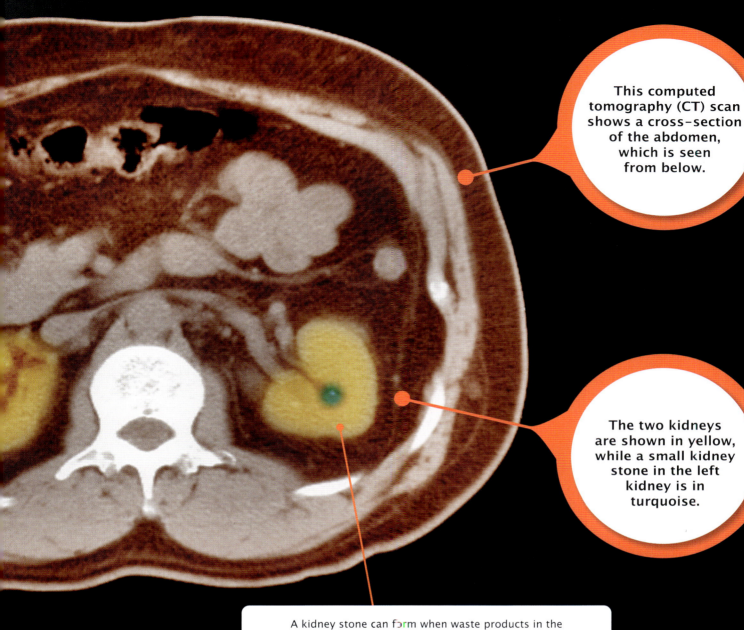

This computed tomography (CT) scan shows a cross-section of the abdomen, which is seen from below.

The two kidneys are shown in yellow, while a small kidney stone in the left kidney is in turquoise.

A kidney stone can form when waste products in the blood collect inside a kidney, developing into a hard lump. Most kidney stones are small enough to be carried out of the body in urine, but larger ones can be treated with medications or surgery. Kidney stones can be prevented by drinking plenty of water.

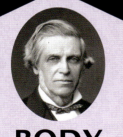

BODY BREAKTHROUGH

Scientist: William Bowman
Breakthrough: Identified the Bowman's capsule
Date: 1842
The story: While studying a kidney under a microscope, the English surgeon William Bowman discovered the nephron's cuplike sac, which is named after him. Two other body structures are also named after Bowman: Bowman's glands, in the nose; and Bowman's membrane, in the cornea of the eye.

DID YOU KNOW? The kidneys also make hormones that stimulate the production of blood cells and regulate blood pressure.

Bladder

The bladder is a muscly, baglike organ that stores urine until the time is right to release it from the body. In an adult, the bladder can hold more than 2 cups of urine, while a child's bladder usually holds less—and it is best to empty it before it gets anything like that full!

In Urine

Urine is 95 percent water, along with urea, salts, creatinine, ammonia, and products of blood breakdown, which give it a pale yellow shade. Urine's faint smell is a result of ammonia, which is made by helpful intestinal bacteria when digesting protein. A sign that you are not drinking enough is when urine turns dark yellow or smells stronger, both caused by pee containing too much waste and not enough water.

Eating certain foods, such as asparagus, can give urine a harmless smell.

Children older than 8 years old should drink 8 glasses of water a day, plus more in hot weather.

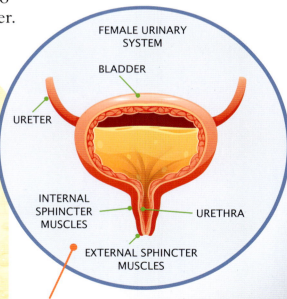

FEMALE URINARY SYSTEM
BLADDER
URETER
INTERNAL SPHINCTER MUSCLES
URETHRA
EXTERNAL SPHINCTER MUSCLES

The internal sphincter muscles are smooth muscle (see page 56), so you cannot consciously control them. The external sphincter muscles are skeletal muscle, so you can consciously squeeze them to stop urine from leaking.

Squeeze and Release!

Two sets of muscles work together to keep urine in the bladder between bathroom trips: The internal sphincter muscles of the bladder neck and urethra, and the external sphincter muscles. When your bladder is full, nerves in its walls send signals to your brain to find a toilet. To empty your bladder, the brain signals the bladder muscles to tighten and the sphincter muscles to relax. Urine passes out of the body through the urethra.

DID YOU KNOW? The inside of the bladder's wall has folds called rugae, which stretch out as the bladder fills with urine.

BODY BREAKTHROUGH

Scientist: Anna Broomall
Breakthrough: Invented a lithotrite
Date: 1879
The story: Broomall invented a tool for crushing bladder stones, which are mineral lumps that can form when the bladder is not completely emptied of urine for a long period. She also worked to improve care for mothers and babies during pregnancy and birth, starting the first maternal health clinic in the United States in 1888.

The body needs water to make blood liquid enough to flow; to maintain the health of cells, muscles, skin, and joints; to aid digestion; to make sweat to cool you down; and to make urine.

Around 15 percent of the water we drink is lost in the air we breathe out.

Around 21 percent of the water we drink is lost through the skin, much of it as sweat.

Around 60 percent of the water we drink is lost in urine, while 4 percent is in feces.

133

Chapter 5
Defending the Body

Your body is always on guard, ready to ward off attacks by germs that could make you ill. Although you are surrounded by millions of these germs, your body has barriers—from skin to mucus, spit, and tears—to deal with most of them before they can harm you. Even if germs make it past your defensive barriers, your body has lots of other weapons to do battle.

The Immune System

It is the job of the body's immune system to defend you against germs including viruses, bacteria, and fungi. The immune system is a body-wide network of organs and cells. The most important weapons of the immune system are white blood cells, which travel through the blood and lymphatic vessels, as well as moving into tissues to the site of an infection. When white blood cells recognize an invader, they fight to destroy it.

Your skin is your first line of protection against most types of infection. But it is important to keep it clean. Washing your hands thoroughly helps prevent the spread of colds, flu, food poisoning, and many other illnesses. A good tip is to count slowly to 20 while you wash them.

DID YOU KNOW? Your body is laden, both inside and out, with trillions of harmless or even helpful bacteria, but a few can cause disease.

Staying on Guard

Your defensive systems remain active even after they have dealt with an infection or injury. It is just as important to make sure you can heal, recover fully, and—perhaps—not suffer from the same infection a second time. For example, white blood cells remember how they won against a particular invader, so it will be easier to see off that type of attack next time.

Your nose is always making gooey mucus. Mucus stops lots of germs from going any further into your body and making you ill.

Your tears contain antibodies that can destroy germs if they get into your eyes. Antibodies are proteins made by the immune system. They attach themselves to attackers and either neutralize them or attract the attention of special cells that digest the attackers.

Germ Warfare

Germs are tiny, harmful organisms. All germs are so small that you cannot see them with the naked eye. That is why you need to be extra careful to protect yourself from them.

Types of Germs

Most of the germs that make you unwell are either living things called bacteria, fungi, and protozoa—or viruses (see page 138), which are non-living entities.

Bacteria		These one-celled living things are everywhere around you and even inside you! However, less than 1 percent of all bacteria species can cause disease in humans. For example, if *Streptococcus pneumoniae* bacteria enter alveoli in the lungs, they can cause a disease called pneumonia, which results in coughing, chest pain, and fever.
Fungi		These tiny relatives of mushrooms often live in damp places. Of at least 2 million different fungi, only around 300 can cause disease, if they land on the skin or are breathed in. If *Trichophyton rubrum* fungi invade skin cells on the feet, they can cause the common disease athlete's foot, which results in itching and flaking skin.
Protozoa		These one-celled living things feed on other microorganisms or living material. Most are harmless, but some cause disease if they get inside the body. For example, *Toxoplasma gondii* protozoa cause toxoplasmosis, a flu-like illness that can be more serious in pregnant women.

The bites of female *Anopheles gambiae* mosquitoes can pass *Plasmodium protozoa* from one person to another.

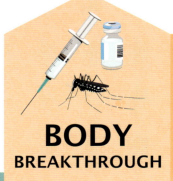

BODY BREAKTHROUGH

Scientists: Mehreen Datoo, Adrian Hill, and team at Oxford University, England
Breakthrough: Developed a vaccination against malaria
Date: 2023
The story: Aiming to reduce the world's 600,000 annual deaths from malaria, the team developed the R21/Matrix-M malaria vaccine (see page 234), which teaches the immune system to fight *Plasmodium* protozoa. Children in Côte d'Ivoire and South Sudan were the first to receive it.

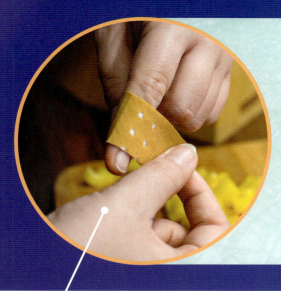

Protect Yourself!

You can pick up germs almost anywhere! They could be in the food you eat, on door handles, or on phone screens. Germs can be in the air you breathe if someone has spread germs by coughing or sneezing. When you eat, germs from your hands can go in your mouth. Rubbing your eye with a dirty finger can spread germs into it.

Your skin stops many germs from entering your body. However, one of the most common ways for germs to attack is through wounds, like cuts or scrapes. That is why it is important to dab a cut with antiseptic to clean it, and to cover it while it heals.

Malaria-causing *Anopheles* mosquitoes are mainly found in tropical parts of the world.

Infection with some species of *Plasmodium* protozoa causes malaria, a disease that results in fever, vomiting, and even death. Infection can be prevented by medications and by avoiding mosquito bites by using insect repellent and sleeping under a mosquito net.

DID YOU KNOW? One of the most common bacterial infections in humans is of the urinary tract (bladder and urethra) by *Escherichia coli*, which causes a burning feeling when peeing.

Viruses

A virus is a biologically active entity, but it is not alive. It is not made from a cell but is built from a piece of DNA (or RNA) wrapped up in a coat made of proteins. The viral DNA is parasitic, and it takes over the machinery of cells to make copies of itself.

A coronavirus is named for the way it is covered in "spike" proteins. When viewed through a microscope, they look like a crown, or corona, around the outside.

Viral Diseases

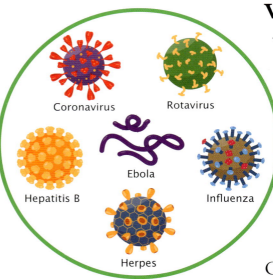

Viruses are organized by their distinctive shapes. All viruses cause diseases in a target organism. Most viruses are harmless to humans, but we still have several viral diseases. Influenza, or flu, is a viral disease. Herpes viruses create several diseases, including chickenpox. Ebola virus is a rare but dangerous infection, while rotavirus attacks the stomach, and hepatitis viruses damage the liver. COVID-19 is caused by a coronavirus.

Infection

A virus is able to bond to its target cell using its protein coat. It then injects its DNA into the cell. The DNA takes over the cell's system for copying its own DNA and makes many copies of itself. The viral DNA's genes carry the instructions for making its coating proteins, and the cell is used to manufacture those. Eventually, the cell is so full of new viruses that it bursts. The viruses then infect the next cell.

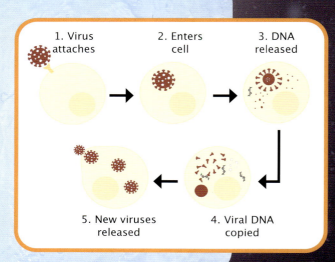

DID YOU KNOW? The viruses that cause the common cold are only 20 nanometers across. That means that 50,000 of them could line up on a pinhead.

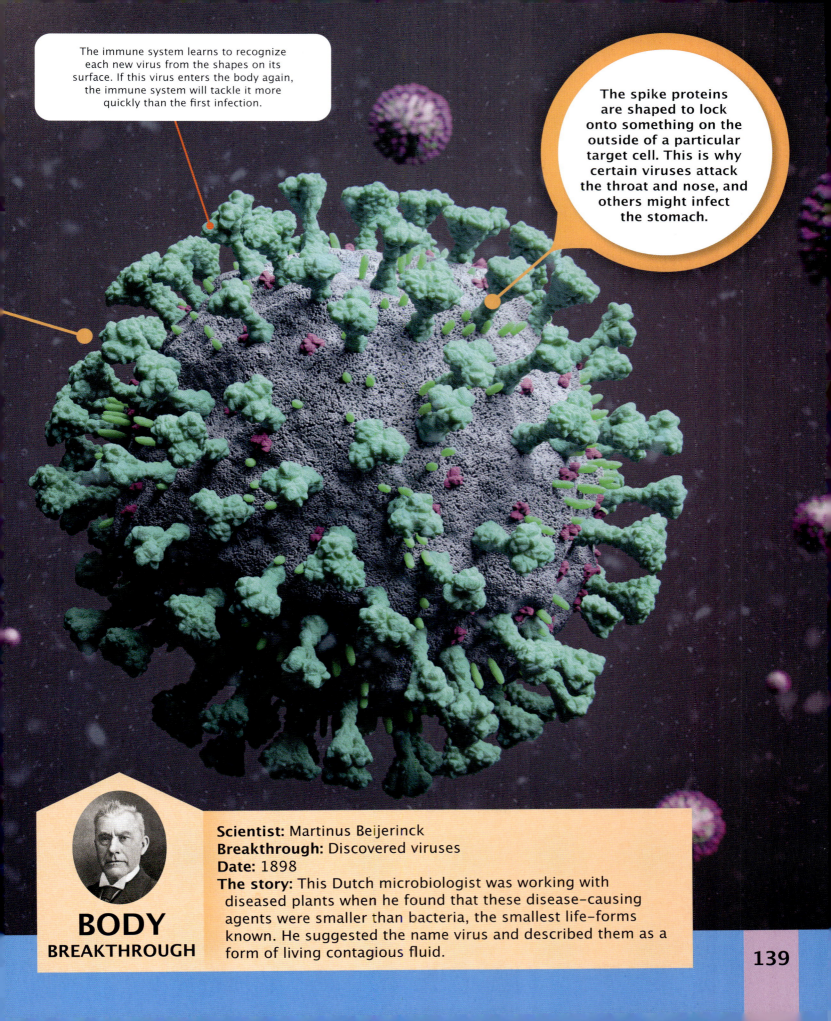

The immune system learns to recognize each new virus from the shapes on its surface. If this virus enters the body again, the immune system will tackle it more quickly than the first infection.

The spike proteins are shaped to lock onto something on the outside of a particular target cell. This is why certain viruses attack the throat and nose, and others might infect the stomach.

BODY BREAKTHROUGH

Scientist: Martinus Beijerinck
Breakthrough: Discovered viruses
Date: 1898
The story: This Dutch microbiologist was working with diseased plants when he found that these disease-causing agents were smaller than bacteria, the smallest life-forms known. He suggested the name virus and described them as a form of living contagious fluid.

139

Rapid Response

Even with your skin protecting you, and your own good work to stay clean, germs can enter your body. That is when your immune system starts to fight back. It gets rid of some germs almost as soon as they arrive. And if germs do get past and start to make you ill, your body does its best to limit the damage.

A sneeze is your body's way of getting an irritating—or attacking—object out of your nose and mouth.

Mighty Mucus

Cup-shaped cells in your nose, called goblet cells, are always making mucus, even when you are well. Mucus is mostly water and a gel-making molecule called mucin. Mucus stops the skin inside your nose from drying out, helps you smell things, and stops lots of germs from going further into your body. If you have a cold, the mucus gets thicker and stickier, so it can more easily trap and flush out the invader.

A runny nose can be one of the first signs of having a cold.

Powerful Vomiting

Sometimes, germs enter your body on food or drink. If your body recognizes the invaders, it tries to get rid of them quickly by throwing up. This action is controlled by your brainstem (see page 174), without your conscious thought. The stomach, esophagus (foodpipe), and lower esophageal sphincter (the ring of muscle at the top of the stomach) are all relaxed during vomiting. The diaphragm (see page 49) and abdominal muscles contract to force out the stomach contents.

You may feel a bit unwell after vomiting because it is such a violent act, but you will probably soon begin to feel a little better! For the first three or four hours after vomiting, sip small amounts of water every 15 minutes, to make sure you stay hydrated but do not trigger more vomiting.

140   **DID YOU KNOW?** In 2013, using black pepper and volunteers, Canadian scientists calculated that a sneeze travels at 18 km/h (11 mph).

From the brainstem, signals travel along the nerves to tell muscles in your diaphragm, chest, and throat to work together to make a sudden blast of air.

A sneeze can expel 100,000 germs! Make sure you do not give them to anybody else by covering your mouth and nose with a thick tissue. If you do not have a tissue, sneeze into the bend in your elbow.

BODY BREAKTHROUGH

Scientist: Lydia Bourouiba
Breakthrough: Discovered how far a sneeze travels
Date: 2020
The story: Using high-speed video, Bourouiba studied how far particles from a sneeze can travel. Her assessment was that particles reach up to 8 m (27 ft) away, depending on turbulence within the sneeze cloud, airflow, and ventilation systems within a room.

White Blood Cells

White blood cells, or leukocytes, help to defend the body against infection by tracking down and destroying invaders. Unlike red blood cells, which remain in the bloodstream, white blood cells also travel in lymph (see page 146) and can move from vessels into the body's tissues to fight an infection.

White Blood Cells in Action

Some white blood cells—including neutrophils, monocytes, and mast cells—"swallow" invaders (see "Phagocytosis"). Others release substances such as toxic proteins, which destroy invaders; antitoxins, which neutralize invaders' harmful effects; chemical messengers such as histamine, which widens blood vessels to increase the flow of blood (and white blood cells); and antibodies (see page 144), which lock on to invaders.

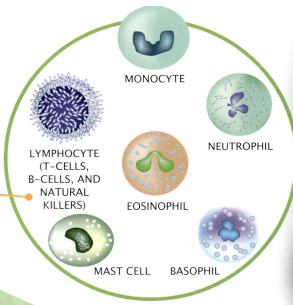

There are many types of white blood cell. Each has its own way of overcoming pathogens. A pathogen is any disease-causing micro-organism or agent, such as a virus, bacterium, protozoa, or fungus.

4. Chemicals released by the helper T-cells tell this B-cell which antibody (see page 144) will defeat the pathogen.

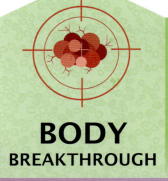

BODY BREAKTHROUGH

Scientists: Washington University and Siteman Cancer Center, USA
Breakthrough: Started trials of natural killer cell therapy
Date: 2016
The story: The team tested a new treatment for cancer in which natural killer cells (a type of lymphocyte that releases toxic chemicals called cytokines) are given to patients. Cancer is a disease where cells grow and reproduce uncontrollably.

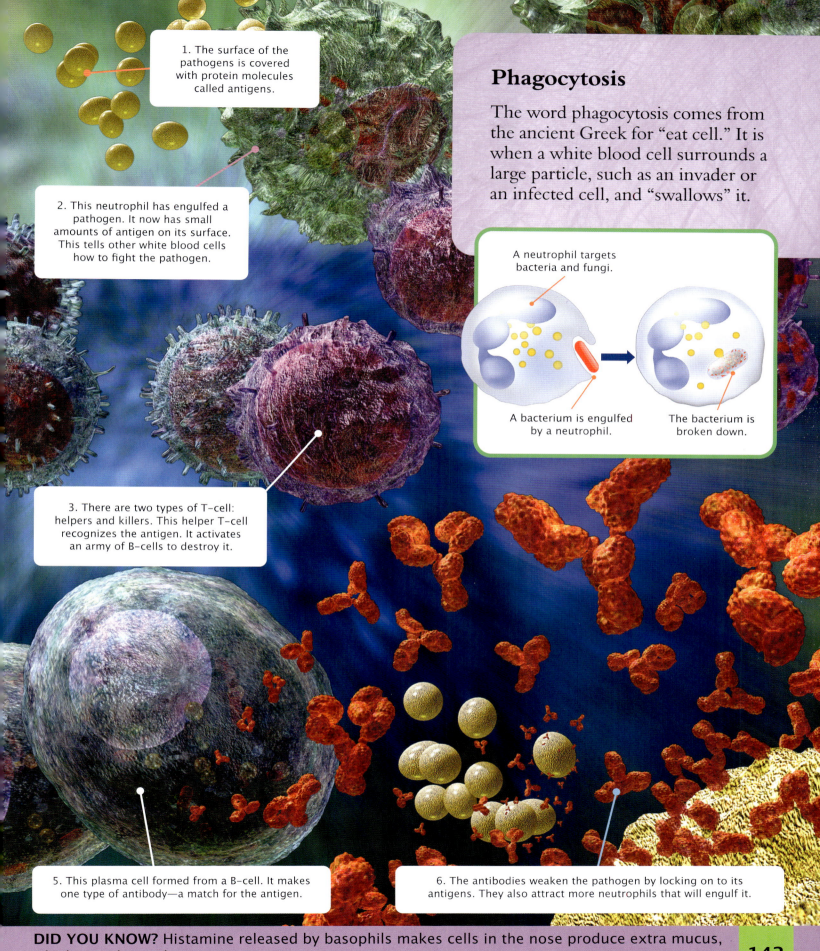

1. The surface of the pathogens is covered with protein molecules called antigens.

2. This neutrophil has engulfed a pathogen. It now has small amounts of antigen on its surface. This tells other white blood cells how to fight the pathogen.

Phagocytosis

The word phagocytosis comes from the ancient Greek for "eat cell." It is when a white blood cell surrounds a large particle, such as an invader or an infected cell, and "swallows" it.

A neutrophil targets bacteria and fungi.

A bacterium is engulfed by a neutrophil.

The bacterium is broken down.

3. There are two types of T-cell: helpers and killers. This helper T-cell recognizes the antigen. It activates an army of B-cells to destroy it.

5. This plasma cell formed from a B-cell. It makes one type of antibody—a match for the antigen.

6. The antibodies weaken the pathogen by locking on to its antigens. They also attract more neutrophils that will engulf it.

DID YOU KNOW? Histamine released by basophils makes cells in the nose produce extra mucus, which can also make you sneeze.

143

Antibodies

Antibodies are Y-shaped proteins made by white blood cells called B lymphocytes, or B-cells. Antibodies attach to the surface of bacteria, viruses, fungi, and protozoa. This neutralizes the invaders or helps white blood cells to identify them.

Once locked on, antibodies can prevent a virus—such as this SARS-CoV-2 virus, which causes coronavirus (COVID-19)—from entering a healthy cell and causing infection.

B-Cells

Antibodies are made when a B-cell comes into contact with an antigen (short for "**anti**body **gen**erator"), which are "markers" on the surface of an invader. This makes the B-cell divide and clone itself, making two different types of B-cells: plasma cells and memory cells (see "Not Again"). Plasma cells release up to 2,000 antibodies per second into your blood and lymphatic system, each antibody designed to lock on to that particular antigen.

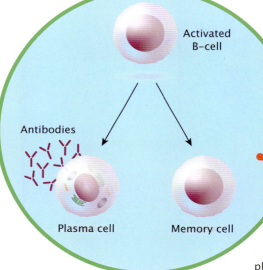

An activated B-cell makes plasma cells and memory cells. Plasma cells make antibodies.

BODY BREAKTHROUGH

Scientist: Paul Ehrlich
Breakthrough: Named antibodies
Date: 1891
The story: A German physician and immunologist (specialist in the immune system), Ehrlich named and investigated antibodies. Along with Emil von Behring, he transferred blood serum (blood plasma, without blood cells or clotting factors) with antibodies to fight the dangerous bacterial infection called diphtheria.

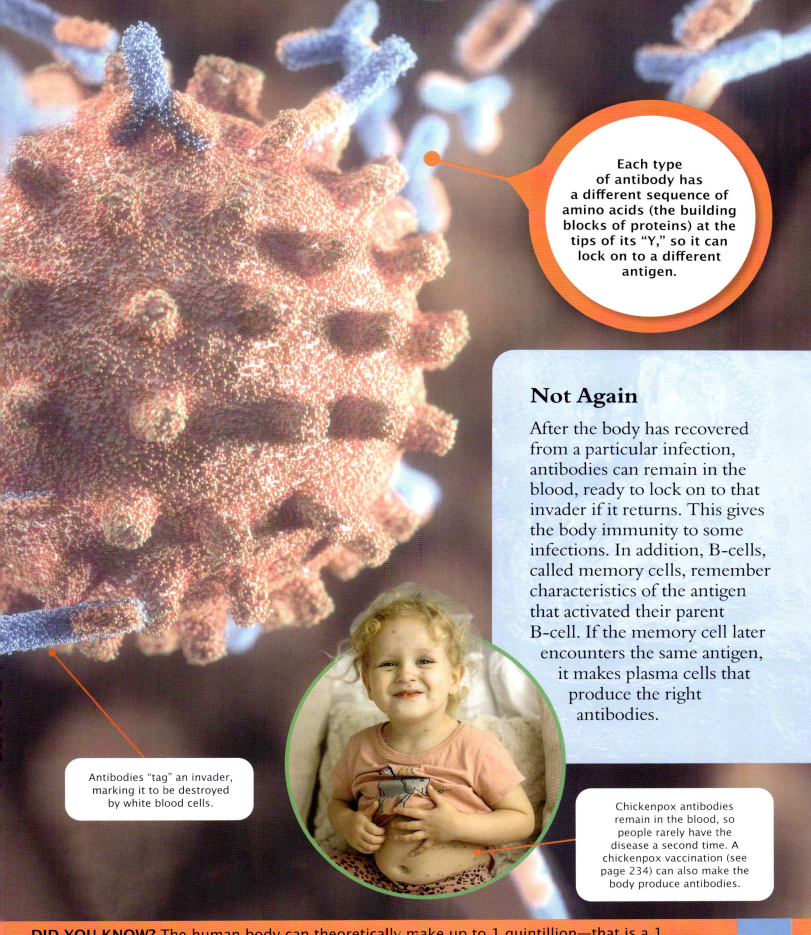

Each type of antibody has a different sequence of amino acids (the building blocks of proteins) at the tips of its "Y," so it can lock on to a different antigen.

Not Again

After the body has recovered from a particular infection, antibodies can remain in the blood, ready to lock on to that invader if it returns. This gives the body immunity to some infections. In addition, B-cells, called memory cells, remember characteristics of the antigen that activated their parent B-cell. If the memory cell later encounters the same antigen, it makes plasma cells that produce the right antibodies.

Antibodies "tag" an invader, marking it to be destroyed by white blood cells.

Chickenpox antibodies remain in the blood, so people rarely have the disease a second time. A chickenpox vaccination (see page 234) can also make the body produce antibodies.

DID YOU KNOW? The human body can theoretically make up to 1 quintillion—that is a 1 followed by 18 zeros—unique antibodies.

145

Lymphatic System

Blood is not the only fluid running through your body! The lymphatic system is often called your body's "drainage network." But the clear or whitish liquid flowing slowly through it—called lymph—also contains infection-fighting white blood cells.

When you are fighting an infection, your lymph nodes—particularly on the side of the neck or under the arms—may become swollen as white blood cells rush to the area.

Fighting Infection

Lymph flows through lymphatic vessels. Lymph moves slowly because it is not pumped by a large organ in the same way as your blood. Your muscles squeeze it along, and it passes through around 600 small masses of tissue, called lymph nodes, along the way. These nodes are packed with white blood cells that identify harmful germs in the lymph and destroy them.

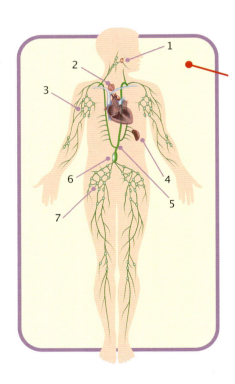

LYMPHATIC SYSTEM
1. Tonsils contain T-cells and B-cells.
2. Thymus gland is where T-cells mature.
3. Armpit nodes filter lymph from the arms and breast, and drain it from the chest wall.
4. Spleen stores monocytes that can turn into phagocytic cells.
5. Thoracic duct is the largest lymph vessel.
6. Cisterna chyli receives lymph from the lower body.
7. Groin nodes filter lymph from the lower body.

BODY BREAKTHROUGH

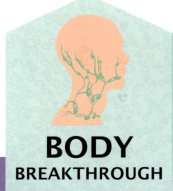

Scientists: Olaus Rudbeck and Thomas Bartholin
Breakthrough: Discovered the lymphatic system
Date: 1652
The story: Working independently, these two scientists discovered part of the lymphatic system and its workings. Rudbeck presented his findings to Queen Christina of Sweden in April or May of 1652, while Danish physician Bartholin published his work in December, resulting in an argument about who was first.

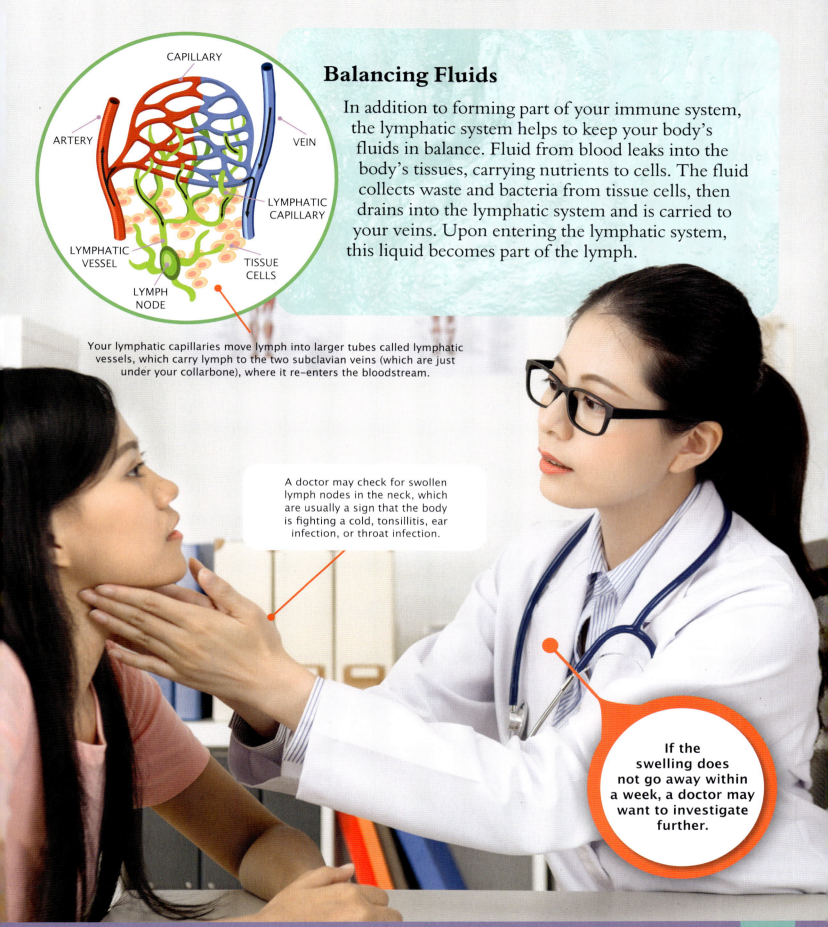

Balancing Fluids

In addition to forming part of your immune system, the lymphatic system helps to keep your body's fluids in balance. Fluid from blood leaks into the body's tissues, carrying nutrients to cells. The fluid collects waste and bacteria from tissue cells, then drains into the lymphatic system and is carried to your veins. Upon entering the lymphatic system, this liquid becomes part of the lymph.

Your lymphatic capillaries move lymph into larger tubes called lymphatic vessels, which carry lymph to the two subclavian veins (which are just under your collarbone), where it re-enters the bloodstream.

A doctor may check for swollen lymph nodes in the neck, which are usually a sign that the body is fighting a cold, tonsillitis, ear infection, or throat infection.

If the swelling does not go away within a week, a doctor may want to investigate further.

DID YOU KNOW? An adult's body usually makes around 2 liters (0.5 US gallons)—more than 8 cups—of lymph fluid.

147

Allergies

Not all foreign substances that enter the body are harmful. Sometimes, the immune system overreacts to a harmless invader, known as an allergen, such as pollen or particular foods. This overreaction is called an allergic reaction.

An autoinjector "pen" delivers a dose of adrenaline (also called epinephrine) if someone is exposed to an allergen.

Having a Reaction

People may be born with an allergy to a substance or they may develop one due to factors in their environment that make their immune system oversensitive, such as air pollution from cars. The first step in an allergic reaction is when the allergen enters the body—through the nose, mouth, or eyes—or, in some cases, touches the skin. White blood cells release histamine, which causes swelling, itchy skin, red eyes, and a runny nose. In rare cases, so much histamine is released that it causes anaphylaxis. This dangerous condition affects the heartbeat and constricts the airways.

Food allergies—to foods such as peanuts, eggs, and milk—are among the most common allergies in children.

Treatment for Allergies

An allergic reaction can be eased with an antihistamine medication, which stops the body responding to histamine. Anaphylaxis can be treated with an immediate injection of the hormone adrenaline, which opens the airways and maintains heartbeat. Specialist doctors can treat some allergies—such as hay fever, insect bites, and dust mites—using allergen immunotherapy, which gradually exposes people to larger amounts of the allergen.

Some people react to breathing in the droppings of dust mites, relatives of spiders just 0.2 mm (0.008 in) long, which live among house dust.

Hay fever is caused by an allergy to plant pollen. At certain times of year, the air holds many tiny grains of pollen, which are produced by the male parts of flowering plants, then blown to other plants so they can produce seeds.

148

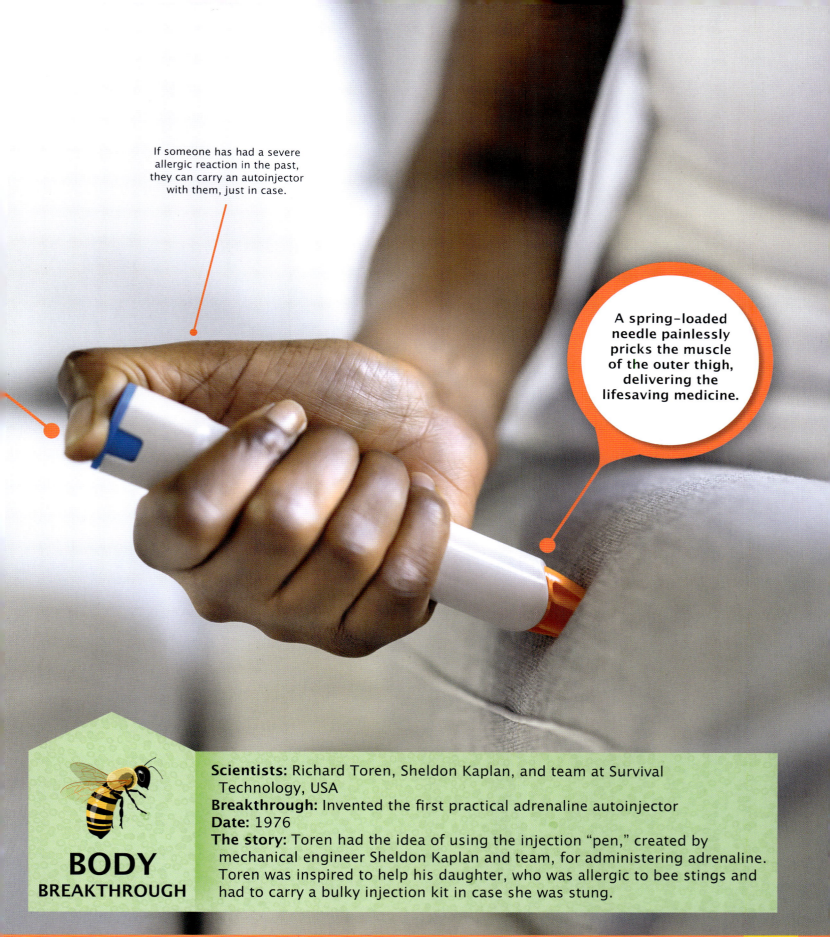

If someone has had a severe allergic reaction in the past, they can carry an autoinjector with them, just in case.

A spring-loaded needle painlessly pricks the muscle of the outer thigh, delivering the lifesaving medicine.

BODY BREAKTHROUGH

Scientists: Richard Toren, Sheldon Kaplan, and team at Survival Technology, USA
Breakthrough: Invented the first practical adrenaline autoinjector
Date: 1976
The story: Toren had the idea of using the injection "pen," created by mechanical engineer Sheldon Kaplan and team, for administering adrenaline. Toren was inspired to help his daughter, who was allergic to bee stings and had to carry a bulky injection kit in case she was stung.

DID YOU KNOW? Breathing in allergens may worsen asthma, which is a common lung condition that causes swelling of the airways, making breathing more difficult.

Suffering the Symptoms

When you catch a cold or develop the flu, you begin to feel uncomfortable in various ways. Yet, unpleasant as these symptoms are, they are usually signs that your immune system is acting to get rid of the virus.

You often sweat during a fever, to make sure that your body does not get too hot.

Symptoms of a Cold

A cold—caused by one of 200 viruses infecting the lining of the nose, throat, sinuses, and larynx (voicebox)—makes your nose stuffed up or runny. This is because you are making extra mucus to flush out the infection. Your joints and muscles may begin to ache. This is a sign that your immune system is releasing lots of white blood cells, as well as chemicals called interleukins that carry messages between them. This activity causes inflammation and leaves you feeling achy.

Rhinoviruses are the most common group of viruses to infect humans. They are the most likely causes of a cold.

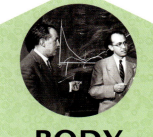

BODY BREAKTHROUGH

Scientists: Thomas Francis (left) and Jonas Salk
Breakthrough: Developed the first influenza vaccine
Date: 1945
The story: The first vaccination (see page 234) against flu viruses was developed by Francis and Salk, who were virologists (experts in viruses) at the University of Michigan. The vaccine was tested on the US Army, then offered to the public from 1945.

DID YOU KNOW? Caused by an influenza virus, the flu may have symptoms including fever, tiredness, runny nose, sore throat, coughing, muscle aches, headache, and vomiting.

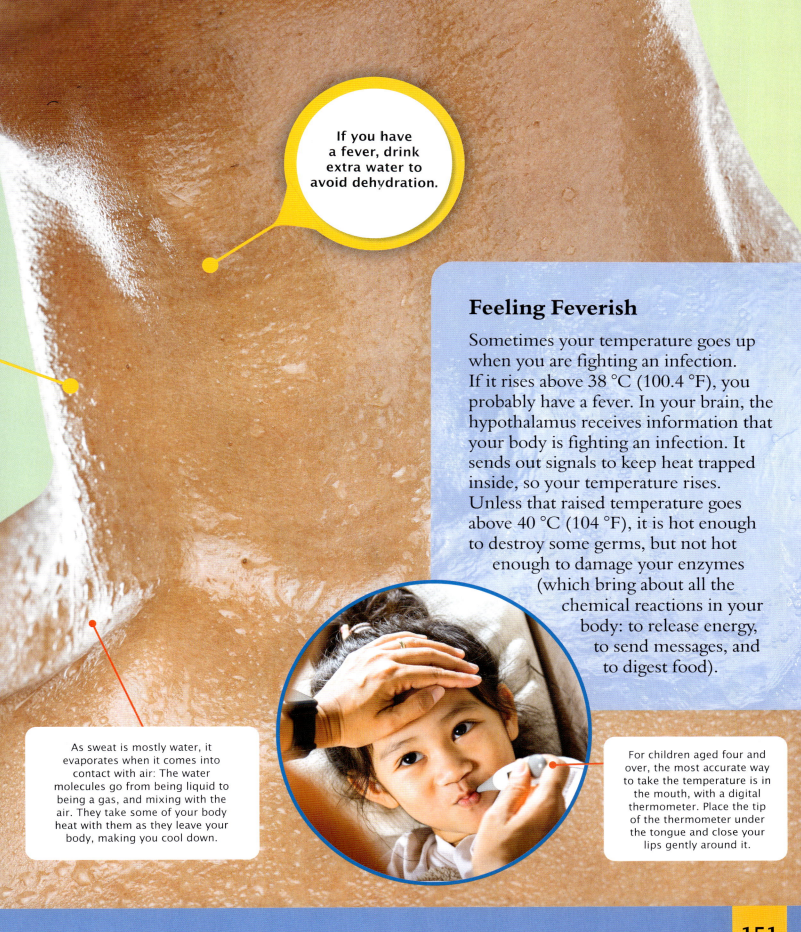

If you have a fever, drink extra water to avoid dehydration.

Feeling Feverish

Sometimes your temperature goes up when you are fighting an infection. If it rises above 38 °C (100.4 °F), you probably have a fever. In your brain, the hypothalamus receives information that your body is fighting an infection. It sends out signals to keep heat trapped inside, so your temperature rises. Unless that raised temperature goes above 40 °C (104 °F), it is hot enough to destroy some germs, but not hot enough to damage your enzymes (which bring about all the chemical reactions in your body: to release energy, to send messages, and to digest food).

As sweat is mostly water, it evaporates when it comes into contact with air: The water molecules go from being liquid to being a gas, and mixing with the air. They take some of your body heat with them as they leave your body, making you cool down.

For children aged four and over, the most accurate way to take the temperature is in the mouth, with a digital thermometer. Place the tip of the thermometer under the tongue and close your lips gently around it.

Body Repairs

Our body has an amazing ability to heal itself after it has been damaged. Wounds and broken bones repair themselves in anything from days to weeks. We can even grow new tissue for our organs, thanks to the astonishing properties of stem cells.

This white line on the X-ray shows where the fracture was. Now it has healed.

Clots and Scabs

When an injury breaks the skin, we bleed—and that blood helps us heal. Tiny cells called platelets (see page 88) stick to the damaged tissue and cling together, slowing the flow of blood. At the same time, the wound releases chemicals that make blood thicken around the platelets and form a scab, which stops germs getting inside the body. However, if you get a deep cut, you might need stitching up by a doctor or nurse. Most modern stitches dissolve once they have done their job.

Scabs start to form less than 10 seconds after you cut yourself.

This X-ray image of a ten-year-old child's wrist and lower arm bones was taken three weeks after the bone was broken.

Fractured bone will try to heal in whatever position it ends up. The doctors made sure that the ends of the bone were lined up, then placed the child's arm in a rigid cast and supportive sling while it healed.

BODY BREAKTHROUGH

Scientists: James Till and Ernest McCulloch
Discovery: Stem cells
Date: 1963
The story: In their experiments on mouse bone marrow, Till and McCulloch came up with some of the first evidence of stem cells—cells that can form many types of tissue. Today we use stem cells in regenerative medicine.

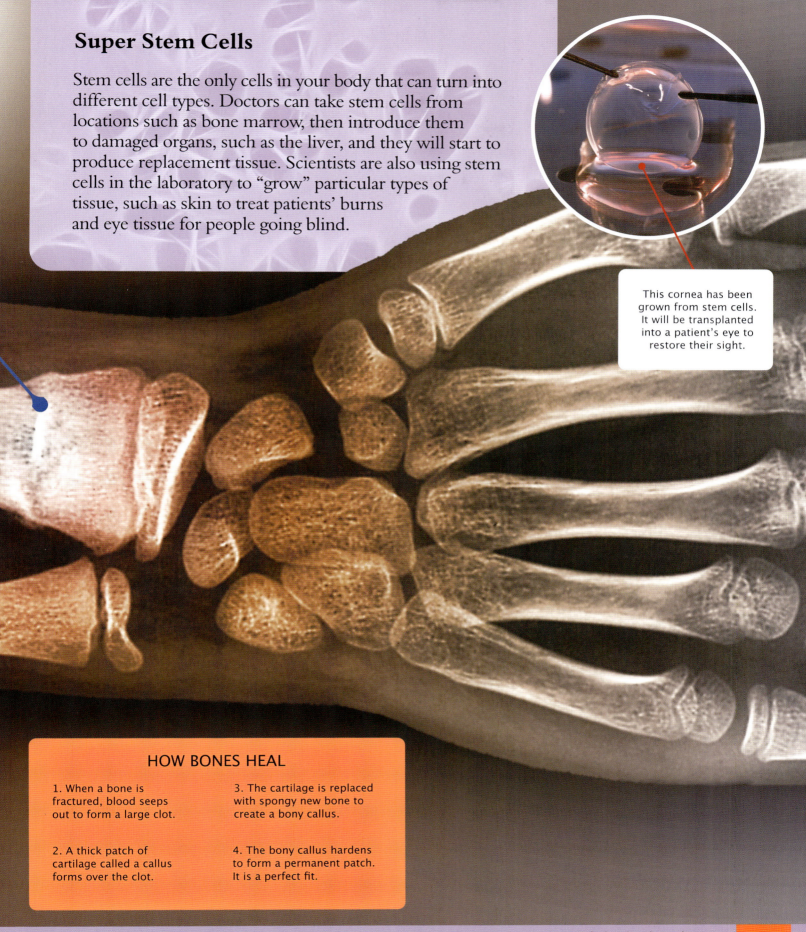

Super Stem Cells

Stem cells are the only cells in your body that can turn into different cell types. Doctors can take stem cells from locations such as bone marrow, then introduce them to damaged organs, such as the liver, and they will start to produce replacement tissue. Scientists are also using stem cells in the laboratory to "grow" particular types of tissue, such as skin to treat patients' burns and eye tissue for people going blind.

This cornea has been grown from stem cells. It will be transplanted into a patient's eye to restore their sight.

HOW BONES HEAL

1. When a bone is fractured, blood seeps out to form a large clot.

2. A thick patch of cartilage called a callus forms over the clot.

3. The cartilage is replaced with spongy new bone to create a bony callus.

4. The bony callus hardens to form a permanent patch. It is a perfect fit.

DID YOU KNOW? The tongue and mouth lining are the fastest-healing parts of the body—they can heal from minor damage in just hours.

Chapter 6

Brain and Senses

Like the conductor of an orchestra, your brain is making decisions and guiding you all the time. Different areas of your brain concentrate on special jobs. Some of those jobs need quick action, like telling your body which muscles to use when you are running or swimming. Others, like doing your homework, take more time.

The Brain

Your brain is responsible for your conscious thoughts: It enables you to think, talk, move, learn, and remember. But without you being conscious of its work, your brain is also constantly receiving messages from other organs and the senses, and then sending out commands to keep your body safe and well. Your brain relies on your senses to give it information about the world around you. Your senses are like scouts, constantly sending reports back to headquarters. What you see, hear, taste, smell, and touch helps your brain decide how to guide you—and what to remember.

The outer portion of the brain, called the cerebral cortex, is where most of your conscious thinking happens.

DID YOU KNOW? Neurons range in length from 0.0004 cm (0.00016 in) for most neurons in the brain to 1 m (3.3 ft) for a neuron that runs from the toe to the end of the spinal cord.

The Nervous System

Your brain, spinal cord, and nerves make up your nervous system. The nerves and spinal cord link the brain to other parts of your body. The nervous system is like a network of busy roads, with traffic constantly going both ways. Your senses and organs send information along nerves to your brain. Your brain uses the nervous system to send messages to your muscles and organs.

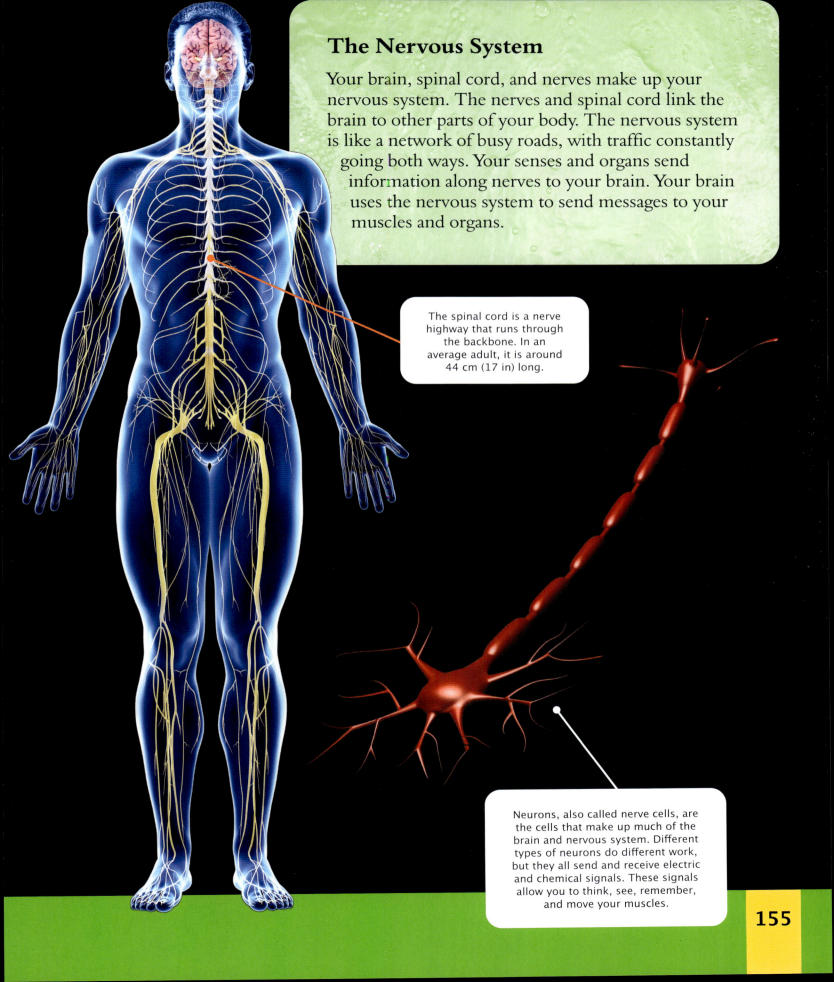

The spinal cord is a nerve highway that runs through the backbone. In an average adult, it is around 44 cm (17 in) long.

Neurons, also called nerve cells, are the cells that make up much of the brain and nervous system. Different types of neurons do different work, but they all send and receive electric and chemical signals. These signals allow you to think, see, remember, and move your muscles.

In Control

The brain controls your body and your mind. An adult brain weighs around 1.4 kg (3 lb), and contains 100 billion neurons. Each neuron can have thousands of connections with other neurons. This makes the brain one of the most complex structures that we know of in the universe.

Wired Up

The brain receives signals from every part of the body, and sends signals back that tell the body what to do. These "messages" ping through the brainstem, along the spinal cord, spreading out into the body.

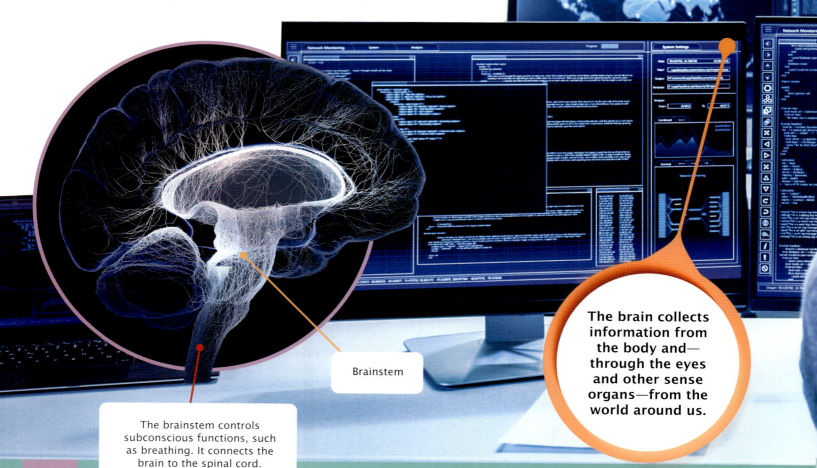

The eight bones that make up the skull surround and defend the delicate brain.

Brainstem

The brainstem controls subconscious functions, such as breathing. It connects the brain to the spinal cord.

The brain collects information from the body and—through the eyes and other sense organs—from the world around us.

BODY BREAKTHROUGH

Scientist: Thomas Willis
Breakthrough: Made a map of the brain
Date: 1664
The story: Thomas Willis, an academic and doctor in Oxford, England, published a book with more than 200 diagrams of the structure of the brain. It was the first book to use the word "neurology," meaning the science of the nervous system. Willis's names for different areas of the brain are still used today.

Protective Layers

The brain does not touch the skull. It floats in cerebrospinal fluid, a liquid that is rich in oxygen from the bloodstream. Three bag-like membranes hold and cushion the brain—the dura mater, arachnoid mater, and pia mater.

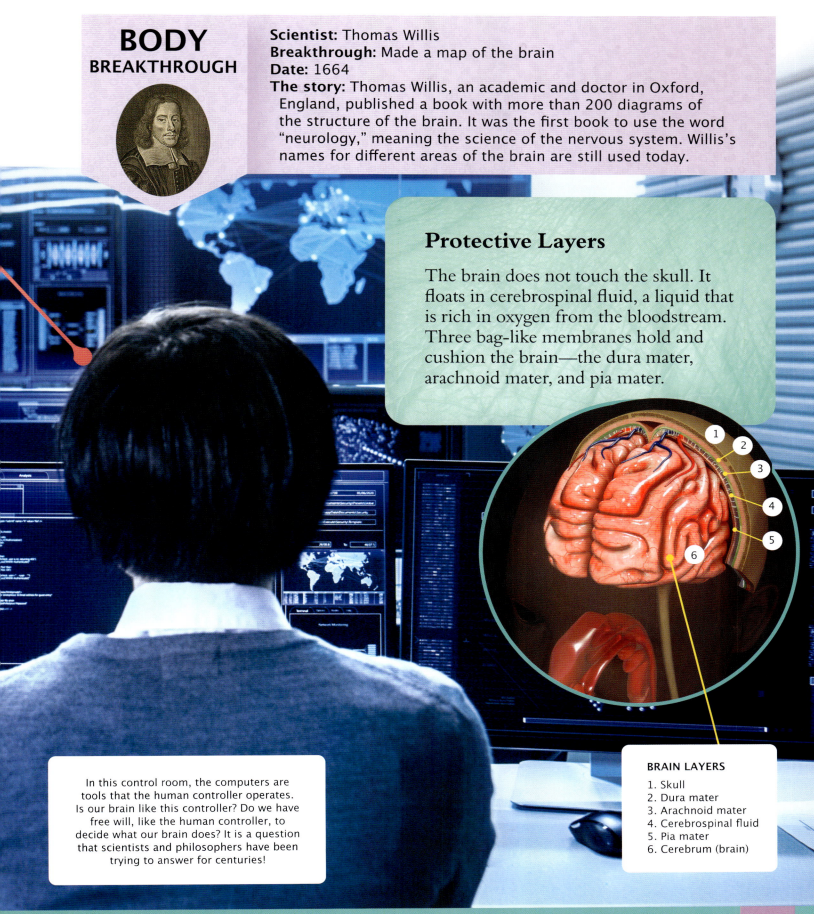

BRAIN LAYERS
1. Skull
2. Dura mater
3. Arachnoid mater
4. Cerebrospinal fluid
5. Pia mater
6. Cerebrum (brain)

In this control room, the computers are tools that the human controller operates. Is our brain like this controller? Do we have free will, like the human controller, to decide what our brain does? It is a question that scientists and philosophers have been trying to answer for centuries!

DID YOU KNOW? Just 2 percent of our body weight, the brain consumes more than 20 percent of our energy needs!

157

Consciousness

The building blocks of the human brain are similar to those of other animals. But we are different from most other animals, as we have "consciousness." Consciousness is your awareness of your thoughts, memories, and feelings. We could say that consciousness is self-awareness—or the way we notice ourselves experiencing an experience!

This performer's drawn-on frown is a symbol. Our ability to use symbols is part of being conscious.

Consciousness and the Brain

Some scientists believe that understanding how the brain works will answer all the questions we have about how consciousness is made. They can now map which parts of the brain are used for different types of conscious activity (see pages 168–169). Yet British neuroscientist Anil Seth says that the ultimate question about consciousness is why a particular brain activity results in a particular conscious experience—rather than just figuring out that it does.

Nature and Nurture

Consciousness functions only when the brain is working, so it depends on the brain we are born with ("nature"). Outside influences ("nurture"), such as diet and learning, also affect how the brain develops. This means that consciousness is built from a mix of nature and nurture.

Some people believe our consciousness is part of a spiritual force that exists beyond us. We might use meditation or other rituals to connect to this spiritual force.

Having consciousness lets us overcome our natural fears, so we can enjoy the thrill of activities such as skydiving.

Part of self-awareness is knowing that we are looking at ourself when we see our reflection in the mirror.

158

BODY
BREAKTHROUGH

Scientist: Melanie Klein
Breakthrough: Play therapy
Date: 1932
The story: Melanie Klein was trained by fellow Austrian Sigmund Freud, founder of psychoanalysis. Psychoanalysts treat mental illness by finding the fears that lurk in a patient's unconscious mind. Children are too young for the usual "talking therapy," so Klein developed play therapy, a method still used to help children make sense of how they feel, think, and behave.

Humans love storytelling. Our minds organize information into stories, in which one event causes the next.

DID YOU KNOW? Humans, great apes, dolphins, magpies, and a few other animals can pass the mirror test, which is recognizing that the animal reflected in a mirror is yourself.

Inside the Brain

The brain has three main parts: cerebrum, cerebellum, and brainstem. The outer, and largest, part of the brain is the cerebrum. The cerebrum's deeply wrinkled surface, called the cerebral cortex, is where most of your conscious thinking takes place. It is divided into left and right halves, known as hemispheres, which are connected to each other by a bundle of nerves called the corpus callosum.

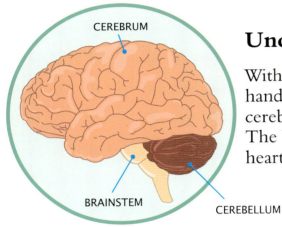

Unconscious Activities

Without you noticing, your cerebellum and brainstem handle much of your brain's unconscious work. The cerebellum helps with coordinating your movements. The brainstem controls your vital functions, such as heartbeat and breathing.

1. Thalamus
2. Cingulate gyrus
3. Corpus callosum
4. Basal ganglia
5. Hypothalamus
6. Amygdala
7. Hippocampus

Limbic System

The limbic system is a group of structures—including the thalamus, amygdala, hypothalamus, and hippocampus—beneath the surface of the cerebrum. The structures are involved with emotion, learning, and memory.

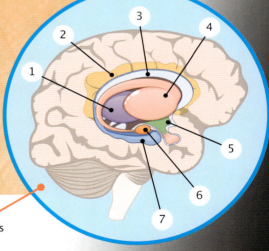

The basal ganglia help with learning, while the cingulate gyrus is involved with motivations.

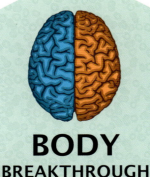

BODY BREAKTHROUGH

Scientist: Roger Sperry
Breakthrough: Carried out split brain experiments
Date: 1981
The story: Some sufferers of epilepsy, a disease that causes dangerous seizures, are cured by surgery that cuts the corpus callosum between the left and right brain. American brain scientist Roger Sperry invited patients who had this surgery to take part in research. He identified "gaps" in their thinking that revealed how the brain's halves work.

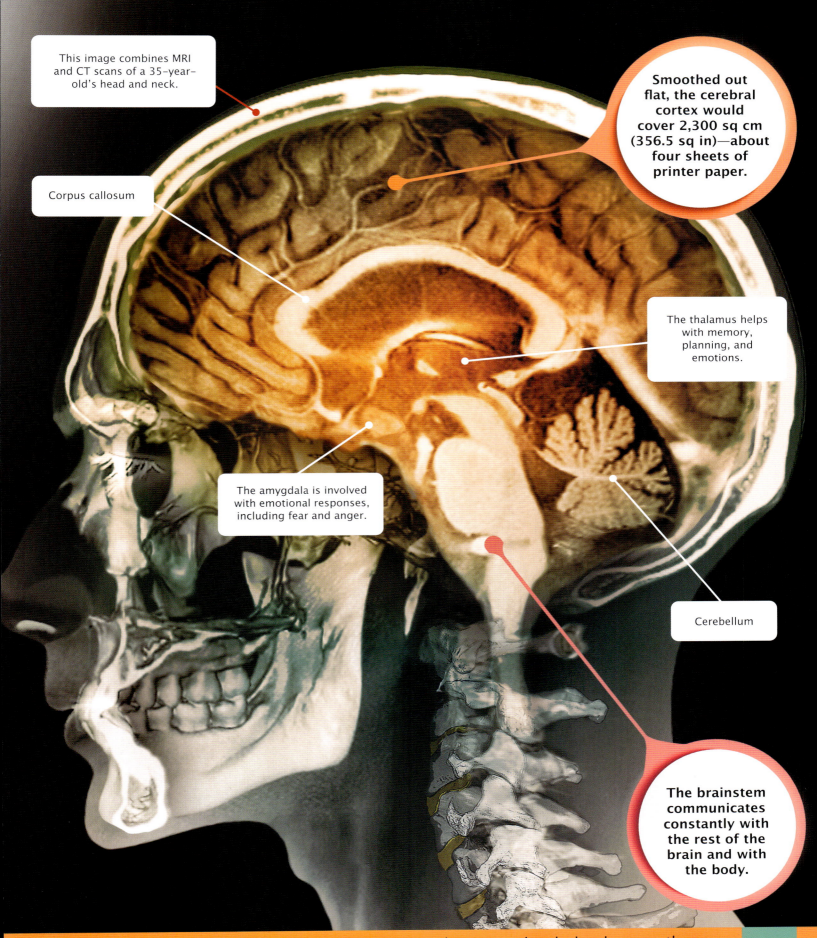

This image combines MRI and CT scans of a 35-year-old's head and neck.

Smoothed out flat, the cerebral cortex would cover 2,300 sq cm (356.5 sq in)—about four sheets of printer paper.

Corpus callosum

The thalamus helps with memory, planning, and emotions.

The amygdala is involved with emotional responses, including fear and anger.

Cerebellum

The brainstem communicates constantly with the rest of the brain and with the body.

DID YOU KNOW? The brain has no pain receptor nerves, but we get headaches because the surrounding tissue—the dura and pia mater—does.

161

Mapping the Brain

Over the last 50 years, we have invented tools to map the living brain. We can now scan and create computer images of brain activity as the brain's owner is thinking and talking. Together with insights from observing animals, these new technologies give us a more detailed understanding of brain function.

Senses and Sensibilities

We have detailed maps of the parts of the brain that handle sense data from the eyes, ears, nose, tongue, and the sensors in our bodies. It is harder to pin down the parts that we use to think—our consciousness.

Different areas of the cerebral cortex detect data—sensory (green) or motor (movement; red and pink). The association areas (purple) make sense of all the data.

This "slice" shows the middle of the brain—the area that is linked to forming memories.

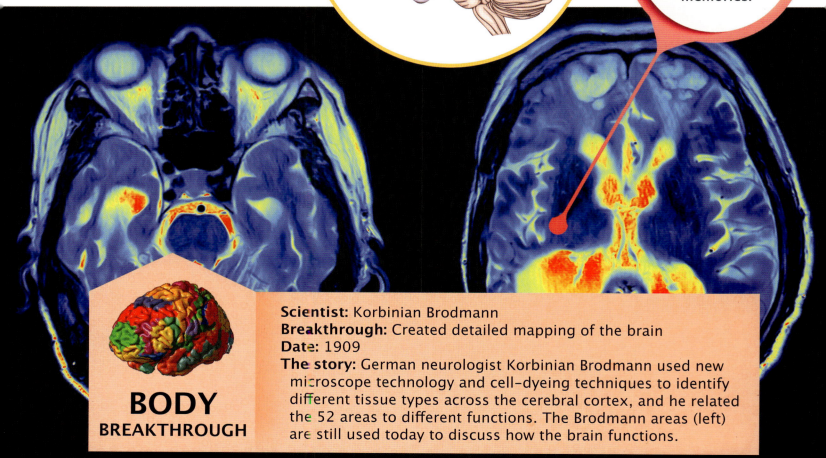

BODY BREAKTHROUGH

Scientist: Korbinian Brodmann
Breakthrough: Created detailed mapping of the brain
Date: 1909
The story: German neurologist Korbinian Brodmann used new microscope technology and cell-dyeing techniques to identify different tissue types across the cerebral cortex, and he related the 52 areas to different functions. The Brodmann areas (left) are still used today to discuss how the brain functions.

DID YOU KNOW? Neurosurgeons use 3D coordinates, called Talairach coordinates, to pinpoint a particular location on their map of the brain.

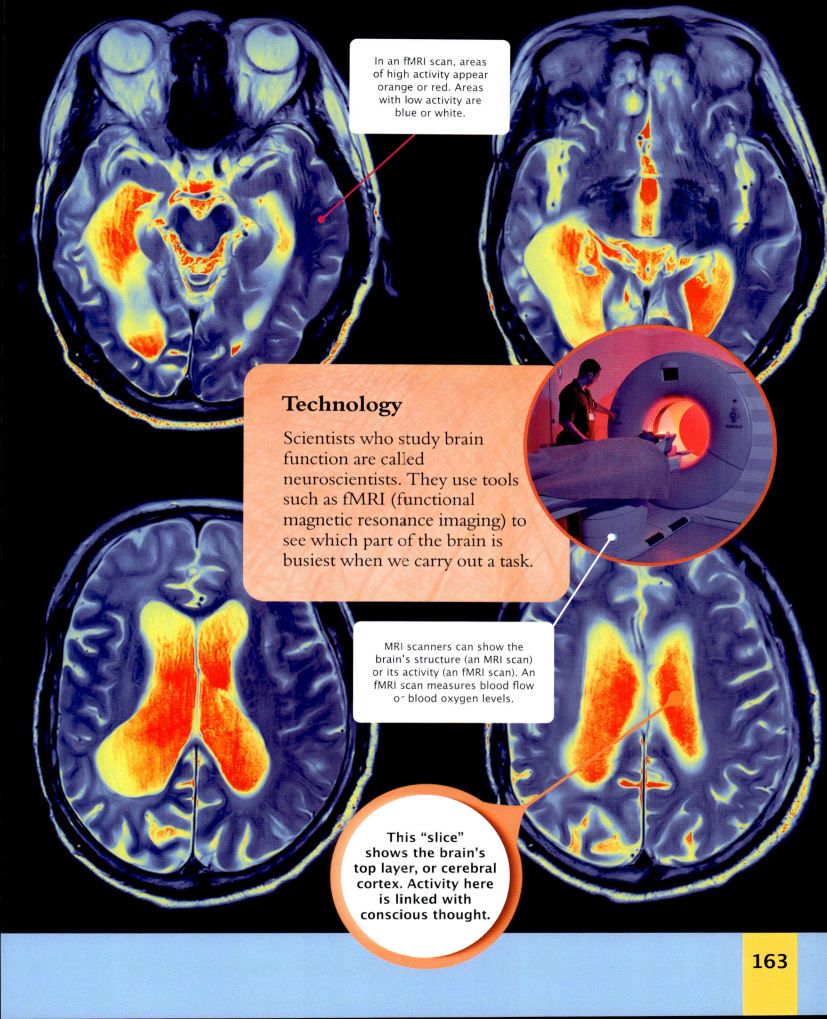

In an fMRI scan, areas of high activity appear orange or red. Areas with low activity are blue or white.

Technology

Scientists who study brain function are called neuroscientists. They use tools such as fMRI (functional magnetic resonance imaging) to see which part of the brain is busiest when we carry out a task.

MRI scanners can show the brain's structure (an MRI scan) or its activity (an fMRI scan). An fMRI scan measures blood flow or blood oxygen levels.

This "slice" shows the brain's top layer, or cerebral cortex. Activity here is linked with conscious thought.

163

Brain Cells

There are two main types of brain cells: neurons (also called nerve cells) and glial cells. Neurons pass on signals to each other, sending messages and creating thoughts. Glial cells give support and nutrients to neurons.

> Sensors in this cap detect electrical activity in the cerebral cortex. They are being used to produce an EEG—a recording of brain activity.

Sending Signals

When a neuron receives a signal, an electrical signal travels down its long fiber, called an axon, heading for the next neurons in the network. Yet neurons do not actually touch each other: Signals are sent across tiny gaps called synapses. At a synapse, the electrical signal is turned into a chemical called a neurotransmitter, which is received by receptors on the next neuron, which turns the signal back into an electrical one.

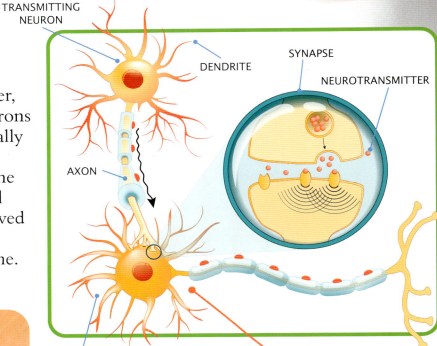

Short branching extensions of the neuron, called dendrites, receive the signal from the transmitting neuron.

Glial Cells

The different types of glial cells include astrocytes, oligodendrocytes, and microglia. Astrocytes help to control blood flow through the brain. Oligodendrocytes wrap the axons of neurons in a fatty substance called myelin, which insulates them so that electrical signals travel more quickly. Microglia destroy damaged neurons and invaders such as bacteria.

> Neurons fire in patterns of electrical activity, called microstates.

> In this micrograph of the cerebellum, neurons are stained green, while glial cells are red.

164

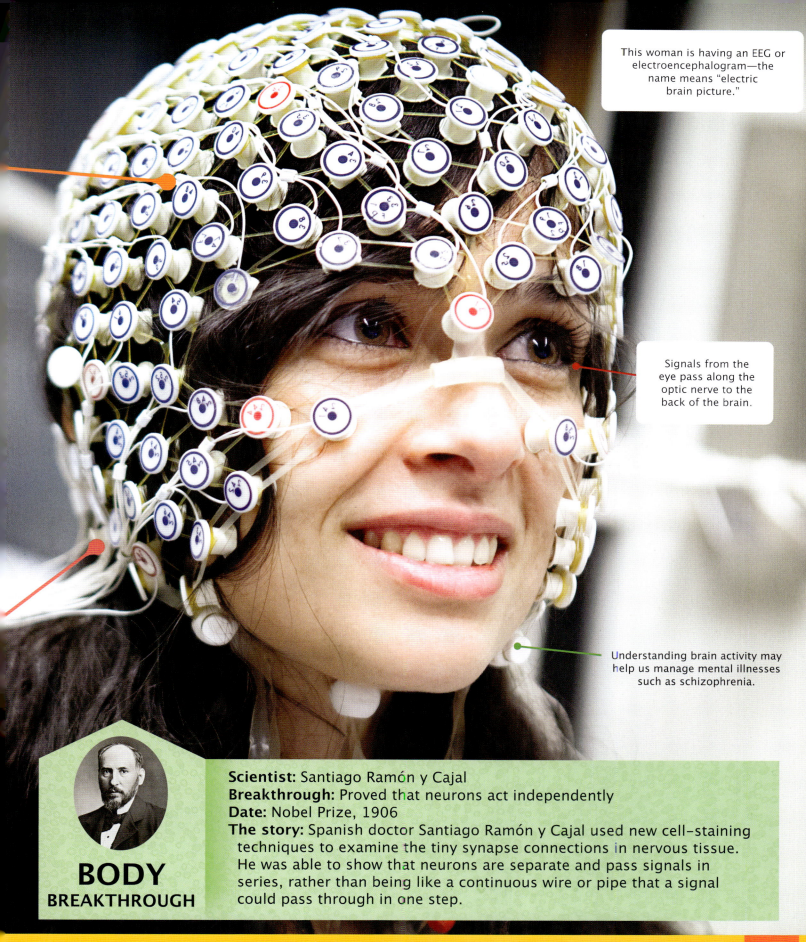

This woman is having an EEG or electroencephalogram—the name means "electric brain picture."

Signals from the eye pass along the optic nerve to the back of the brain.

Understanding brain activity may help us manage mental illnesses such as schizophrenia.

BODY BREAKTHROUGH

Scientist: Santiago Ramón y Cajal
Breakthrough: Proved that neurons act independently
Date: Nobel Prize, 1906
The story: Spanish doctor Santiago Ramón y Cajal used new cell-staining techniques to examine the tiny synapse connections in nervous tissue. He was able to show that neurons are separate and pass signals in series, rather than being like a continuous wire or pipe that a signal could pass through in one step.

DID YOU KNOW? Each neuron in your brain can connect with 2,000 to 11,000 other neurons and can send 1,000 signals per second.

165

Cerebrum

The cerebrum (which means "brain" in Latin) is what makes you into a unique one-and-only you. It is where you think, make decisions, and store memories.

When you are studying, several areas of the cerebrum are working hard.

Cerebral Cortex

The wrinkled surface layer of the cerebrum, around 3 mm (0.12 in) thick, is called the cerebral cortex. This is where most of your higher-level processes take place (see page 168). The cerebral cortex is made of what is often called gray matter because of its shade. Gray matter is largely composed of the bodies of neurons and tiny blood vessels.

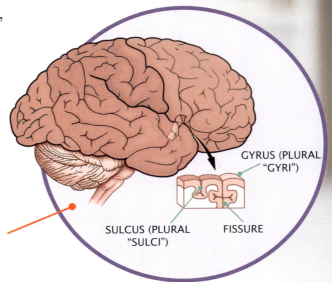

GYRUS (PLURAL "GYRI")
SULCUS (PLURAL "SULCI")
FISSURE

Over millions of years, as our distant ancestors became more intelligent, the cerebral cortex became folded to give it more surface area. Some of the folds run deep into the brain, forming fissures. The largest is the medial longitudinal fissure, which divides the cerebrum into two hemispheres. Ridges are called gyri, while valleys are called sulci.

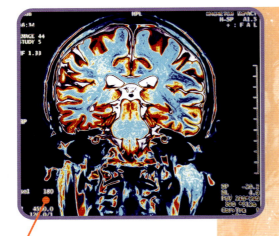

This magnetic resonance imaging (MRI) scan shows the brain from the front. Gray matter is shown in orange, while white matter is in blue.

Beneath the Surface

Below its surface, the cerebrum is made of white matter: glial cells and the axons of neurons, which carry signals from one part of the brain to another. In this region are limbic system structures concerned with emotion and memory, such as the hippocampus (see page 176) and basal ganglia (see page 160). These structures receive information from the rest of the nervous system, make adjustments, and then pass it on to other areas of the brain.

DID YOU KNOW? The cerebrum is by far the heaviest part of your brain, accounting for nearly 90 percent of its weight.

BODY BREAKTHROUGH

Scientist: Alcmaeon of Croton
Breakthrough: Realized that the brain is the home of intelligence
Date: 5th century BCE
The story: The ancient Greek thinker and scientist Alcmaeon of Croton was the first to write that the brain is the organ of the mind. Earlier scientists (as well as many later scientists) thought that the heart was the home of intelligence.

The cerebral cortex controls reasoning and understanding language, while the hippocampus helps with memorizing.

When you write, you are using the cerebral cortex (for sight, producing language, and commanding movement) and the basal ganglia (for keeping you motivated).

167

Lobes

Each hemisphere of the cerebral cortex is divided into four lobes, or regions, by fissures. Although activities, from talking to dancing, involve several different parts of the brain, scientists have discovered that the four lobes are related to specific functions. They have also discovered that portions of each lobe are focussed on particular activities.

The frontal lobe is involved with complex thinking, speech, and executing movements.

Frontal Lobe

The frontal lobe is the brain's largest lobe. Its prefrontal cortex is involved with important skills, such as planning, reasoning, creativity, controlling emotions, and getting along with other people. The lobe's premotor cortex helps with planning movements, while the primary motor cortex helps to make those movements skilled. The Broca's area coordinates the mouth movements used in speech.

- PREMOTOR CORTEX
- PRIMARY MOTOR CORTEX
- BROCA'S AREA
- PREFRONTAL CORTEX

Temporal Lobe

This lobe's primary auditory cortex receives signals from your ears, then its auditory association area helps you identify whether you are hearing speech, music, traffic, or birdsong. The sensory speech area helps you understand what people are saying. The lobe's olfactory cortex identifies smells.

- PRIMARY AUDITORY CORTEX
- SENSORY SPEECH AREA
- OLFACTORY CORTEX
- AUDITORY ASSOCIATION AREA

The temporal lobe processes signals from the ears and nose.

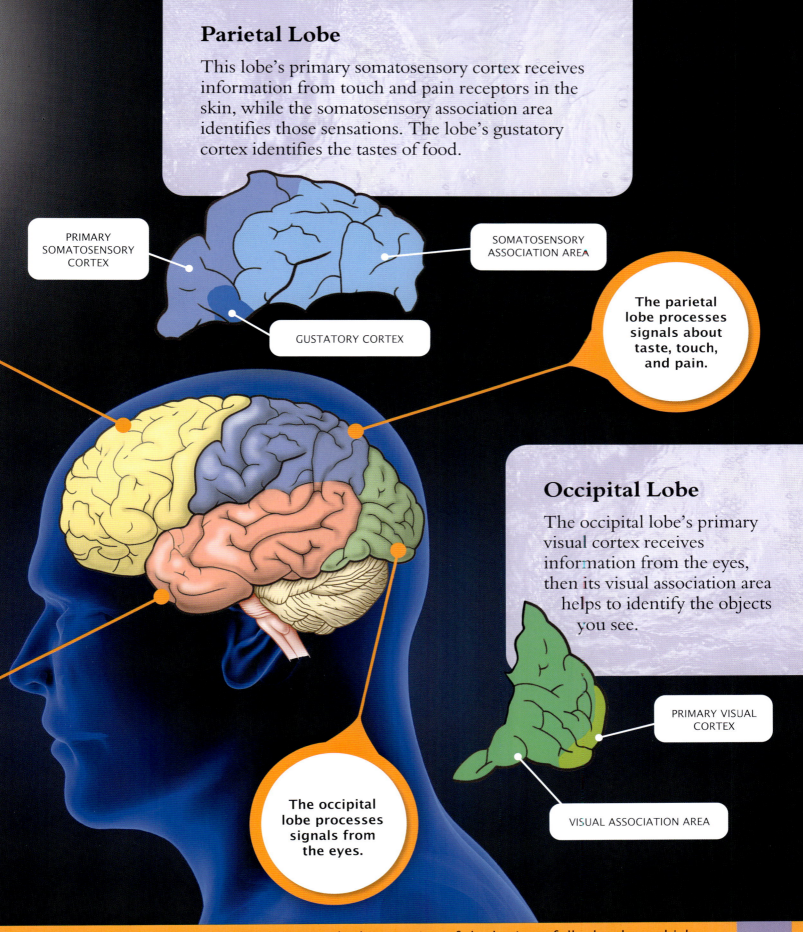

Corpus Callosum

The corpus callosum is a bundle of nerves that links the left and right halves, or hemispheres, of the cerebrum. Each hemisphere has its own four lobes and underlying structures. The corpus callosum enables the two halves to work together.

> In only 10 percent of people, the right hemisphere is dominant, which makes them lefthanded.

Divided in Two

Neuroscientists think the cerebrum is in halves so the hemispheres can specialize in separate processes, but—with the help of the corpus callosum—work together to carry out tasks. The lobes of each hemisphere are not quite mirror images of each other in shape and size (the left hemisphere is larger at the back) and the two hemispheres also have differences in function.

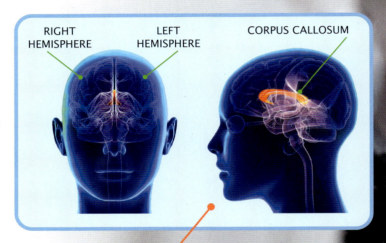

The corpus callosum is a structure found only in humans and other mammals, such as apes and dogs.

Signals travel along the corpus callosum to share information between the two hemispheres, enabling you to run using both sides of your body.

Left or Right

The left hemisphere of the cerebrum controls the movement of the right side of your body, while receiving information from the right ear and right visual field (the right half of what both eyes see). The right hemisphere controls the left side of the body and gets information from the left ear and left visual field. When it comes to thinking, some aspects are handled more by one hemisphere than the other, but both usually do all tasks. Some neuroscientists think the left hemisphere is more practical, while the right side is more creative.

170

Your left hemisphere often focuses on overseeing practical tasks, such as chores.

If the right brain hemisphere is dominant, it makes a person more skilled at performing tasks with their left hand. Only around 1 percent of people are naturally ambidextrous, which means they are equally skilled at using both hands.

BODY BREAKTHROUGH

Scientists: Charlotte Faurie and Michel Raymond at the University of Montpellier, France
Breakthrough: Discovered that the likelihood of lefthandedness is constant
Date: 2004
The story: When studying prehistoric cave paintings made by blowing paint over one hand through a pipe held in the other hand, Faurie and Raymond noted that the rate of lefthandedness was the same 30,000 years ago. They concluded that having right- and lefthanded people in a population is a benefit, as it lets tasks be shared helpfully.

DID YOU KNOW? Around 10 cm (4 in) long, the corpus callosum is made of the axons of around 250 million neurons.

Cerebellum

Located at the back of the brain, the cerebellum has an important role in smoothing and coordinating your conscious movements, from walking to throwing a ball. If someone's cerebellum is damaged, they may move clumsily or unsteadily.

Gymnast Laura Casabuena's cerebellum is very active to coordinate her movements.

Coordinating Movements

The cerebellum does not initiate movement, which is the job of the cerebrum. However, the cerebellum works on the coordination and accuracy of movements. To do its work, the cerebellum receives information direct from the spinal cord about the position of the body and limbs, while also getting information from the cerebrum and brainstem. The cerebellum processes these inputs to fine-tune your conscious movements.

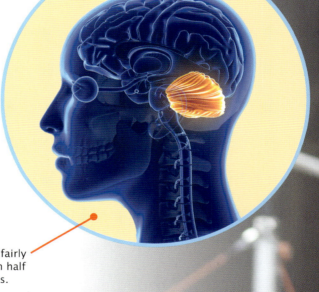

Although the cerebellum is fairly small, it contains more than half of all the brain's neurons.

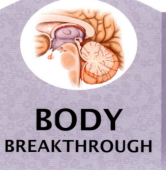

BODY BREAKTHROUGH

Scientists: Birgitte Bo Andersen, Hans Jorgen Gunderson, and Bente Pakkenberg
Breakthrough: Discovered that the cerebellum shrinks with age
Date: 2003
The story: These Danish neuroscientists discovered that the cerebellum loses, on average, around 16 percent of its volume with age. This may partly account for difficulties with balance and movement in some elderly people.

DID YOU KNOW? The right side of the cerebellum controls the right side of your body, by communicating with the cerebrum's left hemisphere.

The cerebellum helps all the skeletal muscles work together.

Signals are also being sent from the cerebellum to the eye muscles, ensuring that her eyes adjust their focus as she moves.

Learning to Walk

The cerebellum also plays a part in learning to perform movements. It is very active when a child is starting to walk, when you are learning a new sport, or when you adjust all your movements as you grow taller.

When learning a new physical skill, you move clumsily until the cerebellum adjusts its commands.

Brainstem

Positioned at the top of the spinal cord, the brainstem is a busy nerve junction, through which pass all signals from and to the brain. The brainstem is truly the core of your brain—it regulates your body's vital processes and your awareness.

Controlling the Essentials

The brainstem regulates your breathing and heartbeat, ensuring that both continue constantly, changing speed when you are exercising. This region also regulates other actions that you do not consciously control, such as sneezing (to expel irritants in the nose), coughing (to expel irritants from the airways), vomiting (to expel harmful substances from the stomach), and swallowing. It tells your saliva glands to produce saliva when you see food or start to eat.

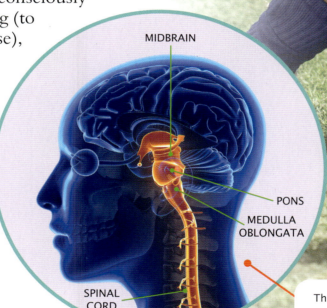

The brainstem is in three main parts: midbrain, pons, and medulla oblongata.

BODY BREAKTHROUGH

Scientists: Massachusetts General Hospital and Boston Children's Hospital, USA
Breakthrough: Mapped brain consciousness
Date: 2024
The story: Using high-resolution imaging, the team mapped a network of neuron pathways, connecting the brainstem and cerebrum, which maintains wakefulness and awareness. This knowledge will help treat conditions such as coma, which is a deep state of unconsciousness usually caused by injury.

The brainstem controls your response to pain, enabling you to bear low levels of it.

The middle portion of your brainstem, called the pons, coordinates your facial expressions, as several cranial nerves—nerves that run from the brain to the face—start here.

Signals to the facial muscles travel through the brainstem, from the cerebrum and cerebellum.

Staying Alert

The brainstem communicates with the hypothalamus (see page 182) to regulate your sleep and your wakefulness. When you are awake and healthy, the brainstem keeps you alert to your surroundings.

The midbrain portion of the brainstem is responsible for your alertness.

DID YOU KNOW? Your brainstem sends signals to adjust the size of your pupil (the black hole at the front of your eye) to adapt to lighting changes.

Memory

Memory is your brain's ability to store information—and then find it again. Without memory, you would not be able to speak, have friendships, or know who you are. A new memory is created by neurons connecting with each other in a new formation.

When you learn a new skill, new connections between neurons are formed.

Store or Lose

Your brain does not remember everything! Most information with no long-term use is never stored. Instead, it is kept at hand for up to a minute in the "working memory," which is in the prefrontal lobe of the cerebral cortex. The hippocampus is responsible for moving information from the working memory to long-term memory. After processing information, the hippocampus either dismisses it or sends it for storage by neurons in different areas of the brain.

While the working memory is essential, it is also quite small, which is why you can remember a five-digit security code while you are entering it, but not a ten-digit one.

Getting Emotional

The more emotional you are about an event—joyful, sad, or fearful—the more likely it is to be stored for ever. Close to the hippocampus is the amygdala, which is responsible for many of your emotions—and also adds emotions to your memories. When it does so, the hippocampus is more likely to store the memory. A part of the brain that processes smells is also nearby, which is why a particular smell may always bring back memories of an event.

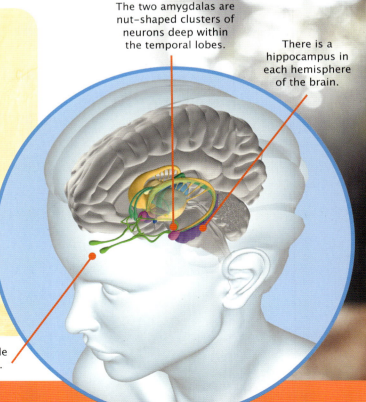

The two amygdalas are nut-shaped clusters of neurons deep within the temporal lobes.

There is a hippocampus in each hemisphere of the brain.

The olfactory bulbs are responsible for linking smells with memories.

176

BODY BREAKTHROUGH

Scientist: Eric Kandel
Breakthrough: Discovered how neurons store memories
Date: 1970
The story: While studying a seasnail with a simple nervous system, Kandel found that, as the snail learned, chemicals changed the structure of the connections between neurons. He discovered that short-term and long-term memories were formed by different chemicals.

The more you practice a skill, the stronger these neuron networks become.

Knowing how to ride a bike is an "unconscious" memory. These are skills (such as using a fork) and habits (such as that you eat lunch at midday). Unconscious memories are harder to lose than conscious ones (such as that Madrid is the capital of Spain).

DID YOU KNOW? Studies have shown that knowing you can access information on the internet makes your brain less likely to store it as a memory.

177

Emotions

From happiness to embarrassment, we feel emotions nearly every minute of every day. Emotions are born in a region at the heart of your brain called the limbic system.

What Are Emotions?

An emotion is usually triggered by an experience. As an emotion takes shape in your brain, various changes take place: in your thoughts, your decisions, your facial expression, your body posture and responses (such as tears or laughter), and even the hormones coursing through your bloodstream (see page 182). These changes are helped along by chemicals in the brain, called neurotransmitters, that encourage different patterns of activity.

Neurotransmitters such as serotonin and dopamine are active in the brain when we are happy, giving a feeling of well-being.

Information from the senses is passed to the limbic system.

By working with our memories, the hippocampus helps us to understand our emotions.

The amygdala processes information from the senses and starts to generate emotions.

The cingulate gyrus links our emotions with our actions, helping us to understand which actions (such as working hard) will lead to emotional rewards (such as pride).

The prefrontal cortex helps us to control and respond to our emotions.

BODY BREAKTHROUGH

Scientists: Laura Carstensen and colleagues
Breakthrough: Discovered how age changes emotions
Date: 1999
The story: By surveying 184 people aged 18 to 94, Carstensen and her colleagues found that, as people increase in age, their ability to regulate—or manage—their emotions also increases. Negative emotions reduced until around the age of 60, at which point the decline stopped.

DID YOU KNOW? Many universal emotions—such as sadness, anger, and relief—can be recognized across the world because of their characteristic facial expressions.

Sometimes sadness lasts for a long time, preventing us from enjoying life. Talking about emotions with family, friends, a teacher, or a healthcare professional is the first step to feeling better.

Why Do We Feel Emotions?

Neuroscientists think that we have evolved to feel emotions because they help with humankind's survival. Fear protects us from harm, while love encourages us to take care of each other. Often, emotions guide us toward behaving kindly, so we can escape the negative feeling of shame. Showing our sadness—particularly through tears—usually makes other people kind to us, just as we try to be kind when others need support.

When we are amused, we have a characteristic facial expression (a smile) and make other bodily responses, such as laughter.

Feeling amusement with friends helps us to bond, which encourages us to work together for everybody's benefit.

Sleep

Along with eating and drinking, sleep is one of your body's essential activities! The average person spends around 26 years of their life asleep. While you sleep, your brain and body rest and carry out essential chores.

Falling Asleep

When signals from the eyes tell the brain it is dark, the pineal gland produces the hormone melatonin, which makes you feel sleepy. As you drift off, your brainstem slows your heartbeat and breathing. Your major organs also slow their work, which leaves your body with more energy for its maintenance tasks. The brainstem and hypothalamus switch off some brain activity, so you are no longer aware of your surroundings.

While brain activity is quieter, the brain clears out toxins that have built up in its tissue.

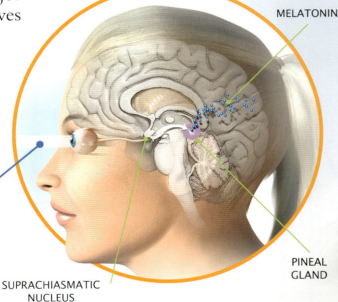

MELATONIN

PINEAL GLAND

SUPRACHIASMATIC NUCLEUS

A group of neurons in the hypothalamus, called the suprachiasmatic nucleus (SCN), controls the body's internal clock, which regulates sleep patterns. When the SCN receives signals that it is getting dark, it signals to the pineal gland to make melatonin.

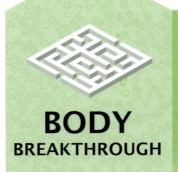

BODY BREAKTHROUGH

Scientists: Researchers from the University of Michigan Medical School, USA
Breakthrough: Discovered how lack of sleep affects memory
Date: 2024
The story: Researchers studied electrical activity in the hippocampus (which stores and finds memories) of rats that explored mazes over the course of several days. Rats with disrupted sleep had weaker hippocampus activity as they tried to remember mazes than rats with plenty of sleep. None of the rats was harmed by the experiment.

DID YOU KNOW? Adults need at least 7 hours' sleep a night, teens need 8 to 10 hours, and school-age children need 9 to 12 hours.

Dreaming

The pons portion of the brainstem kickstarts the periods of sleep in which you dream, known as rapid eye movement (REM) sleep because your eyes tend to move beneath your closed eyelids. You have three to five REM periods during each night's sleep, each one lasting up to an hour, whether or not you remember your dreams when you wake. Neuroscientists believe that, during REM sleep, the brain is storing memories and processing the events of the day. As it does so, it throws up images and ideas—your dreams!

Your hopes and fears may appear in your dreams, but often in an unrecognizable form. Some people say that, if you dream you are falling, you may be afraid of failure.

While your body is resting, it can use energy for repairing and maintaining muscles and other tissues.

As you sleep, your brain sends signals that release hormones, including growth hormones that make you taller.

181

Hormones

Hormones are chemicals that act as messengers in the body. More than 50 different types of hormones regulate all the body's processes, from sleeping and eating to growing and reproducing. The brain controls the release of hormones.

The hormone oxytocin makes you feel happy.

The Endocrine System

Hormones are made in special hormone-producing organs called glands, as well as in other organs that make hormones alongside other work. All these organs are part of the endocrine system, the body's hormone system. The endocrine system is controlled by a brain structure called the hypothalamus, deep inside the cerebrum.

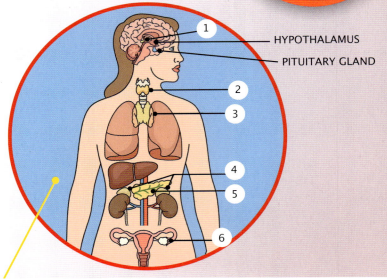

HYPOTHALAMUS
PITUITARY GLAND

1. The pineal gland produces melatonin, which makes you sleepy.
2. The thyroid gland makes hormones that control appetite, speed of digestion, and heart rate.
3. The thymus produces thymosin, which makes white blood cells develop.
4. The adrenal glands produce adrenaline, which gives you a burst of energy when you feel under threat.
5. The pancreas makes insulin, which controls the level of sugar in the blood.
6. In a woman, the ovaries produce hormones that control the reproductive cycle.

In addition to messaging other endocrine glands, the pituitary gland also makes growth hormones, which develop the bones and muscles, making you grow taller.

Sending Signals

The hypothalamus gathers information received by the brain, such as about body temperature and hunger. It then communicates with the nearby pituitary gland by sending it hormones. When the pituitary gland receives these signals, it releases hormones that control many of the other endocrine glands. When glands receive a signal to produce a particular hormone, they release it into the bloodstream. Only cells that are receptive to a particular hormone will respond to it, by starting to behave differently.

The hypothalamus makes oxytocin, which is stored in the pituitary gland and released in large quantities when a mother cuddles her baby.

Your pituitary gland also releases oxytocin when you are playing with friends or family.

BODY BREAKTHROUGH

Scientists: Edward Sharpey-Schafer (left) and George Oliver
Breakthrough: Discovered the first hormone
Date: 1894
The story: Working together, these two British scientists were the first to discover and demonstrate the existence of a hormone: adrenaline. Sharpey-Schafer also came up with the word endocrine, which means "to secrete (make and release) internally."

DID YOU KNOW? A burst of adrenaline is released when you are under threat or just feeling nervous, making your heart beat faster and sending more glucose into the blood.

Nervous System

A nerve is a bundle of long neurons. A network of nerves spreads out from the brain and spinal cord to carry signals to and from all parts of the body. The central nervous system (CNS) is the brain and spinal cord. The network of nerves spreading out from the CNS is called the peripheral nervous system (PNS).

Not in Control

Many signals in our nervous system happen without our control. These keep our body systems running—the digestive system processes food, the lungs breathe, and our blood pressure stays steady. The nerves that transmit these automatic signals make up the autonomic nervous system (ANS).

Twelve pairs of cranial nerves carry signals between the brain and the head, face, neck, and upper body.

The nervous system allows precise movements and feedback from the body.

Thirty-one pairs of spinal nerves branch out from the spinal cord.

Running from the lower back to the toes, the sciatic nerve is our longest nerve.

Forty-three pairs of nerves (cranial and spinal) connect the PNS to the CNS. They transmit signals to and from every part of the body.

BODY BREAKTHROUGH

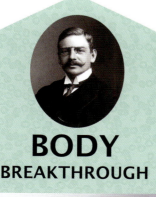

Scientist: Otto Loewi
Breakthrough: Proved that neurons communicate with chemicals
Date: 1921
The story: German chemist Otto Loewi wanted to know if neurons transmit chemical or electrical signals. (Today, we know it is a complex mixture of both!) Loewi electrically stimulated a frog's heart to slow it down. He moved chemicals from it to a second heart, which slowed without electrical stimulus. Loewi had proved the signal was chemical.

DID YOU KNOW? In the early 1970s, scientists confirmed that the neurons of fish and mammals carry signals both chemically and electrically.

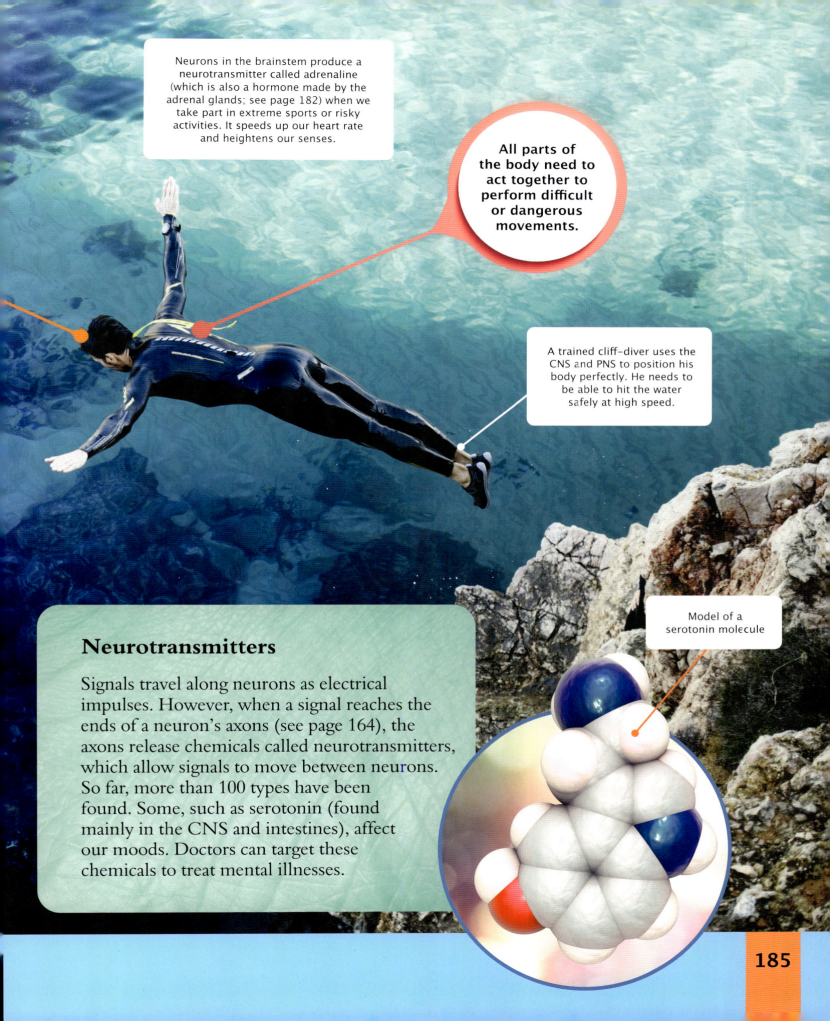

Neurons in the brainstem produce a neurotransmitter called adrenaline (which is also a hormone made by the adrenal glands; see page 182) when we take part in extreme sports or risky activities. It speeds up our heart rate and heightens our senses.

All parts of the body need to act together to perform difficult or dangerous movements.

A trained cliff-diver uses the CNS and PNS to position his body perfectly. He needs to be able to hit the water safely at high speed.

Model of a serotonin molecule

Neurotransmitters

Signals travel along neurons as electrical impulses. However, when a signal reaches the ends of a neuron's axons (see page 164), the axons release chemicals called neurotransmitters, which allow signals to move between neurons. So far, more than 100 types have been found. Some, such as serotonin (found mainly in the CNS and intestines), affect our moods. Doctors can target these chemicals to treat mental illnesses.

185

Sight

You can see because light—from the Sun or a lightbulb—bounces off objects and into your eyes. Your eyes detect patterns of light using light-sensitive cells, called rods and cones. Signals from these cells travel to the brain, which makes sense of them to build a picture of the world around you.

Making Pictures

Light enters the eye through a hole at the front, called the pupil. Light then travels through a clear, curved structure called the lens, which changes its shape to focus the light rays on the back of the eye. Here, there is a light-sensitive layer of tissue called the retina. Special cells (rods and cones) turn the light into electrical signals, which travel along the optic nerve to the brain.

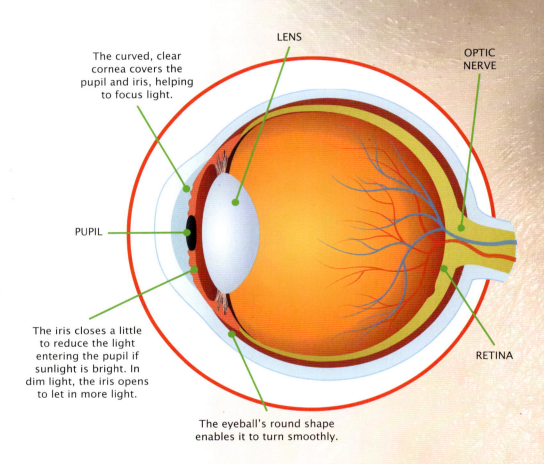

LENS
OPTIC NERVE
The curved, clear cornea covers the pupil and iris, helping to focus light.
PUPIL
The iris closes a little to reduce the light entering the pupil if sunlight is bright. In dim light, the iris opens to let in more light.
RETINA
The eyeball's round shape enables it to turn smoothly.

BODY BREAKTHROUGH

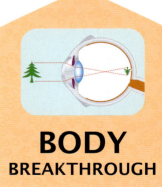

Scientist: René Descartes
Breakthrough: Proved the retina's image is upside down
Date: 1630s
The story: By studying a bull's eyeball, the Frenchman René Descartes proved that, since the front part of the eye is curved, it bends light to create an upside-down image on the retina. The brain processes the information from the retina, making it fit with what it already knows, so we "see" a right-way-up image.

DID YOU KNOW? Each of your eyes has only around 6 million cones, but as many as 120 million rods.

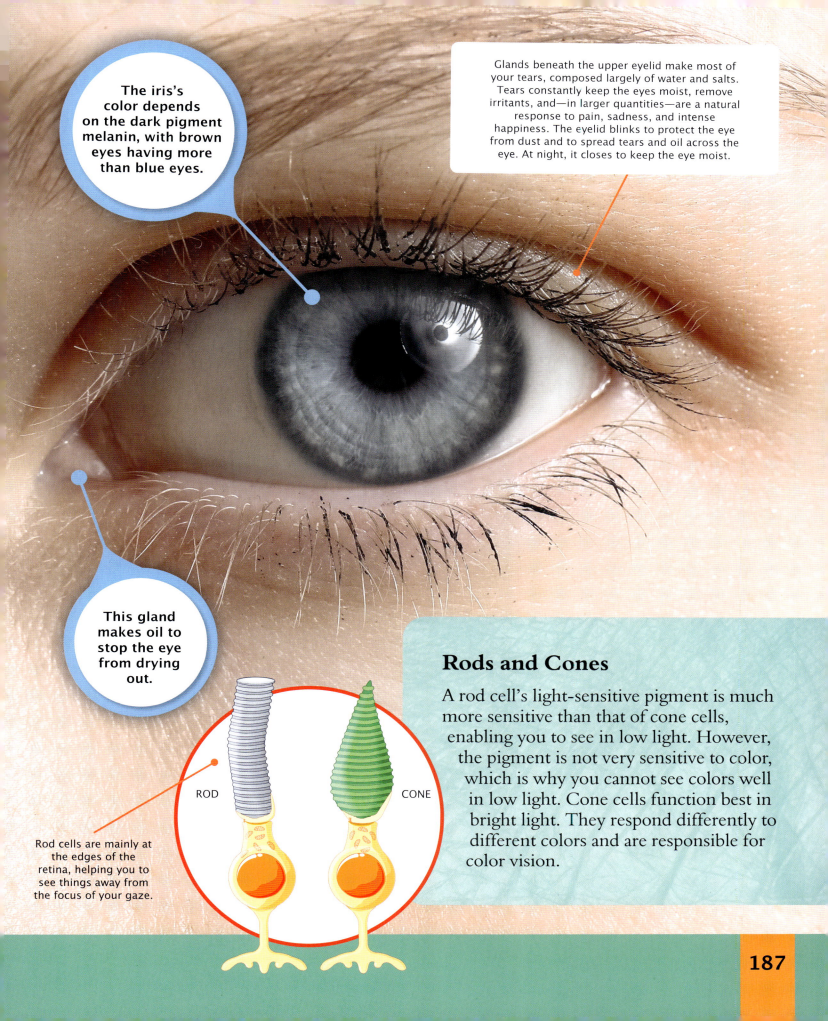

The iris's color depends on the dark pigment melanin, with brown eyes having more than blue eyes.

Glands beneath the upper eyelid make most of your tears, composed largely of water and salts. Tears constantly keep the eyes moist, remove irritants, and—in larger quantities—are a natural response to pain, sadness, and intense happiness. The eyelid blinks to protect the eye from dust and to spread tears and oil across the eye. At night, it closes to keep the eye moist.

This gland makes oil to stop the eye from drying out.

Rod cells are mainly at the edges of the retina, helping you to see things away from the focus of your gaze.

ROD

CONE

Rods and Cones

A rod cell's light-sensitive pigment is much more sensitive than that of cone cells, enabling you to see in low light. However, the pigment is not very sensitive to color, which is why you cannot see colors well in low light. Cone cells function best in bright light. They respond differently to different colors and are responsible for color vision.

187

Smell

Your sense of smell helps you to enjoy food and to notice hazards. Smells are detected by receptors inside the nose, which send signals to the brain, where information is processed and sometimes stored as a memory.

> A smell is carried by a tiny molecule: a collection of atoms.

How Do You Smell?

Once smell-producing molecules enter your nostrils, they are dissolved in (mixed into) the mucus (snot) that coats the lining of your nose. This helps the molecules to be detected by special cells, called olfactory receptors, near the back of the nose.

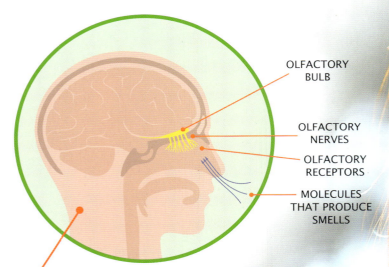

- OLFACTORY BULB
- OLFACTORY NERVES
- OLFACTORY RECEPTORS
- MOLECULES THAT PRODUCE SMELLS

Olfactory receptors send signals along the olfactory nerves to two areas, one at the front of each brain hemisphere, called the olfactory bulbs. These help to decide what kind of molecules are forming the smell.

BODY BREAKTHROUGH

Scientists: Linda Buck and Richard Axel
Breakthrough: Identified how olfactory receptors behave
Date: 1991
The story: Biologists Linda Buck and Richard Axel identified how different olfactory receptors change when particular molecules attach to them, causing them to send electrical signals to the olfactory bulbs. An olfactory receptor is a sensitive cell in the nose lining, with hairlike projections that trap mucus and the smell-producing molecules floating in it.

Smell molecules are given off much more easily by some substances, such as flowers and food, than by others.

Smell molecules are light enough to be carried through the air.

Cherry blossom is the national flower of Japan. Its vanilla-like smell is caused by the molecule coumarin, which is made of carbon, hydrogen, and oxygen atoms.

Responding to Smell

From the olfactory bulbs, information about a smell then travels to parts of the brain connected with emotion and memory (see page 176). This is why smells can make you feel disgust, happiness, or even remind you of another time you experienced them. Information is then sent to the part of the brain where you do your thinking: the cerebral cortex. If you smell smoke, your cortex decides to raise the alarm.

If food smells like it is decaying, the cerebral cortex will decide not to put that food into your mouth.

DID YOU KNOW? Different types of olfactory receptors detect different smells, enabling the brain to tell the difference between up to 1 trillion smells.

Taste

When you put food in your mouth, your sense of taste helps you to identify and enjoy it. Around 500,000 taste receptor cells let you know if a food tastes good or bad, which makes you want to eat it—or spit it out!

Taste Buds

If you stick out your tongue and look in the mirror, you will see hundreds of small bumps on the tongue's surface, which are called papillae. Most of these bumps contain hundreds of taste buds, each of which contains 50 to 100 taste receptor cells. Taste buds are also found on the roof and sides of the mouth and in the throat.

TONGUE
MICROVILLI
TASTE BUD
TASTE RECEPTOR CELL
NERVE

Taste receptor cells have hairlike extensions called microvilli that extend into the mouth to pick up tastes.

Your understanding of a food's taste is helped by smell signals from the nose and visual signals from the eyes.

Five Tastes

Taste receptor cells can identify five tastes: sweetness, sourness, saltiness, bitterness, and umami (also called savoriness). Most foods are a unique mixture of these tastes. Different types of taste receptors respond best to only one or two of the five tastes. When a taste receptor meets a food molecule that triggers it to react, it sends a signal along a nerve to the brain. The brain processes information from the thousands of receptor cells.

While sweet and umami tastes usually make us want to eat more, sour or bitter tastes can provoke disgust. Strongly bitter tastes warn us something could be poisonous.

BODY BREAKTHROUGH

Scientist: Kikunae Ikeda
Breakthrough: Discovered the basis of umami
Date: 1908
The story: This Japanese chemist discovered the chemical basis of the taste he named umami: the molecule monosodium glutamate. Ikeda decided that humans enjoy the umami taste because it is linked with protein, a necessary part of our diet. Umami can be tasted strongly in meat soups and stews, mushrooms, cheese, and soy sauce.

Touch signals from the facial nerves tell you about a food's texture and temperature.

The senses of taste and smell combine at the throat, where the nose cavity meets the mouth. These two senses are very similar, as they both respond to chemical molecules.

DID YOU KNOW? Your sense of taste is helped so greatly by your sense of smell that, when your nose is clogged by a heavy cold, your food tastes dull and is harder to identify.

191

Hearing

Your ears enable you to hear sounds, from speech to singing and traffic to tambourines. All sounds are made by vibrations, which is shaking so tiny we usually cannot see it. These vibrations travel through the air—or through water—and into your ears.

What Is Sound?

When you bang a drum, you make the skin of the drum vibrate. This makes the surrounding air molecules vibrate. When a molecule vibrates, it makes the molecules that are touching it vibrate. The vibration travels through the air—toward your ear—in the form of a wave. Each molecule vibrates less than the one before, which is why sounds get quieter the farther they travel.

The rim of the outer ear, called the helix, forms a curving structure that captures sound waves.

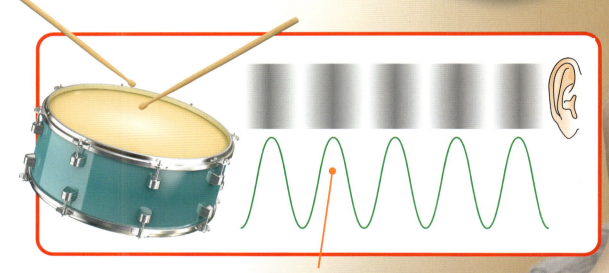

A sound wave is a little like a wave on the ocean, with tightly packed molecules making the peaks of the wave and lightly packed molecules making the troughs of the wave.

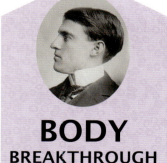

BODY BREAKTHROUGH

Scientist: Miller Reese Hutchison
Breakthrough: Invented the first electric hearing aid
Date: 1895
The story: American engineer Miller Reese Hutchison invented an electric hearing aid for his friend Lyman Gould. Like modern hearing aids, the device amplified (or increased) sounds, so they could be heard more easily. A modern hearing aid also adjusts to the user's type of hearing loss and the level of background noise.

DID YOU KNOW? One of the loudest sounds ever heard was the 1883 eruption of Indonesia's Krakatoa volcano, which could be heard 4,800 km (3,000 miles) away.

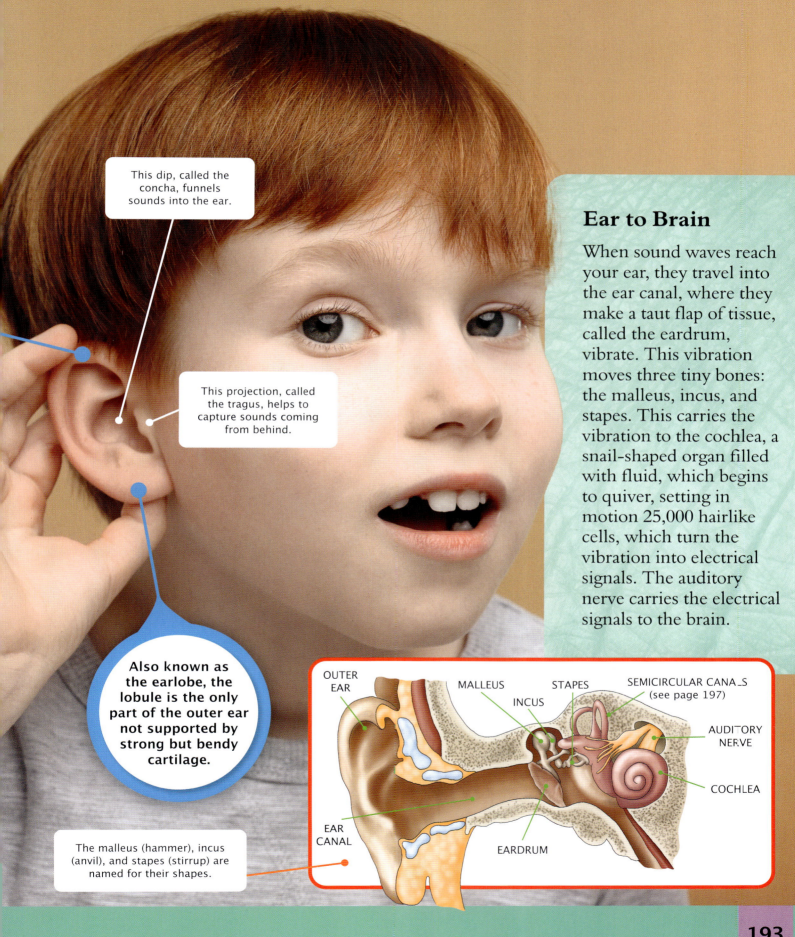

This dip, called the concha, funnels sounds into the ear.

This projection, called the tragus, helps to capture sounds coming from behind.

Also known as the earlobe, the lobule is the only part of the outer ear not supported by strong but bendy cartilage.

The malleus (hammer), incus (anvil), and stapes (stirrup) are named for their shapes.

Ear to Brain

When sound waves reach your ear, they travel into the ear canal, where they make a taut flap of tissue, called the eardrum, vibrate. This vibration moves three tiny bones: the malleus, incus, and stapes. This carries the vibration to the cochlea, a snail-shaped organ filled with fluid, which begins to quiver, setting in motion 25,000 hairlike cells, which turn the vibration into electrical signals. The auditory nerve carries the electrical signals to the brain.

OUTER EAR · MALLEUS · INCUS · STAPES · SEMICIRCULAR CANALS (see page 197) · AUDITORY NERVE · COCHLEA · EARDRUM · EAR CANAL

193

Touch

Your sense of touch makes use of receptors in your skin, which collect information not just about touch but about pain and temperature, too. Touch is not only important for understanding the world:—kindly touch also comforts us.

Types of Touch Receptors

Receptors called mechanoreceptors respond to different types of touch. The most sensitive are Merkel's disks and Meissner's corpuscles, in the top layers of skin. Merkel's disks are good at sensing continuous pressure and coarse textures. Meissner's corpuscles are good at sensing vibration and fine textures. Deeper in the skin and along joints and muscles are Ruffini's corpuscles and Pacinian corpuscles. They sense deep vibrations and the stretching of skin, which is helpful during activities such as catching a ball.

There are four main kinds of mechanoreceptors in the skin.

MEISSNER'S CORPUSCLE
PACINIAN CORPUSCLE
RUFFINI'S CORPUSCLE
MERKEL'S DISKS

Receptors in the skin send signals about the pressure, texture, and temperature of the dog.

BODY BREAKTHROUGH

Scientist: Louis Braille
Breakthrough: Invented the Braille system of writing
Date: 1824
The story: Frenchman Louis Braille invented his system of writing for people with visual impairments, so they can read using their fingertips. Braille uses tiny bumps to represent letters, numbers, and punctuation. Meissner's corpuscles are the mechanoreceptors that enable people to feel these fine details.

Signals from the skin allow the brain to understand the dog's shape, furriness, and warmth.

In response to these touch signals, the brain generates happy feelings.

Temperature and Pain

Thermoreceptors respond to temperature. They are in highest numbers on the face and ears, which is why these areas feel cold most quickly. You also have over 3 million pain receptors, in your skin, muscles, bones, blood vessels, and organs. They can create a sharp pain in response to cuts, scrapes, and burns, making you move away from the source of pain immediately; or create a dull ache to remind you of a bruise or sprain so you rest the damaged area until it heals.

Cold receptors stop sending signals when skin temperature drops below 5 °C (41 °F), giving a feeling of numbness.

DID YOU KNOW? Merkel's disks and Meissner's corpuscles are found in large numbers on the palms, fingertips, soles of the feet, tongue, and face, making these body parts very sensitive.

Balance and Coordination

We all know about the five senses of touch, sight, hearing, taste, and smell, but what about the others? Our vestibular system—based on information from our inner ear—provides our sense of balance, while proprioception makes our movements coordinated instead of clumsy.

Body Awareness

Proprioception tells us where our body is so we can walk down stairs without a handrail or use a pencil with the right amount of force. It comes from proprioceptors in muscles, joints, tendons, and ligaments all over the body. Our brain—particularly the brainstem, cerebellum, and parietal lobe—constantly combines these proprioceptive signals with vestibular information from the inner ear so we can keep our balance.

Astronauts in space experience weaker gravity than on Earth. They feel unbalanced for a few days until their vestibular system adapts to their new environment. When they return to Earth, they feel disorientated until they readjust again.

BODY BREAKTHROUGH

Scientist: Anna Jean Ayres
Breakthrough: Sensory integration (SI) therapy
Date: 1979
The story: People with sensory processing disorder (SPD) experience sensations too strongly or hardly at all. US occupational therapist Anna Jean Ayres developed a program to treat SPD to help sufferers cope with everyday sensations. Tailor-made sensory activities could calm people with SPD and, in some cases, even "rewire" their brain.

Proprioceptors in the performer's hands and arms tell her how hard to grip the pole.

Sight is important for balance. We stay steadier if we fix our eyes on a spot just in front of us.

Balance is helped by the inner ear's three semicircular canals (see page 193), which face in three different directions. As fluid in the canals swishes against hairlike cells, the vestibular system can detect turning movement in three dimensions.

Dizziness

Our inner ear keeps track of our body's movement on different planes (up-and-down, forward-backward, and side-to-side), turns, and rolls. If these vestibular signals do not match what our eyes see, our proprioceptors feel, and our brain expects, we become dizzy.

The pole lowers the girl's center of balance to make balancing easier. Stretching our arms to the sides works the same way.

Proprioceptors in each foot's 33 joints—as well as its muscles, tendons, and ligaments—feed the brain information about where the performer is in space.

Riders on a rollercoaster experience speed and motion through their vestibular system.

DID YOU KNOW? In 1974, French high-wire artist Philippe Petit walked a wire between New York's Twin Towers, 400 m (1,000 ft) above the ground.

Language and Communication

Humans use many tools to share ideas and feelings, so we can live and work together. We communicate with our bodies and our facial expressions. We also learn a language that helps us to think and to swap ideas and stories. Our ability to use language is a big part of who we are.

Making Words

Humans make precise sounds, called phonemes, to build words and sentences. We use our teeth, tongue, breath, and larynx (voicebox) to make phonemes, just like we use our fingers to write or type the letters of an alphabet.

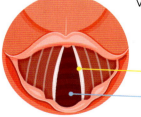

Our breath passes through the voicebox in the throat. If our vocal cords are open and relaxed, we are silent. If they stretch tight, the breath makes them vibrate and produce sound.

VOCAL CORDS TIGHT
VOCAL CORDS OPEN
WINDPIPE (TRACHEA)

Breathing silently

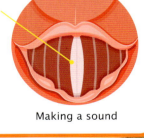

Making a sound

BODY BREAKTHROUGH

Scientist: Paul Broca
Breakthrough: Discovered Broca's area
Date: 1861
The story: French surgeon Paul Broca found that two patients who could not speak had damage in the same area of their brain (see also page 168). This was the first scientific evidence for the idea that each human ability happens in a specific part of the brain. His theory helped to launch neuroscience.

DID YOU KNOW? After 2 million responses, testyourvocab.com found that the average eight-year-old already knows 10,000 words.

Some body language may be special to our culture, and some is shared by all humans.

Body language is not just gestures. It is also how we position our body in relation to others.

We interpret not just the words in speech, but also the pitch changes that convey meaning and emotion.

Body Language

Some scientists argue that most of what we "say" is not through words—it is the messages we send and receive through body movements. We can certainly use words to communicate over distance or time. But to connect fully with each other, we often prefer to be together.

Body language can be "closed" or "open." Crossed arms or legs may communicate that we are holding back.

Body language can show what a speaker is not telling us—and even reveal if they are lying.

199

Living Mindfully

We can make the most of the time that we are alive by looking after our body. It has certain physical requirements, such as air, water, food, and sleep. Just as importantly, we need to look after our mental well-being and fulfill our spiritual and emotional needs.

The Good Life

There is not one single guidebook to meaningful human existence—there are hundreds! In our time on this planet, human beings have established multiple religions, philosophies (ways of thinking), and moral frameworks (ways of acting) to live by. Many tell us the same thing—to be selfless and loving, show gratitude, and live in the present moment.

Meditation and yoga allow our minds to go quiet. They may help us to control stress and anxiety.

Self-care helps to improve mental well-being, but we may need outside help, too. If we have serious worries, we should talk to someone we trust.

Empathy is the ability to feel others' pain or fear. It helps us understand what other people need.

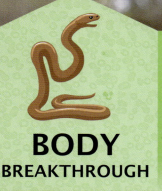

BODY BREAKTHROUGH

Scientist: Sheila Coulson
Breakthrough: Found the earliest evidence of religion
Date: 2006
The story: When archeologist Sheila Coulson discovered carvings on a snake-shaped rock, she was able to push back the time that humans were first carrying out rituals to around 70,000 years ago. Myths, religions, and rituals are a uniquely human way of making sense of the world.

DID YOU KNOW? To meditate, sit in a comfortable position, focus on your gentle breathing, and then imagine you are in a beautiful, happy place.

Past, Present, and Future

It is not healthy to dwell in the past … but it is good to learn from our mistakes. And it is not good to worry excessively about the future … but it is good to have goals and a sense of direction. Being in the present does not mean we should ignore our responsibilities.

Our planet is an amazing gift. It is our responsibility to look after it for future generations.

We cannot change the past, and the future is not here yet. The only moment we can control is right now. By meditating, we can pause and enjoy it.

Chapter 7

Stages of Life

Your body changes throughout life, during the fast-growing years of childhood and adolescence and into adulthood and old age. Your rate of learning is fastest in the first three years of life, but the process of gaining skills and knowledge continues through every year.

Developing Body

Between the ages of 8 and 15, the body starts to go through puberty, when sex hormones bring about physical changes. For girls, these include growing breasts and starting their periods. For boys, changes include broadening shoulders and a deepening voice. Both boys and girls grow quickly in height, produce body hair, and may get pimples caused by the skin making too much oil. Puberty readies the body for sexual reproduction. However, most adults wait many more years to feel emotionally and practically ready to bring a new life into the world, while plenty of adults choose not to have their own biological children.

At the beginning of puberty, brain cells called neurons are gaining and losing up to 25 percent of their connections every week. For adults, that number drops to 10 percent. This is why adolescence is a perfect time for learning new ideas and developing new interests.

202

Developing Brain

By the age of two, the brain has tripled in weight since birth. Many children are able to use 300 words and understand hundreds more. By the age of seven, the brain has reached 95 percent of its final weight. This is why the early school years are a time of rapid learning, not just in reading, writing, mathematics, and sports, but also in building friendships and working together with others. By around the age of 25, the brain has fully developed its ability to plan and to control emotions. However, the ability to pay attention continues to improve until the age of 45.

Exercising regularly, eating a varied diet, and enjoying the company of family and friends can slow the aging process, helping us to feel healthier for longer.

DID YOU KNOW? By the age of 2, most children are able to throw a ball, but most will not be able to catch a ball until after the age of 3.

Different Bodies

Like all other living things, humans are able to reproduce. Like many plants and other animals, humans reproduce sexually. This is when a female cell joins with a male one. In humans, a female cell is called an ovum (egg), while a male cell is called a sperm.

Female Organs

If a baby has two X chromosomes (see page 29), one from its mother and one from its father, it is usually born with female reproductive organs. Glands called ovaries store immature female sex cells, called ova (eggs), until they are ready. A baglike organ called the uterus, or womb, can carry and protect a growing baby during pregnancy. After reaching puberty (see page 214), a female body makes sex hormones that signal to the ovaries to release eggs. These hormones also bring about changes in the body, such as growing breasts.

Growing thicker facial hair and body hair is triggered by the main male sex hormone, testosterone.

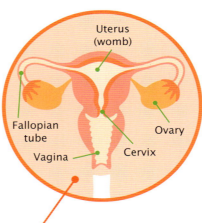

The cervix, or neck of the womb, protects the reproductive organs. It opens slightly during menstruation, also known as a "period." This is when, roughly once a month during a woman's reproductive years, the body sheds an unfertilized (unused) egg, along with some of the lining of the uterus.

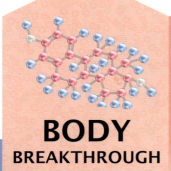

BODY BREAKTHROUGH

Scientist: Edgar Allen
Breakthrough: Discovered estrogen
Date: 1929
The story: He discovered the first of a group of female sex hormones known as estrogen. These play an important role in the menstrual cycle, by triggering the ovaries to release an egg. Estrogen levels rise during puberty, then drop as a woman approaches menopause, the time (usually between the ages of 45 and 55) when her periods stop.

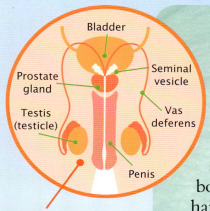

The prostate gland and seminal vesicles help to produce semen.

Male Organs

If a baby has an X and a Y chromosome (see page 29), an X from its mother and a Y from its father, it is usually born with male reproductive organs. After reaching puberty (see page 214), a male body makes sex hormones that trigger the body to make sperm. These hormones also bring about other changes in the body, such as developing a lower voice and growing thicker body hair. Sperm is made in two glands, called testicles or testes, which are held in a sac called the scrotum. Sperm can be released from the penis, after being mixed with fluids to make a liquid called semen.

The pituitary gland, at the base of the brain, makes sex hormones that kickstart our reproductive systems.

Growing breasts and gaining body fat on the hips are effects of a group of female sex hormones called estrogen.

DID YOU KNOW? Across the world, for every 100 babies that are born with female organs, around 105 are born with male organs.

Life Begins

During her reproductive years, a woman ovulates (releases a ripe egg from an ovary) each month. If the egg is fertilized by a sperm, it forms a zygote. If the zygote attaches itself to the lining of the uterus (womb)—which will contain and nourish it—it will develop into an embryo.

Cell Division

About 30 hours after fertilization, the zygote splits into two identical cells. The cells keep dividing to become a cluster called a morula (Latin for "mulberry"). The morula grows and changes, becoming a blastocyst. Now it is ready to bed into the uterus lining.

> When a woman is hoping to have a baby, she may watch out for the day in each month when she ovulates.

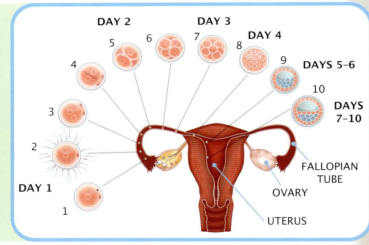

EGG TO EMBRYO
1. Unfertilized egg
2. Sperm fertilizes egg
3. Zygote (egg fused with sperm)
4. Dividing zygote
5. Two-cell stage
6. Four-cell stage
7. Eight-cell stage
8. Morula (cluster of cells)
9. Blastocyst
10. Embryo (implanted blastocyst)

Ovulation usually takes places around 12 to 20 days after the start of a woman's last period. An egg can survive for 12 to 24 hours after ovulation. If it does not meet a sperm during this time, it will be absorbed by the uterus lining, then shed in the woman's next period.

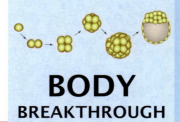

BODY BREAKTHROUGH

Scientist: Jean Purdy
Breakthrough: First embryologist
Date: 1977
The story: Along with gynecologist Patrick Steptoe and biologist Bob Edwards, British nurse Jean Purdy was part of the pioneering team responsible for the first IVF baby, Louise Brown, who was born in July 1978. Purdy worked in the laboratory, fusing eggs and sperm and growing embryos in controlled conditions, ready to implant into the mother.

ICSI is a method used in IVF. The sperm is injected directly into the egg using a microneedle (shown on the left in this image).

Test-Tube Technology

IVF (in vitro fertilization) is when eggs are removed from the ovaries and fertilized by sperm in a laboratory instead. Two to five days later, one or two blastocysts are placed in the mother's uterus to grow and develop.

This SEM scan shows sperm moving through the uterus. Tufts of tiny hairs called cilia help to waft the sperm on their way.

When a woman ovulates, one—or, sometimes, both—of her ovaries releases an egg (ovum).

DID YOU KNOW? When a baby girl is born, she has around two million follicles, which are fluid-filled sacs in the ovaries that contain immature eggs.

207

Pregnancy

The journey from the release of a single-celled egg to the birth of a baby takes about 40 weeks. Once the blastocyst is firmly fixed in the wall of the uterus, it develops into an embryo. When all the major organs have formed, it is called a fetus.

> Ultrasound scans are used to see how a baby is developing inside its mother's womb.

In the Womb

The fetus develops in the amniotic sac, a "bag" that contains amniotic fluid that helps cushion it. An organ called the placenta grows, attached to the wall of the uterus. The placenta is joined to the tube-like umbilical cord, which delivers oxygen and nutrients from the mother's blood to the baby.

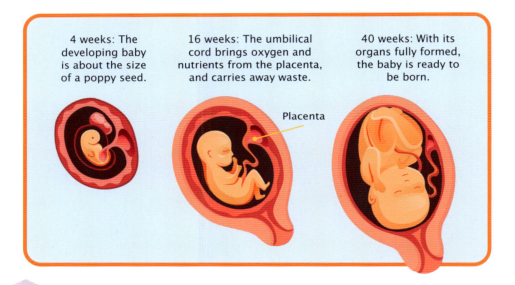

4 weeks: The developing baby is about the size of a poppy seed.

16 weeks: The umbilical cord brings oxygen and nutrients from the placenta, and carries away waste.

40 weeks: With its organs fully formed, the baby is ready to be born.

Placenta

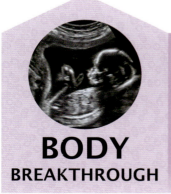

BODY BREAKTHROUGH

Scientists: Ian Donald and Tom Brown
Breakthrough: Ultrasound scans of developing babies
Date: 1956
The story: The first ultrasound scanner, based on a device used by shipbuilders, was developed by Tom Brown, an engineer, and Ian Donald, an obstetrican (doctor specializing in pregnancy and birth). The technique bounces sound waves at the developing baby and builds up a picture from the "echoes"—rather like bats' sonar.

DID YOU KNOW? Born in Liverpool, UK, in 1983, the Walton sextuplets were the world's first surviving multiple birth of six baby girls.

This ultrasound scan shows twin fetuses developing in their own amniotic sacs. In just one percent of twin pregnancies, the fetuses share a sac.

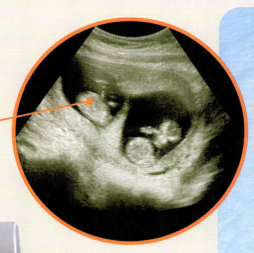

Twins and More

Non-identical twins develop if two eggs are fertilized by two different sperm. Identical twins, who share the same genes, develop from one fertilized egg that splits. Twins and multiple births of three or more babies are most likely to be born to older mothers, women with twins in their family, or women having IVF (see page 207).

By 20 weeks of pregnancy, an ultrasound scan can show a baby waving its hands and sucking its thumb.

After 20 weeks of growing, a developing baby may be around 26 cm (10 in) long. It is probably kicking, punching, and turning.

209

Birth and Baby

In the last weeks of pregnancy, hormones start off gentle squeezes (contractions) of the mother's uterus. This is practice for the stronger ones that will push the baby out. In most cases, the baby's head moves down into the pelvis at this time—about 96 percent of babies are born head first.

Into the World!

Physicians, nurses, and midwives often divide birthing a baby into three stages. During the first stage, strong contractions of muscles in the uterus pull on its narrow outer end (the cervix) until it is fully open. This process that can take many hours. Then comes the second stage, when the baby is pushed down through the cervix and out through the vagina. The third stage is delivering the placenta.

A fetal monitor records the contractions, as well as the baby's heartbeat, which is usually 120–160 beats per minute (bpm).

Babies are born coated with a greasy white substance called vernix. It helped to "waterproof" them in the womb.

The "Apgar" score is a quick check on the baby's health. The midwife marks each of the following 0, 1, or 2 (7 or more is a good overall score):

Appearance (skin shade), **p**ulse (heart rate), **g**rimace response (reflexes), **a**ctivity (muscle tone), and **r**espiration (breathing).

FIRST STAGE		SECOND STAGE		THIRD STAGE
	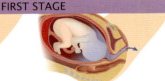	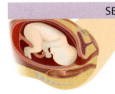	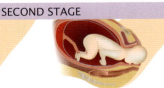	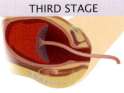
1. The baby's head presses on the softening cervix.	2. The cervix dilates (widens). The amniotic sac ruptures ("waters break").	3. The cervix dilates until it is about 10 cm (4 in) wide.	4. The baby is pushed out through the vagina.	5. The placenta is pushed out.

The lungs are one of the last organs to finish forming. The baby gets to test them with their first breath of air!

Newborn Baby

A newborn can hear, smell, taste, and feel. Its eyes can only focus on objects up to 25 cm (10 in) away, but this is around the distance of its parents' faces when it is held. A newborn also has an important skill: the ability to suck. When the roof of a baby's mouth is touched, by a breast or baby bottle, it sucks automatically. Its main form of communication is crying, which it does to show it is hot, cold, tired, hungry for milk, or wants a cuddle.

The average newborn is around 50 cm (20 in) long and weighs around 3.2 kg (7 lb).

DID YOU KNOW? The placenta forms when the embryo implants. It grows from a few cells that split away and burrow deep into the wall of the uterus.

Childhood Milestones

> From birth to two, the brain triples in weight. Mastering a new ability builds fresh neural pathways in the brain.

Human babies are the most helpless in the animal kingdom. As newborns we cannot hold up our head or coordinate our movements. Everyone is different, but most of us can sit unsupported and grasp a toy by about six months. Over the coming months, we learn to crawl, walk, and talk.

Great Leaps

In our first year we progress from an all-milk diet to solid foods. Our body grows physically stronger, but we develop emotionally, too—we become aware of our own feelings and other people's. By two-and-a-half, we are using more than 300 words and can understand about 1,000. With language, we can understand more rules and develop our social skills.

In this X-ray, the red areas show adult teeth ready to replace baby teeth. Adult teeth come through from the age of six.

> A one-year-old can grasp, hold, reach, wave, clap, and pinch. These are called fine motor skills.

> Moving around helps babies and children to gain body awareness and coordination.

BODY BREAKTHROUGH

Scientist: Maria Montessori
Breakthrough: Learning through play
Date: 1909
The story: Believing that traditional education dulled natural curiosity and squashed independence, Italian doctor Maria Montessori came up with a method that encouraged children to learn through play and practical tasks. Pupils explored topics in a "prepared environment"—an orderly classroom space equipped with carefully designed materials.

Going to School

At school, we learn to read, write, and count. We also develop other life skills, such as being able to form friendships, and having the discipline to do things even when we do not want to. We meet people from different backgrounds and cultures, and learn to respect other viewpoints.

At school we are taught how to work together, or collaborate. Hopefully we develop interests that will continue into adulthood.

Sitting up, pulling up to standing, and "cruising" are all preparations for solo walking. Most of us take our first steps at 9 to 12 months.

DID YOU KNOW? There is a theory that a person's adult height is double their height aged two-and-a-half ... but it is not always exactly correct!

Adolescence

Adolescents have greater freedom and choice than younger children. They decide who to spend time with, and may pair up with a boyfriend or girlfriend.

The process of turning from a child into an adult is called adolescence. It can start as early as 10 and go on into our 20s, but most changes occur in our teens. Puberty, when the body becomes able to reproduce, is a part of adolescence.

Signs of Puberty

At the start of puberty, girls begin to make more of the sex hormones estrogen and progesterone. They begin menstruation (having monthly periods) and their breasts develop. Boys produce the sex hormone testosterone, which triggers sperm production, broadening of the chest and shoulders, and a deepening of the voice. Both sexes grow extra body hair.

Hormones released during puberty can make the skin produce too much oily sebum. It clogs pores and causes pimples and acne.

Marking the Moment

Many cultures celebrate the end of childhood with ceremonies or rituals. These help adolescents to focus on their new adult responsibilities, and to build up their strength and resilience.

On the Pacific islands of Vanuatu, boys dive off a 30-m (100-ft) tower the year they hit puberty.

214

BODY BREAKTHROUGH

Scientist: Sarah-Jayne Blakemore
Breakthrough: Understanding the teenage brain
Date: 2018
The story: British neuroscientist Sarah-Jayne Blakemore has studied changes to the brain during adolescence. She has shown that rewiring of the brain affects how teenagers behave, interact, and make decisions. It also explains why teenagers often push boundaries, take more risks than adults—and even why they struggle to get up in the morning!

Testosterone bulks out boys' bodies. It also thickens their vocal cords so they vibrate at a lower frequency, which lowers the voice.

Hormones make moods switch suddenly. It is normal to feel on top of the world one minute, then low the next.

About 95 percent of US teens have access to a smart phone. Social media help us connect, but can expose us to bullying or dangerous situations.

DID YOU KNOW? There are more than 1.8 billion youths aged 10 to 24 in the world—a larger proportion of the world population than ever before.

Adulthood

As adults, we take on new roles and responsibilities. In some parts of the world, young adults stay in their parents' home or do not leave until they marry. Elsewhere, they move out. Most of us must make money to support ourselves.

There are over 100 million construction workers worldwide.

How We Work

The work we do determines how much we earn, our status in society, and how we organize our time. The sooner we leave school, the more likely we are to have an unskilled, manual job. Further education costs money, but in return we may end up with a higher salary and—perhaps—a more fulfilling job.

A college degree is not essential for having a successful working life—but it is a huge achievement.

These workers from Bangladesh are in Dubai, in the United Arab Emirates (UAE). They can earn higher wages here and send money home to their families.

BODY BREAKTHROUGH

Scientists: Derk-Jan Dijk, Simon Archer, and team, Surrey Sleep Research Unit
Breakthrough: Effects of shift work
Date: 2014
The story: Dijk and Archer studied 22 shift-workers to see why night shifts cause physical and mental health problems. They found that some genes are programmed to work at particular times of the day. Disrupting the body's natural rhythm puts our organs out of synch.

DID YOU KNOW? Worldwide, around 24 percent of employed adults work in factories and construction, 26 percent work in farming, and 50 percent work in offices, schools, and hospitals.

Time Off

Leisure is the time when we are not working or carrying out domestic tasks. We spend it on the things we like doing, such as meeting up with family and friends, taking part in sports, or pursuing hobbies. We also need time to rest and unwind.

Going to the movies is a popular leisure pursuit, but numbers are falling because of TV on demand.

There are nearly 8 million migrant workers in UAE. Most are from India, Bangladesh, or Pakistan.

Construction workers in Dubai work long hours in the glaring sun. Average summer temperatures are around 40 °C (104 °F).

Family Life

Some of us are raised by one parent or carer without sisters or brothers. Some of us grow up with lots of siblings in huge extended families, where several generations live together in the same home. There are many different types of family.

Marriage

Not everyone chooses to share their life with one partner. Those who do often make a commitment to each other in front of their family and friends in a wedding or civil partnership ceremony. Some of us have arranged marriages, where older family members select our husband or wife.

Having Children

Some people cannot or do not want to have children. For those who do, there are many family set-ups. Children may be raised by foster, adoptive, or step-parents rather than their biological mother and father. Where IVF or surrogacy are involved, children may never know who donated the egg or sperm that gave them half their genes.

A Hindu bride and groom wear red. Every culture and religion has its own wedding traditions.

Grandparents pass on wisdom and memories, and give emotional support. If they can, they may provide childcare and financial help.

Where both partners are male, they can become fathers through adoption or surrogacy, where a woman carries and gives birth to a baby for them.

Family gives us many of our values and beliefs. It is where we form our first relationships with others.

Mothers are getting older. In the United States, the average age to have a first child was 21 years in 1970. Today, it is more than 27 years.

Scientist: Margaret Sanger
Breakthrough: Opening the first birth-control clinic
Date: 1916
The story: American nurse Margaret Sanger saw the health risks of unwanted pregnancies. Contraception was against the law but in her clinic Sanger gave women the diaphragm, a contraceptive device that formed a barrier over the cervix. Sanger was arrested many times until family planning began to be legalized in the United States, from 1938.

BODY
BREAKTHROUGH

DID YOU KNOW? Family size varies around the world. On average, Portuguese mothers have one child, Americans two, and Nigerians six.

Old Age

Joints can become less mobile with age. The skeleton weakens and we are more likely to break bones if we fall.

Humans are the longest lived of land mammals, and our average life span (73 years worldwide) is still increasing. According to the United Nations, old age begins at 65, but experiences and expectations of it are very different around the world.

Pros and Cons

Our cells can divide (see page 18) only 40 to 60 times. Cell division slows from the age of 30, but the effects are not usually felt for many more years. When there are not enough new cells to replace dead cells, tissues and organs begin to work less well. However, there are many positive effects of aging! Research shows that older people are happier and more resilient than younger adults. In many societies, they are respected for their wisdom and experience.

Following a healthy lifestyle can slow down the physical effects of aging. This karate master in Okinawa, Japan, is 75 years old.

What Next?

How we approach our death depends on our personality, spiritual beliefs, and culture. To cope with the death of a loved one, we go through a process called grief. Rituals sometimes help with this.

Laying flowers on a gravestone is one way to remember a loved one and come to accept their death.

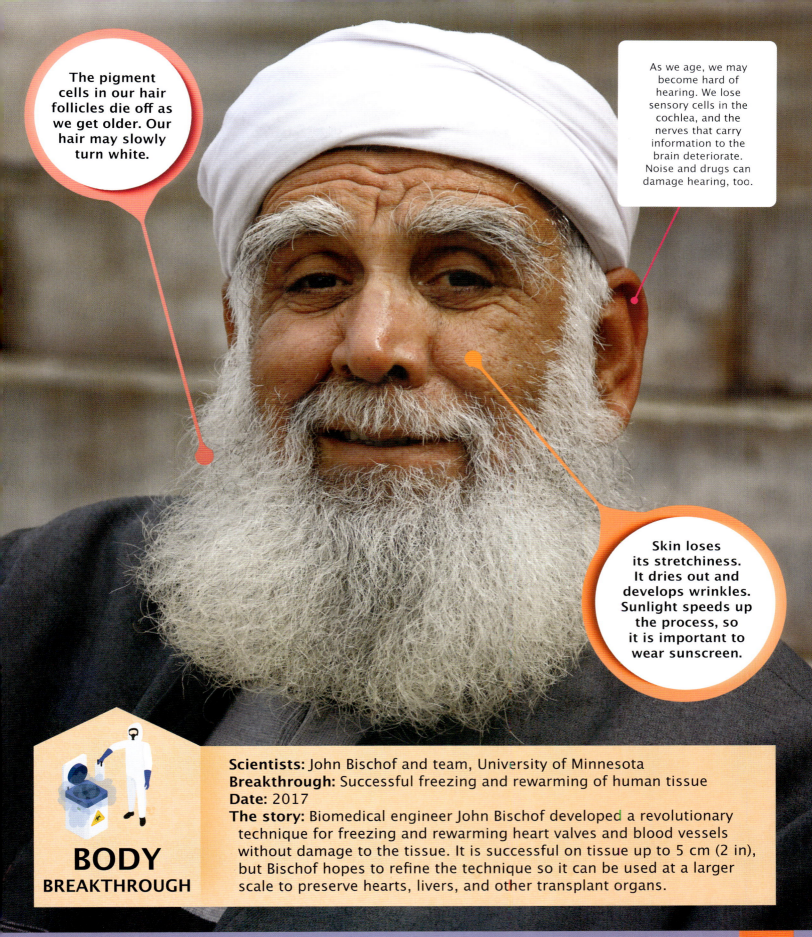

The pigment cells in our hair follicles die off as we get older. Our hair may slowly turn white.

As we age, we may become hard of hearing. We lose sensory cells in the cochlea, and the nerves that carry information to the brain deteriorate. Noise and drugs can damage hearing, too.

Skin loses its stretchiness. It dries out and develops wrinkles. Sunlight speeds up the process, so it is important to wear sunscreen.

BODY BREAKTHROUGH

Scientists: John Bischof and team, University of Minnesota
Breakthrough: Successful freezing and rewarming of human tissue
Date: 2017
The story: Biomedical engineer John Bischof developed a revolutionary technique for freezing and rewarming heart valves and blood vessels without damage to the tissue. It is successful on tissue up to 5 cm (2 in), but Bischof hopes to refine the technique so it can be used at a larger scale to preserve hearts, livers, and other transplant organs.

DID YOU KNOW? Japan has the world's highest life expectancy (the average number of years a person can expect to live): around 87 for women and 82 for men.

Chapter 8
Medicine

Medicine is the science of keeping people healthy and of caring for the sick or injured. As a science, medicine is based on study, experiment, and fact. Medical professionals work hard to identify diseases and injuries, to treat them—and to prevent them.

Medical Professionals

Medical care is given by highly trained doctors, nurses, and other professionals, each with their own areas of expertise. For example, if someone's heart were struggling to pump blood, they would seek the help of a doctor, also known as a physician. Doctors study anatomy (the structure of the body) and physiology (how body structures work), as well as diseases and their latest treatments. A doctor who specializes in treating the heart, called a cardiologist, might be asked to give their particular advice. A physiotherapist could also join the team, suggesting exercises to strengthen the heart. A change in diet might be suggested by a nutritionist, who studies how the food we eat affects our health.

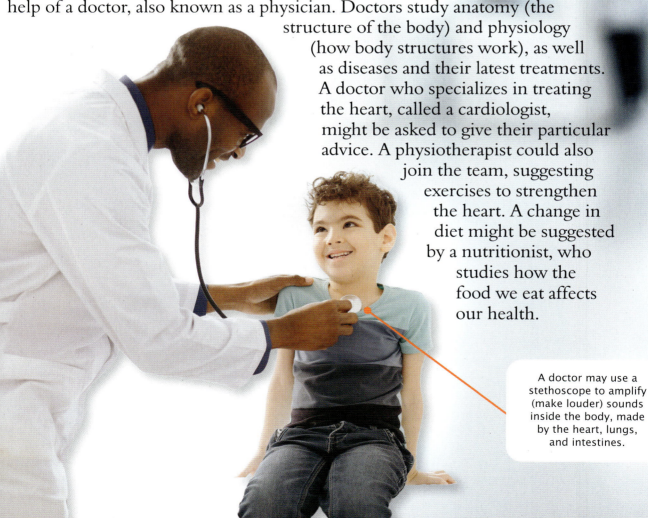

A doctor may use a stethoscope to amplify (make louder) sounds inside the body, made by the heart, lungs, and intestines.

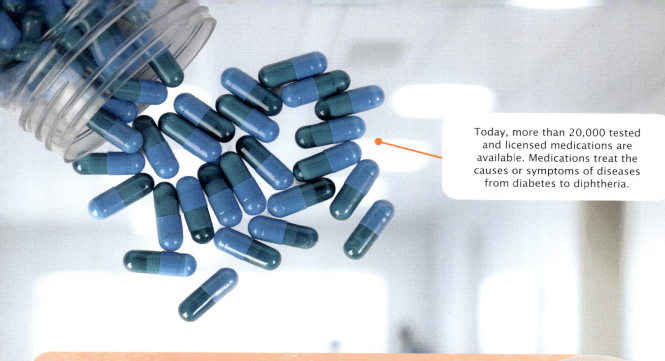

Today, more than 20,000 tested and licensed medications are available. Medications treat the causes or symptoms of diseases from diabetes to diphtheria.

Diagnosis

The ancient Greek doctor Hippocrates (c.460–370 BCE) was one of the first to believe that illness had a physical cause. He was a great influence on later doctors. Like today's doctors, he diagnosed (identified the nature of) an illness after carefully examining his patients and taking note of their symptoms (evidence of disease, such as fever or swelling). Today's doctors can also use medical tests to help with diagnosis. These range from identifying the substances in blood and pee to medical imaging that allows a glimpse inside the body.

X-rays and computerized tomography (CT) scans use a form of energy called X-rays. When the body is placed between an X-ray source and a photographic film, an image forms. Bones absorb X-rays, creating lighter areas on the image. Softer tissue lets X-rays pass through, leaving darker areas on the image.

DID YOU KNOW? In ancient Egypt, healers used magic spells and prayed to gods and goddesses to help their patients.

Medications

A medication is a drug that treats or prevents disease or discomfort. Some medications are prescription drugs, which a pharmacist will supply only on the order of a doctor or nurse. Weaker medications—such as some painkillers and indigestion medicines—can be bought without a prescription.

Ancient Medicines

From ancient times, healers chose herbs to make medicines. While some herbal medicines did more harm than good, others were effective. Some modern medicines are still made with chemicals that come from plants, including the Madagascar periwinkle, which helps treat cancer, and the opium poppy, which can ease pain.

Galantamine is a chemical extracted from daffodils (left) and snowdrops (right). It can slow down the damage to an elderly person's brain caused by diseases such as Alzheimer's.

Lenalidomide is an immunotherapy medication used to treat myeloma, a type of blood cancer.

Immunotherapy stimulates the immune system to attack cancer cells.

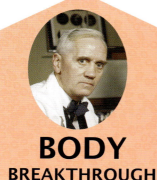

BODY BREAKTHROUGH

Scientist: Alexander Fleming
Breakthrough: Discovered penicillin
Date: 1928
The story: A Scottish physician and biologist, Fleming discovered that the *Penicillium rubens* fungus releases chemicals that kill bacteria which cause infections of the eyes, throat, and lungs. This led to the production of penicillin, the first effective antibiotic.

Cancer is a disease that makes abnormal cells grow and multiply. It begins when some genes in a cell become abnormal. Today, treatments for cancer are becoming more and more effective.

Modern Medicines

When doctors started to use microscopes in the 19th century, they began to understand that some illnesses—from food poisoning to malaria—are caused by microorganisms. During the 20th century, the study of even smaller objects—such as the DNA molecules in cells—led to the development of new medicines. Today, medicines can: destroy microorganisms, such as antibiotics that kill bacteria; replace missing substances in the body, such as vitamins or hormones; treat cancer by stopping cancerous cells from dividing; or target the brain, which doctors now know controls the body systems.

A child with a long-lasting bacterial infection of the middle ear (behind the eardrum) may be given an antibiotic called amoxicillin.

DID YOU KNOW? Non-prescription painkillers work by reducing the strength of pain signals being sent along nerves to the brain.

225

Studying Anatomy

Without anatomy—the science of studying the body—we would have no clue what the parts of the body do, or how to treat them if they go wrong. The first anatomy "book" was a papyrus written in Egypt in 1600 BCE, but our curiosity about the body's make-up dates back to prehistoric times.

Ways of Seeing

From the 1600s, anatomists no longer relied on just the naked eye—they had microscopes for a magnified view. Inner organs could only be seen after death, however, when a body could be cut open. X-rays (see page 223), CT, PET, and MRI scans have made it possible to look inside living bodies.

Anatomical drawings can reveal surprising details. These tendons move the fingers, which do not contain any muscles.

A computed tomography (CT) scan fires X-rays through the body from many angles and then joins together the resulting images to make a 2D or 3D image.

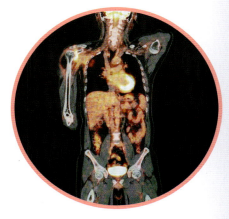

In positron emission tomography (PET), a radioactive chemical called a radiotracer is injected into the bloodstream. Scanning for the tracer gives detailed images of organs, tissue, and even electrical activity.

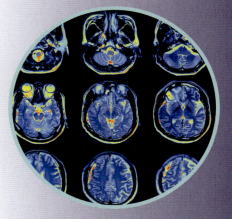

During a magnetic resonance imaging (MRI) scan, magnets make tiny particles in the body, called protons, line up. The protons in different types of tissue line up at different speeds, which creates an image showing organs, tissues, and bones.

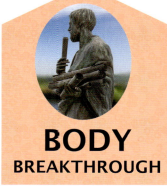

BODY BREAKTHROUGH

Scientist: Aristotle
Breakthrough: Comparative anatomy
Date: c. 350 BCE
The story: Greek philosopher Aristotle studied and compared the bodies of different animals. He believed that their similarities and differences would show him how all bodies worked, including the human body. The approach gave Aristotle lucky insights, but also made him draw some wrong conclusions about the body.

DID YOU KNOW? The 16th-century Flemist anatomist Andreas Vesalius used to dissect the corpses and body parts of hanged criminals.

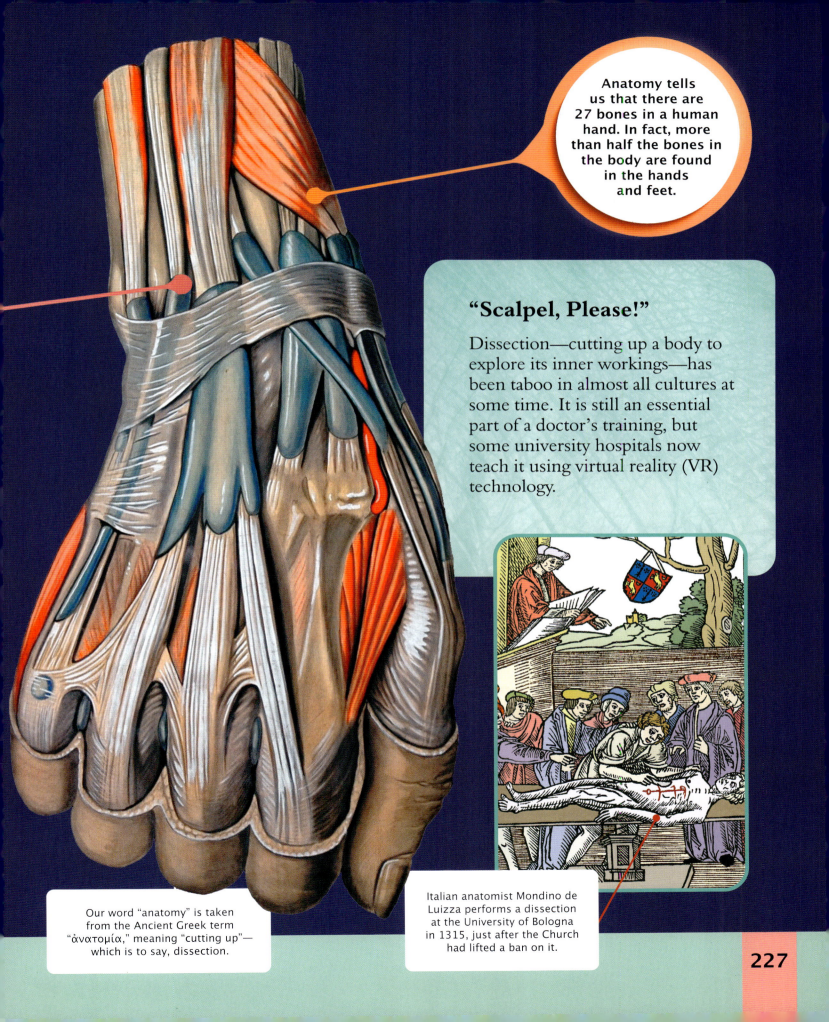

Anatomy tells us that there are 27 bones in a human hand. In fact, more than half the bones in the body are found in the hands and feet.

"Scalpel, Please!"

Dissection—cutting up a body to explore its inner workings—has been taboo in almost all cultures at some time. It is still an essential part of a doctor's training, but some university hospitals now teach it using virtual reality (VR) technology.

Italian anatomist Mondino de Luizza performs a dissection at the University of Bologna in 1315, just after the Church had lifted a ban on it.

Our word "anatomy" is taken from the Ancient Greek term "ἀνατομία," meaning "cutting up"— which is to say, dissection.

227

Surgery

Surgery, also called an operation, is when a team of highly trained doctors and nurses use tools to work on a patient's body. They may treat an injury, remove unhealthy tissue, fix the functioning of an organ—or even replace an organ, which is called a transplant.

Before surgery, doctors and nurses wash their hands and put on caps, masks, and gloves so that microorganisms cannot infect the patient.

Common Surgeries

One of the most commonly performed surgeries is a cesarean section, in which a baby is taken safely out of its mother's womb by making a cut in her abdomen. Other common surgeries include the removal of an appendix, called an appendectomy; cataract surgery, which removes a cloudy lens from the eye; and biopsies, which take a small amount of tissue to check for disease.

Across the world, around one-fifth of babies are born by cesarean section.

Totally Painless

During an operation, doctors trained in the use of anesthetics give the patient a local anesthetic, which numbs the body part that will be operated on, or a general anesthetic, which enables the patient to sleep through the operation painlessly. Anesthetics include the gas nitrous oxide, which is breathed in, and propofol, which is injected.

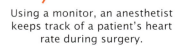
Using a monitor, an anesthetist keeps track of a patient's heart rate during surgery.

DID YOU KNOW? The earliest evidence of surgery was found on a 31,000-year-old skeleton in a cave on the island of Borneo. Part of the lower leg had been removed.

228

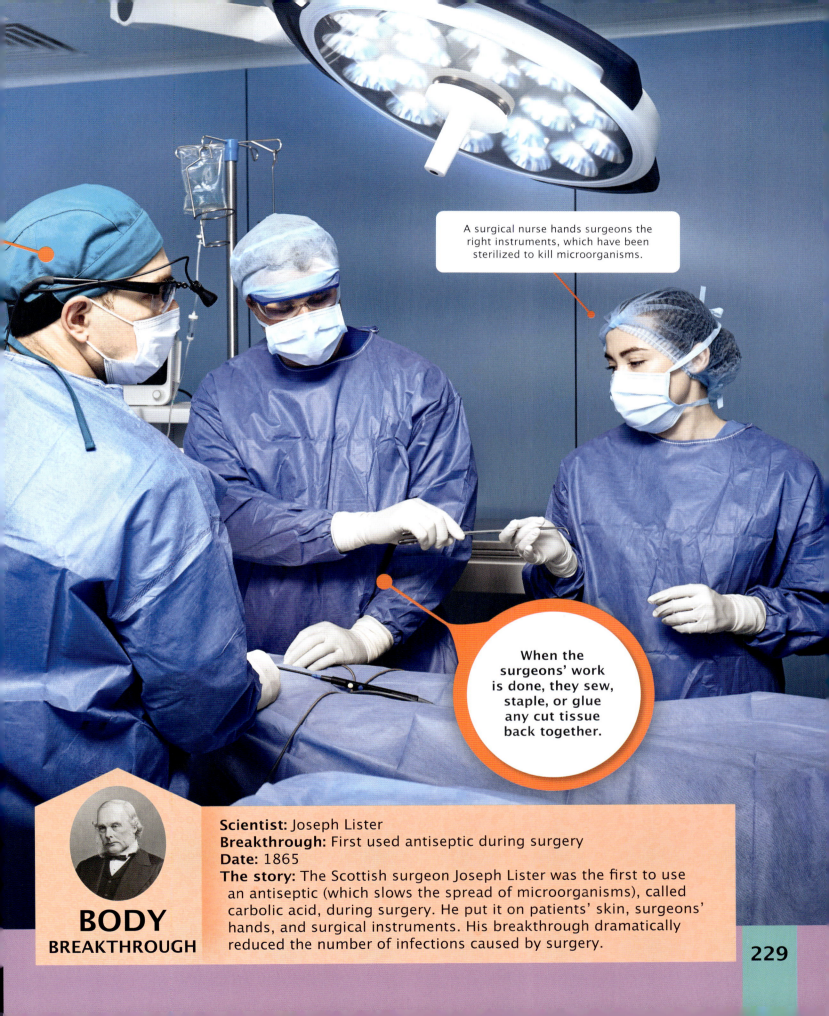

A surgical nurse hands surgeons the right instruments, which have been sterilized to kill microorganisms.

When the surgeons' work is done, they sew, staple, or glue any cut tissue back together.

BODY BREAKTHROUGH

Scientist: Joseph Lister
Breakthrough: First used antiseptic during surgery
Date: 1865
The story: The Scottish surgeon Joseph Lister was the first to use an antiseptic (which slows the spread of microorganisms), called carbolic acid, during surgery. He put it on patients' skin, surgeons' hands, and surgical instruments. His breakthrough dramatically reduced the number of infections caused by surgery.

229

Replacement Parts

From false teeth and wooden legs to lifelike robotic arms, we have used replacement body parts, or prostheses, for thousands of years. If accident or disease stops an organ or limb functioning, a prosthesis can usually do the job. And, thanks to modern materials and technology, it can be hard to tell from the real thing!

Mechanical Stand-Ins

A pacemaker is a device that is fitted inside the chest. It produces electrical pulses that make the heart beat steadily. It is a kind of mechanical spare part that copies a body function. Dialysis machines and ventilators are used to replace the function of kidneys and lungs.

This biobank stores human stem cells. In the future, they may be used to grow lifesaving new organs.

These blood stem cells will be used as living transplants. Their recipient will grow new blood cells.

This heart–lung machine is a temporary stand-in. It is used during surgery to take over from the patient's heart and lungs.

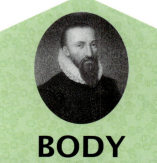

BODY BREAKTHROUGH

Scientist: Ambroise Paré
Breakthrough: Designed prosthetic limbs that could move
Date: c. 1550
The story: French army surgeon Ambroise Paré noticed that soldiers who had lost a limb often became severely depressed. He designed functional replacement limbs—his false legs bent at the knee and his arms at the elbow. Paré even invented a mechanical hand with jointed fingers that could grip.

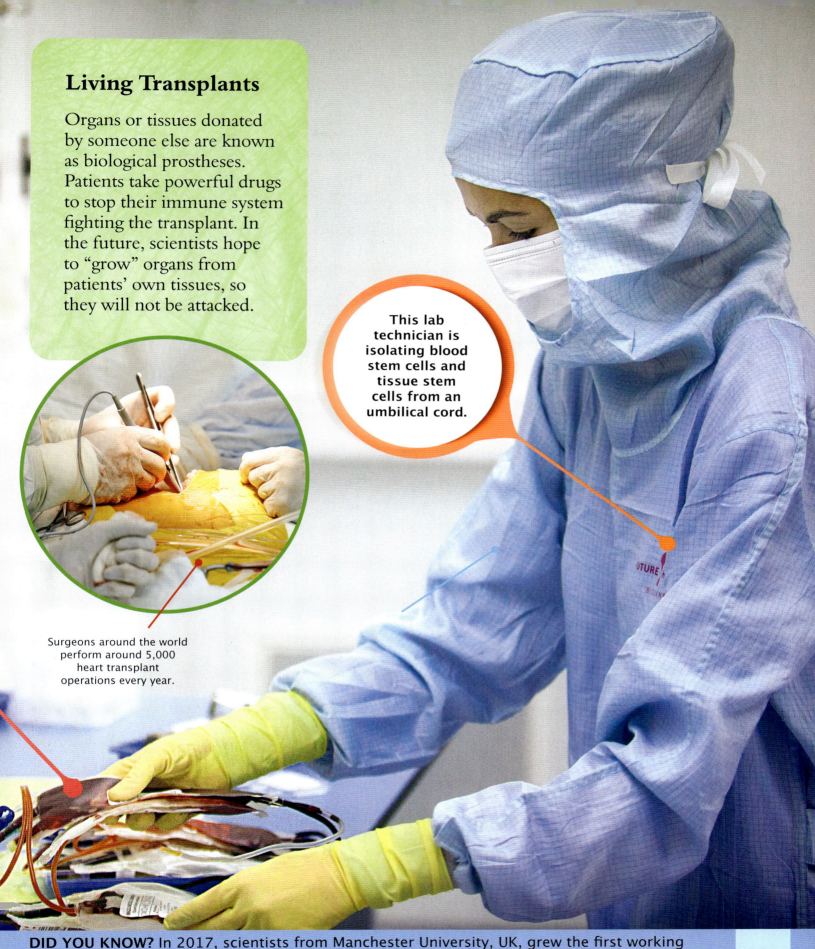

Living Transplants

Organs or tissues donated by someone else are known as biological prostheses. Patients take powerful drugs to stop their immune system fighting the transplant. In the future, scientists hope to "grow" organs from patients' own tissues, so they will not be attacked.

This lab technician is isolating blood stem cells and tissue stem cells from an umbilical cord.

Surgeons around the world perform around 5,000 heart transplant operations every year.

DID YOU KNOW? In 2017, scientists from Manchester University, UK, grew the first working "mini-kidney" from human stem cells.

231

Blood Medicine

Blood is no good at keeping secrets—it gives doctors all sorts of clues about patient health. Testing for sugars, proteins, and other substances reveals how well the heart, liver, or other organs are working. Certain diseases show up in the blood, too, such as cancers, anemia, diabetes, and heart disease.

Blood Groups

Our immune system does not attack its own red blood cells because it recognizes the antigens on their surface. Within any blood group (A, B, AB, or O), the markers match. Red blood cells from a different blood group have different protein markers and usually trigger an immune response.

Putting blood from one person (the donor) into another is called a transfusion. It saves lives, but can also be fatal if the donor's blood group does not match the recipient's. The exception is blood group O, which is compatible with all the other groups.

> Today, diabetics can self-test to check glucose levels in their blood. If there is too much, they need an injection of insulin.

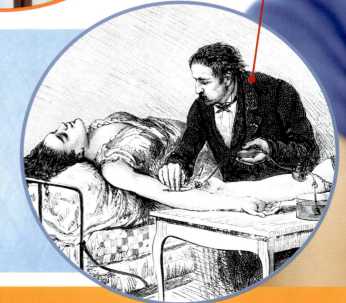

Before 1916, when blood storage became a reality, transfusions were direct. In this 1882 engraving, blood from the donor goes straight into the patient.

The Need for Blood

Blood transfusions help patients who lose a lot of blood after surgery or an injury. Human patients first received donor blood in 1667—but from sheep, not other people! By the 1800s, doctors were performing human-to-human transfusions. However, they did not know about blood groups, so patients often reacted badly.

Fingerstick devices can collect a droplet of blood for testing. They contain a sharp, sterile needle that pierces the skin.

The resulting drop of blood will be put on a test strip. A portable meter will measure its glucose levels.

Scientist: Karl Landsteiner
Breakthrough: Classified the major blood groups
Date: 1901-2
The story: Austrian biologist Karl Landsteiner identified blood groups A, B, and O (which he called C) in 1901, and AB in 1902. He realized blood transfusions must be from compatible groups—otherwise, the patient's antibodies would fight the "alien" blood and their red blood cells would clump together in dangerous clots.

BODY BREAKTHROUGH

DID YOU KNOW? Eighty-five percent of us have Rh positive blood (our red blood cells have the antigen Rh). The rest of us are Rh negative.

Vaccinations

Vaccinations prevent you becoming seriously ill with particular diseases. They usually work by giving the body weakened or inactive parts of a pathogen (something that causes disease). This helps the immune system develop protection against the disease without making you ill. Vaccinations are given as injections, nasal sprays, or drops in the mouth.

A vaccination against polio is given to young children as drops in the mouth.

Race Against Time

In 2020, there was a race against time to produce a vaccine against the virus that causes COVID-19, which had led to a pandemic (when a disease has spread across the world). At record-breaking speed, several vaccines had been developed by the end of the year. Rather than using a weakened version of the pathogen, some of the vaccines worked by a new method, using mRNA (messenger ribonucleic acid), which gives cells instructions to make proteins.

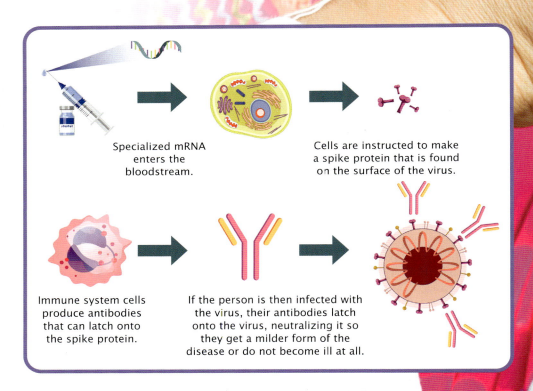

Specialized mRNA enters the bloodstream.

Cells are instructed to make a spike protein that is found on the surface of the virus.

Immune system cells produce antibodies that can latch onto the spike protein.

If the person is then infected with the virus, their antibodies latch onto the virus, neutralizing it so they get a milder form of the disease or do not become ill at all.

BODY BREAKTHROUGH

Scientist: Lady Mary Wortley Montagu
Breakthrough: Introduced a form of vaccination to the West
Date: 1717
The story: Mary Wortley Montagu's brother had died of smallpox and her face was pockmarked by it. Living in Istanbul, she came across a local practice to protect against the disease—rubbing pus from a blister in a mild case into a scratch on an uninfected person. She used the technique—variolation—on her own children.

The first successful polio vaccine was developed in 1950.

In the 1940s, polio killed or paralyzed over 500,000 people every year. Today, polio has been almost wiped out.

Herd Immunity

When a large percentage of a population has been vaccinated against a disease, the population has herd immunity. This means that, even if someone has not been vaccinated, they are unlikely to catch the disease because they have less chance of meeting an infected person. This helps people with serious health problems who cannot get a vaccine because even a weakened version of the pathogen could harm them.

A flu vaccine can be sprayed up a child's nose, which just feels a little tickly. This makes a child less likely to pass on flu to elderly relatives, who might become seriously ill.

DID YOU KNOW? Today, in much of the world, we can be vaccinated against deadly diseases including polio, tetanus, whooping cough, diphtheria, hepatitis B, and meningitis.

Chapter 9

Health and Fitness Primer

To keep your body and brain as healthy and happy as possible, you can take four steps. The first is to eat as balanced a diet as you can. The second is to get the sleep you need. The third is to try to exercise regularly. And the fourth is—to have fun!

A balanced diet includes plenty of fruits, vegetables, and whole grains, such as brown rice and brown bread.

Eat Well

The saying "you are what you eat" is surprisingly true. The minerals, vitamins, and other nutrients in your food are absorbed into your body, becoming part of it. That is why it is important to eat a healthy, balanced diet to give your body the building materials it needs. But it is fine to eat pizza or ice cream as a treat—as long as you eat lots of other healthy foods, too.

Sleep Well

Important changes take place in your brain—and in the rest of your body—as you sleep. Scientists know a lot about the benefits of sleep from studying people who do not sleep enough. Lack of sleep makes a person more likely to catch colds, so we know that sleep has an effect on your immune system. People who go for several days without sleep usually become very confused. It seems that the right amount of sleep is vital to help your brain remain in control. Doctors say that, during the school years, you need between 8 and 12 hours of sleep a night.

Sleep affects production of the hormone that controls how you grow, so it seems that having enough sleep helps you to grow at a normal rate.

Exercise Regularly

Exercise helps to keep your body running smoothly. Exercise, such as playing sports or dancing around your bedroom, also helps you to stay at a healthy weight. Doctors say you should aim for an hour's exercise per day, but any exercise is better than none. Regular exercise strengthens your muscles, joints, heart, and lungs.

As you exercise, you breathe harder and your heart beats faster, so that more oxygen can reach your muscles to keep your body moving. As you get fitter, your body starts to work much harder and for longer.

Take a Break

It is just as important to make time for having fun with family and friends—as well as to wind down by doing things you enjoy, from playing with a pet to reading. Feeling sad or stressed tend to make us sleep poorly, eat poorly, and less likely to bother with exercise. Feeling happy and relaxed has the opposite effect—it helps you to lead a healthy lifestyle!

When you have fun, the brain releases the hormone oxytocin, which makes you feel happy.

DID YOU KNOW? A New Zealand couple in their 60s set a world record by running a marathon (42 km or 26.2 miles) every day in 2013.

The Force of Fitness

Everybody's body needs regular exercise and activity to help it stay healthy and work properly. Find out exactly what fantastic fitness means for you!

Epic Exercise

The **five main benefits of exercise:**

1. Stronger muscles
Lifting exercises make muscle cells contract, and that makes them **stronger** and **bigger**.

2. Stronger bones
Exercise that involves moving around, like tennis, dancing, and walking, helps make **strong tissue** inside bones.

3. Less chance of being overweight
Exercise burns up calories, which is the energy we get from food and drinks. Too many calories can make the body **overweight**.

4. Lower chance of illness
For example, less unwanted body fat means the **pancreas** has a better chance of controlling a chemical called **insulin**—reducing our risk of type 2 diabetes.

5. Less likely to have high blood pressure
High blood pressure puts stress on organs such as the **heart, kidneys, and brain**. Exercise also helps make the heart stronger and pump more blood.

Exercise that increases our **heart rate** (the speed at which it beats) is particularly good for the heart.

During activity, **we breathe faster** and **take in more oxygen.** The **heart** pumps more **blood** around the body.

There are three main types of exercise:

Endurance exercise, like running and swimming.

Strength exercise, such as weightlifting and push-ups.

Flexibility exercise, including yoga and gymnastics.

Health experts say that the average child between 5 and 18 years old should **exercise for around 60 minutes each day.**

Some sports and activities can combine all **three of the exercise types. Swimming** is a good example of this.

This could be **walking** or **cycling** to school, **activities in the schoolyard,** or **after-school sports** such as tennis or hockey

When a person exercises, their body releases chemicals called **endorphins**, which make them feel good. So, **happiness** is another benefit of regular exercise.

The average adult should have between **20 and 25 minutes of exercise each day.**

239

On the Menu

To stay healthy, your body needs you to eat a balanced diet of all the right types of food, with lots of variety. Take a look at what should be on the perfect menu!

Nutrients in different foods keep our bodies **strong** and **healthy**. There are **four types of nutrients:**

1. Carbohydrates
They make energy and are in foods like bread, potatoes, rice, and pasta.

2. Fats
These are **fats** and **oils** in things like fish and butter, which give us energy.

3. Proteins
They make **new cells** and **repair old cells**. Beans, milk, meat, and eggs have lots of protein.

4. Vitamins and **minerals**
These **help cells** and can **prevent illness**. Broccoli has **vitamins C and K**.

Minerals help the **body grow, make cells work,** and **keep bones and teeth strong.**

There are **21 essential minerals**, including **calcium, iron,** and **magnesium**. Vegetables, milk, and small fish, such as sardines, are packed with minerals.

Experts say that around **70%** of energy should come from **carbohydrates,** and around **30%** from **fats**.

240

Experts recommend that we eat plenty of fruit and vegetables each day to stay healthy.

Some types of foods have been called "superfoods," because people claim that they have special powers to keep you healthy. They include **onions, kale, nuts, and salmon.**

These are good for you, but the best thing to stay healthy is to eat a wide variety of different foods.

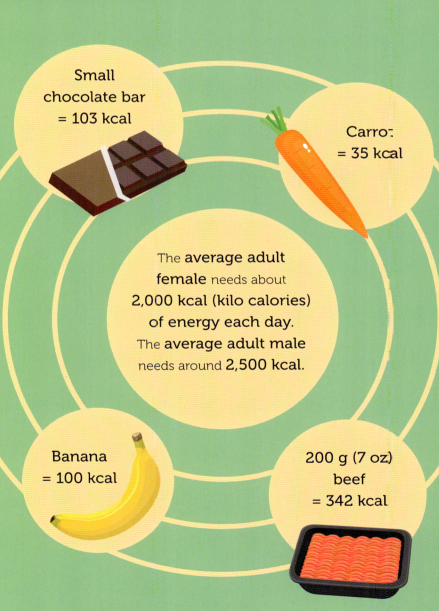

Small chocolate bar = 103 kcal

Carrot = 35 kcal

The **average adult female** needs about **2,000 kcal** (kilo calories) of energy each day. The **average adult male** needs around **2,500 kcal**.

Banana = 100 kcal

200 g (7 oz) beef = 342 kcal

241

Energy Boost

Our brilliant bodies can do all kinds of energetic activities, but we all feel tired sometimes. This could mean that we need to get more energy from the things we eat and drink.

Every part of the human body needs energy to work. We get this energy from food.

Energy Types

Our bodies use **digested food** to make a chemical called **adenosine triphosphate (ATP)**. ATP supplies energy for all our cells. There are **three different types of ATP energy:**

**1.
ATP-PC**
Energy for **high-intensity movements** and **exercises**, such as **sprinting**, lasting for about **10 seconds**.

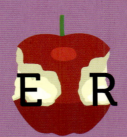

**2.
Aerobic phosphorylation**
A **slow-release energy** for activities such as **walking** and **swimming** that take a longer time.

**3.
Anaerobic glycolysis**
Energy that powers the body in heavy exercise, such as **boxing** for **2–3 minutes**.

Hunger Pain

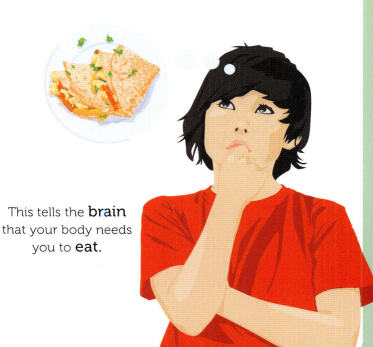

The sense of being hungry is controlled by the brain.

When you have used up your last meal, your empty **stomach** sends a signal through the **vagus nerve to the brain.**

This tells the **brain** that your body needs you to **eat**.

When the body hasn't eaten enough food to turn into energy, we can feel dizzy, faint, and out of breath.

A chemical called **lactic acid** can make parts of the body **painful during exercise**. It can be a **burning feeling**.

The lactic acid builds up in muscles, because they have been working hard and need to get more oxygen.

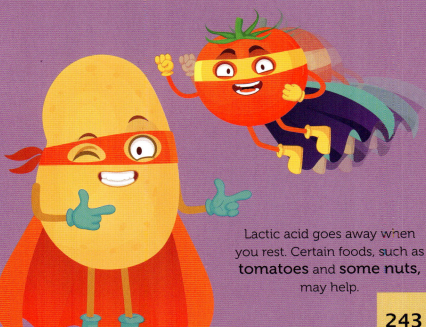

Lactic acid goes away when you rest. Certain foods, such as **tomatoes** and **some nuts**, may help.

243

Sleep Talking

We need to move around to stay healthy—exercising and finding food are essential for our survival. But we also need to stop and sleep every day. Sleep recharges our batteries—it prepares us for the next day's activities.

Hours of sleep

Babies can sleep for **14–15 hours** a day.

Children between 5 and 13 years old may sleep for around **10–12 hours** a day.

Adults often only sleep for about **7–8 hours** a day.

Years of age

Scientists are not totally sure why the body needs sleep, but we know sleep enables us **to recover and rest.**

zzzzzzzZ

Snooze or Lose

Sleep is **very important for the brain** to sort out connections it has made and things it has learned.

The brain also clears any **waste and unwanted information** while the body sleeps.

In comparison, a koala bear can sleep for **18 hours** a day!

If a person misses **one night's sleep,** they will feel **bad-tempered and clumsy.**

After missing **two nights of sleep,** they will struggle to **think properly.**

Going for **five nights without sleep** could make someone see things that are **not really there!**

When we sleep, the walls of the **throat relax and narrow.** This can lead to **snoring.**

Snoring can be as loud as 80 decibels, which is about as noisy as a vacuum cleaner!

Food for Thought

Some foods and drinks are rich in chemicals that help us fall asleep at the end of the day.

Nuts are packed with tryptophan, which helps the brain make sleep-inducing chemicals like serotonin and melatonin.

Milk also contains tryptophan. Having a milky drink may make you feel sleepy and relaxed.

Bananas are high in potassium and magnesium, which help our muscles relax.

Timeline of Discoveries

We know much about the body and how to look after it, thanks to all the hard work and discoveries made around the world by doctors and scientists throughout history.

Early 1500s
Over 500 years ago, Italian artist and scientist **Leonardo da Vinci** sketched and made important notes about how the body worked. This is called **anatomy**.

1796
Edward Jenner's experiment on a 12-year-old in England successfully made a **vaccine** against the disease **smallpox**.

1849
Elizabeth Blackwell became the **first female doctor** in the United States. In 1857, she helped set up the **New York Infirmary for Women and Children**.

1628
William Harvey, an English doctor, published a book explaining, for the first time, that the **heart pumped blood around the body**.

1816
The **stethoscope** was invented in France by **René Laennec**. It enables a **doctor** to listen to a person's heartbeat.

1861
The French scientist **Louis Pasteur** discovered that **germs caused illness**. His work led to better knowledge of diseases like **cholera** and **anthrax**.

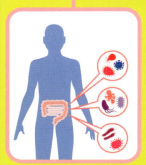

246

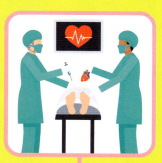

1941
Howard Florey, an Australian, and Ernst Chain, from Germany, developed **penicillin** even further. Their work meant that it could be given to **soldiers during World War II**.

1967
Christiaan Barnard, from South Africa, performed the first heart transplant. A **heart transplant** is when a heart from a recently dead person is placed inside a living person.

1895
German physicist **Wilhelm Röntgen** discovered **X-rays**, which enabled doctors to **see bones** and **organs inside the body**.

1881
After hearing about the international aid work of Swiss humanitarian **Henry Dunant's Red Cross**, American, **Clara Barton** went to Europe to serve as a Red Cross nurse in the **Franco-Prussian war**. This inspired her to set up the **American Red Cross**.

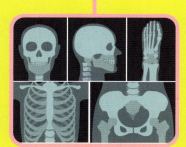

1951
English scientist **Rosalind Franklin** did lots of work in the early 1950s that was essential in helping us to understand **DNA**.

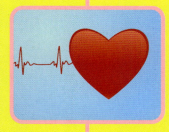

1928
The famous Scottish doctor **Alexander Fleming** was the first person to discover penicillin, which could be used to treat some common illnesses.

1962
Ronald Malt and his team of surgeons in Massachusetts, United States, **reattached the arm of a boy** after he had an accident. It was the first time a limb had been reconnected.

1893
African-American **Daniel Hale Williams**, saved the life of a man with stab wounds by **operating on his heart**. This is thought to be the first successful heart operation.

1950
Canadian surgeons **Wilfred Bigalow** and **John Callaghan** revealed that **hypothermia** (lowering the body's temperature) allowed for **better heart surgery**. They also worked on the **heart pacemaker**.

247

In the Future

Medicine and science have changed so much over the last 100 years and they are advancing all the time. Many more new developments will improve and change human healthcare over the next 100 years, and beyond.

Gene therapy is a technology where genes are used to **treat** or **prevent a disease**. Genes are the body's list of instructions inside every cell.

In the future, **gene therapy** could be used to:

1. Replace a **mutated (faulty) gene** that causes disease with a healthy gene of the same type.

2. Put a new gene into the body to **cure an illness**.

3. Get rid of a **faulty gene** that's not working.

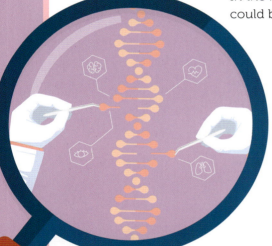

Robotic arms and **equipment** that can do operations are already being used and developed.

A robot arm controlled by a surgeon, is much **steadier and quicker** than a human's arm.

This could mean that **no mistakes** are made in surgery.

A system in the future using an **augmented reality (AR) headset** could let doctors see **organs inside a person's body**.

It could help find and cure problems **very quickly**.

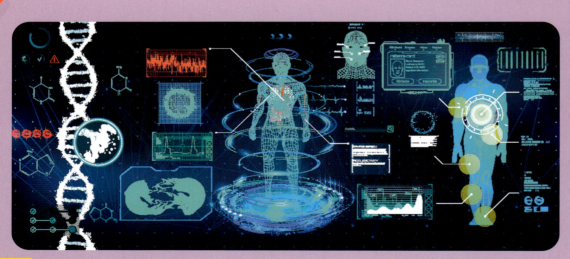

248

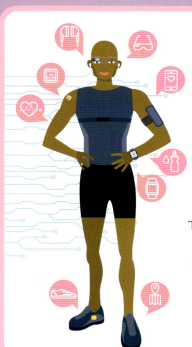

More people will **wear a sensor that detects problems with their body and health**, allowing doctors to receive a message to take medical action if necessary.

This type of medical system is known as **wearable technology.**

Digital contact lenses worn in the eye could help people with **diabetes.**

Sensors in the lens collect information from tears and detect when a **body's blood sugar levels change.**

Medical chatbots will be used a lot more in the future. A **chatbot** is an **automatic computer system that helps people work out what is wrong with them** before they talk to a doctor or nurse.

In the future, **robotic exoskeleton suits** will hopefully help people with severe injuries to **walk again.**

The clever technology **helps move legs, knees, and hips.** These suits could be expensive, though, costing about $40,000 (£32,000).

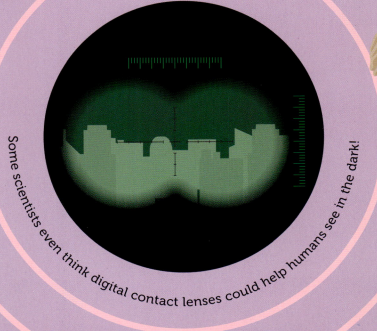

Some scientists even think digital contact lenses could help humans see in the dark!

249

Glossary

ABDOMEN
The part of the body below the chest and above the hips.

ABSORB
To soak up.

ADOLESCENCE
The phase of life, usually from ages 10 to 19, when a person goes through rapid physical and emotional growth.

AMINO ACID
A basic type of molecule that can combine to form proteins.

ANATOMY
The scientific study of the structure of the human body.

ANTIBIOTIC
A medication that is used to kill or damage bacteria.

ANTIBODY
A protein made by the immune system that circulates in the blood. An antibody recognizes an invader, such as a bacterium or virus, and attaches itself to neutralize them.

ANTIGEN
A substance, such as a bacterium, that makes the immune system respond.

ARTERY
A blood vessel that carries blood from the heart toward the tissues.

ATOM
The smallest unit—and tiniest building block—of all things.

BACTERIUM (plural: bacteria)
A tiny living thing with one cell. Some bacteria can cause disease.

BLOOD
The red liquid that travels through blood vessels, carrying materials—including oxygen, nutrients, and waste—around the body.

BLOOD PRESSURE
The force of blood pushing against the walls of arteries.

BLOOD VESSEL
A tube that carries blood around the body.

BODY SYSTEM
A group of linked organs and other body structures that work together to do a task, such as digestion.

BRAINSTEM
The part of the brain that controls essential body functions.

CANCER
A disease in which abnormal (not normal) cells divide uncontrollably.

CAPILLARY
A tiny blood vessel.

CARBOHYDRATE
One of a group of substances, which includes glucose and starch, that can be broken down to release energy in the body.

CARBON DIOXIDE
A substance made of carbon and oxygen atoms. Carbon dioxide is a gas at room temperature. It is made by cells as a waste product, as they break down glucose to release energy.

CARDIAC
Relating to the heart.

CARDIOVASCULAR SYSTEM
The organ system that carries blood around the body.

CARTILAGE
The bendy substance that cushions bone ends in joints, and provides flexibility and support.

CELL
The smallest unit of life and basic building block for all living things.

CEREBELLUM
The part of the brain that controls the body's sense of balance and coordination.

CEREBRAL CORTEX
The surface layer of the cerebrum, where most conscious thinking takes place.

CEREBRUM
The largest part of the brain, divided into halves called hemispheres. It is responsible for functions including thinking, movement, senses, emotions, and memory.

CHROMOSOME
A thread-like structure, composed of DNA, that is found inside the nucleus of most cells. Humans usually have 46 chromosomes.

COLLAGEN
A tough, fibrous protein that gives strength to tendons and other tissues.

COMPOUND
A substance made of identical molecules, each containing atoms of more than one element.

CONDENSE
To change from a gas into a liquid.

CONNECTIVE TISSUE
A tissue that links, supports, or separates other tissues or organs.

CONSCIOUSNESS
Awareness of one's self and one's surroundings.

CONTRACT
To shorten or tighten.

CT (computed tomography)
A technique for taking detailed 2D or 3D images of organs, using X-rays fired from many angles.

DIGESTION
The breakdown of molecules in food into simple nutrients that can be absorbed into the bloodstream.

DNA (deoxyribonucleic acid)
A substance with the structure of a double helix that holds genes and is found in the nucleus of most cells in all living things.

DUCT
A tube that carries materials the body has made.

ELECTROLYTE
A liquid that carries electricity by the movement of ions (atoms or molecules with an electric charge), such as sodium or potassium ions. Some electrolytes are needed to regulate body functions.

ELECTRON
A negatively charged, subatomic particle that travels around the nucleus of an atom.

ELECTRON MICROSCOPE
A machine that uses a beam of particles to make an enlarged image of a tiny object.

ELEMENT
A substance made entirely from one type of atom.

EMBRYO
The name for the developmental stage of an unborn child that follows fertilization, from approximately two to eight weeks.

ENDOCRINE SYSTEM
The organ system that makes and releases hormones, which are chemicals that act as messengers in the body.

ENZYME
A protein that speeds up a chemical reaction, such as breaking up food into smaller molecules.

EVAPORATE
To change from a liquid into a gas.

EVOLVE
To change gradually over time.

FATTY ACID
A basic molecule that can combine to form fats.

FECES (also spelled faeces)
Solid waste that passes out of the body through the anus.

FERTILIZATION
The joining together of the female (egg) and male (sperm) sex cells to produce a zygote that develops into a new living organism.

FETUS (also spelled foetus)
The name for the developmental stage of an unborn child that follows fertilization and being an embryo, from approximately eight weeks until birth.

FUNGUS (plural: fungi)
A living thing that often feeds on decaying material.

GAS
A substance, such as air, that can move freely and has no fixed shape.

GENE
A section of a DNA molecule that gives a particular instruction for making a protein that performs a particular function in the growth or processes of a living thing.

GENETICS
The study of genes and how characteristics are passed down from one generation to the next.

GLAND
An organ that releases a chemical substance, such as hormones, sweat, or semen, into or out of the body.

GLUCOSE
A sugar that is used by cells to produce energy. Glucose is gained by eating carbohydrates.

GLYCEROL
A basic molecule that can combine with fatty acids to form fats.

HIPPOCAMPUS
A part of the brain that has a role in learning and memory.

HORMONE
A chemical messenger made by an endocrine gland. A hormone is carried in the bloodstream to its target tissue or organ, where it brings about a change in behavior.

HYDRATION
The replacement of body liquids that have been lost through sweating, breathing out, pooping, and peeing.

HYPOTHALAMUS
A part of the brain that has a role in releasing hormones and regulating body temperature.

251

IMMUNE SYSTEM
The system of organs, tissues, and cells that fights off pathogens and toxins, prevents infection, and works to protect the body.

IMMUNITY
The ability to resist an infection because the immune system already knows how to defend the body against the invader.

IVF (in vitro fertilization)
A medical technique where an ovum is fertilized by a sperm outside the body in a laboratory, then placed in a woman's uterus.

KERATIN
A tough, waterproof protein found in hair, nails, and the epidermis (upper layer of skin.)

LIGAMENT
A tough strip of tissue that holds bones together in joints.

LIPID
A complex fatty molecule that can perform a range of body functions, including making hormones and cell membranes.

MEIOSIS
A type of cell division that produces sex cells (eggs or sperm) that contain one set of 23 chromosomes.

MEMBRANE
A thin layer of tissue that covers or lines an external or internal body surface.

MENSTRUATION
The process of having a period—shedding the lining of the uterus if no fertilized egg has embedded there. This happens roughly every 28 days in women from puberty.

MICRO-ORGANISM
A living thing too tiny to be seen without a microscope.

MINERAL
A naturally occurring chemical, such as calcium or sodium, that is important for a balanced diet.

MITOSIS
A type of cell division used for growth and repair that results in two cells that are identical to each other and the parent cell.

MOLECULE
A chemical unit made up of two or more atoms bonded together.

MRI (magnetic resonance imaging)
A technique for taking images of soft tissues and hard bones, using magnetic fields and radio waves.

MUCUS
A slimy, protective substance made by glands and membranes.

MUSCLE
A band or bundle of tissue that can contract (shorten) to produce movement.

NERVE
A bundle of neurons that carry messages in the form of electrical signals from the brain to the body and from the body to the brain.

NERVOUS SYSTEM
The organ system that controls everything the body does.

NEURON
Also known as a nerve cell, a cell that transmits electrical and chemical signals inside, to, and from the brain.

NEUROSCIENTIST
A scientist who studies the brain and nerves.

NEUROTRANSMITTER
A chemical made by neurons that enables them to pass on a signal to other neurons or structures.

NUCLEIC ACID
A complex chain-like molecule—such as DNA or RNA (ribonucleic acid)—that carries information in a cell.

NUCLEUS
The central part of a cell, which contains the chromosomes.

NUTRIENT
A substance used by a living thing to survive, grow, and reproduce.

OLFACTORY
Relating to the sense of smell.

ORGAN
A collection of tissues that carries out a particular job or jobs to help a living thing survive.

ORGAN SYSTEM
A group of organs that work together to carry out particular jobs.

ORGANELLE
A structure inside a cell that performs a particular job.

ORGANIC MOLECULE
A group of bonded atoms that includes carbon and hydrogen. All living things are based on organic molecules.

OXYGEN
Found in the air, oxygen is needed by cells so they can make energy. Oxygen is a gas at room temperature.

PARASITE
A living thing that lives on or inside another living thing.

PARTICLE
A tiny portion of matter.

PATHOGEN
A disease-causing organism, such as a bacterium, fungus, or virus.

PIGMENT
A chemical that gives color.

PLANT
A living thing that makes its own food from sunlight.

PLASMA
The liquid part of blood and lymph. It is mainly water but also contains antibodies and proteins.

PROTEIN
A molecule made up of amino acids that can be a structural part of body tissue and can carry out roles in the body from transport to messaging.

PULMONARY
Relating to the lungs.

RADIO WAVE
A form of electromagnetic radiation (energy) used by MRI scanners.

RECEPTOR
An organ or cell able to respond to light, heat, or other stimuli and send a signal to a sensory nerve.

REPRODUCTION
The process by which living things make new living things, known as offspring.

RESPIRATION
The biochemical process in which cells usually combine oxygen and glucose, resulting in the release of carbon dioxide, water, and energy.

RESPIRATORY SYSTEM
The organ system that takes in oxygen and expels carbon dioxide.

SEM (scanning electron micrograph)
A photograph produced by a scanning electron microscope that gives a detailed surface view of an object.

SPECIES
A group of living things that look similar and can reproduce together, such as humans, lions, or English oak trees.

STEM CELL
A cell with the potential to develop into many different types of cells.

SYMPTOM
A feeling or a physical or mental change that is caused by a disease.

TENDON
A strong tissue that connects muscle to bone.

TISSUE
A group of cells with a similar structure and function that work together to do a particular job.

TOXIC
Poisonous or very harmful.

TRANSFUSION
The process of putting new blood into a person's body.

TRANSPLANT
The process of putting a new organ or tissue into a person's body.

URINE
Liquid waste that passes out of the body through the urethra.

VACCINATION
Introducing a medication called a vaccine into the body to produce protection from a disease.

VALVE
A structure that can close a tube or hole so that liquid can flow in only one direction.

VEIN
A tube through which blood travels from the body to the heart.

VENTILATION
The physical process of breathing in oxygen and breathing out carbon dioxide.

VERTEBRA (plural: vertebrae)
One of the small, linked bones that form the spine and have a hole through which the spinal cord passes.

VIRUS
A tiny package of material, which some scientists call living and others call non-living. It can reproduce only inside a living thing and can cause disease.

VITAMIN
One of a group of substances that are found naturally in many foods, and are necessary in small quantities for normal development, functioning, and health.

WATER
A substance made of oxygen and hydrogen atoms. Water is essential to humans and other living things.

X-RAY
A form of energy that can travel through many materials, such as human skin and muscle.

Index

adenosine triphosphate 242
adolescence 214–215
adrenaline 24, 148–149, 182, 183
aerobic respiration 14
aging 172, 178, 220–221
airways 70, 74, 76
alcohol 127
allergies 104, 148–149
alveoli 76, 78–79, 136
Alzheimer's disease 224
amino acids 27, 99, 108, 145
amygdala 160, 161, 176, 178
anaerobic respiration 15
anaphylaxis 148
anatomy 226–227, 246
anesthetic 228
antibiotics 224, 225
antibodies 114, 144–145, 234
antigens 143
antiseptic 229
appendix 124–125
Aristotle 226
arteries 80–81, 82, 95
asthma 149
atoms 9, 10–11
augmented reality 248

babies 182–183, 208, 209, 210–211, 212
bacteria 120, 124–125, 134, 136, 137, 143, 144
balance 196–197
Barton, Clara 247
basal ganglia 160
bases 26–27
bile 98, 110, 122, 126, 127
birth 210–211, 228
birth control 219
Blackwell, Elizabeth 246
bladder 57, 130, 132–133
blood 21, 71, 78, 80–84, 86–91, 123, 126–127, 130, 152, 230, 231, 232–233
blood clots 88, 127
blood groups 232–233

blood pressure 82–83, 94, 238
blood transfusions 89, 232
blood vessels 57, 64, 67, 71, 80–83
body language 199
bone cells 13
bone marrow 42
bones 38, 40–45, 68, 152–153, 193, 220, 238
brain 22, 52–53, 57, 132, 141, 154–198, 203, 215
brainstem 57, 141, 160, 161, 174–175, 180
breathing 74–75, 79, 92, 133, 174, 180, 210
bruises 64

calories 238, 241
cancer 63, 64, 65, 142, 224–225
capillaries 64, 71, 73, 80, 91, 130
carbohydrates 10, 102, 106–107
carbon 10, 11, 107
carbon dioxide 14, 16, 70, 73, 78–79, 90
cardiac muscle 48, 56, 85, 86, 87
cardiovascular system 25, 71, 72–73, 80–95
cartilage 44, 45, 46, 47, 153
cell division 18–19, 28, 30–31, 144, 220
cells 8, 9, 12–13, 14–15, 16–17, 18–19, 26, 28, 30–31, 220, 234
centrioles 12–13
cerebellum 160, 161, 172–173
cerebral cortex 160, 161, 166, 168–169, 178, 198
cerebrum 160, 166–171, 178, 198
childhood 203, 212–213
chromosomes 18, 28–29, 30, 31
cingulate gyrus 160, 178
coccyx 68
colds 68, 140, 147, 148, 150, 236
collagen 19, 44, 45
consciousness 158–159, 174, 175
coordination 172–173
corneas 153
corpus callosum 160, 170–171
coughing 76, 77, 174
COVID-19 138–139, 144–145, 234
Crick, Francis 27
CT (computed tomography) 161, 226
cytoplasm 12

Dalton, John 10
Daly, Marie Maynard 108
Darwin, Charles 37
death 220
dentists 116–117
diabetes 128–129, 232–233, 238, 249
diagnosis 223
diaphragm 75, 140, 141
diet 94, 102–113, 236, 240–241
diffusion 16, 78
digestive system 24, 96–129, 182
diseases 95, 104, 128–129, 136, 137, 138–139, 140, 144, 145, 147, 150–151, 222, 223, 224, 225, 234–235, 246
DNA (deoxyribonucleic acid) 12, 18, 26–27, 28–29, 30, 34, 35, 36, 138, 247
doctors 222, 223, 224
dreams 181
drinking 67, 132–133

ears 69, 168, 170, 192–193, 197, 225
eggs (human) 13, 30–31, 204, 206, 207, 209
elements 10
embryos 208
emotions 160, 168, 170, 176, 178–179, 187, 189, 215
endocrine system 24, 128–129, 182–183
endocytosis 17
endoplasmic reticulum 12–13
endorphins 239
energy 14–15, 98–99, 106–107, 110
enzymes 19, 98, 106, 108, 110, 114, 115, 118, 128
epiglottis 74, 114
epilepsy 160
epithelial cells 13, 20–21, 122, 123
esophagus (foodpipe) 96, 98, 114, 118–119
evolution 36–37, 68
exercise 54–55, 92–93, 203, 237, 238–239
exocytosis 17
eyebrows 69
eyes 56, 153, 169, 170, 173, 175, 180, 186–187, 228

facial expressions 175, 178, 179
families 100–101, 218–219

fat (body) 62, 99, 110, 111
fats (in diet) 102, 108, 109, 110–111
fatty acids 99, 110
feces (poop) 120, 121, 123, 133
fertilization 206, 207
fetuses 208, 209, 210
fever 151
fiber (in diet) 106, 107
fingerprints 62
Fleming, Alexander 224, 247
flus 68, 148, 150, 235
food 94, 96, 97, 100–113, 236, 240–241
fractures 44, 45, 152–153
Franklin, Rosalind 27, 247
fungi 136, 143, 144

gallbladder 98, 123
gas exchange 78–79
gene therapy 34, 35, 248
genes 26–27, 28, 32–37, 138, 248
genetics 28, 32–37
germs 136–139
glands 20, 22, 24, 25, 62, 69, 114, 115, 146, 182, 187, 204, 205
glial cells 164, 166
glucose 14, 15, 70, 99, 106, 115, 126, 128, 231, 232
glycerol 99, 110
Golgi apparatus 12–13, 17
goose bumps 66
growth 25, 44–45, 173, 181, 182, 214, 236

hair 39, 58–59, 66, 109, 221
handedness (right or left) 171
hand-washing 134
hay fever 148
hearing 168, 170, 192–193, 211, 221
heart 71, 72, 80, 81, 82, 83, 84–87, 92, 93, 94–95, 174, 230
heart rate 82, 83, 92, 93, 174, 180, 228
Heimlich, Henry 118
hemispheres (of brain) 170–171
hemoglobin 27, 89, 90
hippocampus 160, 176, 178, 180
Hippocrates 120, 223
histamine 16–17, 142, 143, 148

homeostasis 66–67
hormones 24, 25, 127, 128–129, 148, 178, 180, 181, 182–183, 202, 204, 205, 210, 214, 215, 236, 237
hunger 182, 243
hydrogen 10, 11, 107
hypothalamus 151, 160, 175, 180, 182, 183
hypothermia 247

immune system 64, 65, 134–151, 224, 234–235
immunotherapy 224
indigestion 101
influenzas see flus
insulin 25, 128–129, 182, 238
integumentary system 39, 58–67
intercellular matrix 20
intestines 20–21, 98, 107, 120–125
intolerances 104
involuntary muscles 56–57, 132, 174, 184
IVF (in vitro fertilization) 206, 207, 218

Jenner, Edward 246
joints 46–47, 150, 196, 220

karyotypes 29
keratin 58, 60
kidneys 130–131

lactic acid 15, 125, 243
lactose 104, 105
language 167, 168, 198–199
larynx (voicebox) 198
learning 160, 173, 176–177, 203, 212, 213
leukocytes see white blood cells
ligaments 50, 196
limbic system 160, 166, 176, 178
lipids 10, 11, 102, 110–111
Lister, Joseph 229
liver 98, 110, 123, 126–127
lobes (of brain) 168–169
lungs 70, 72–79
lymphatic system 25, 134, 144, 146–147
lysosomes 12

malaria 136–137
mammals 36

mast cells 16–17
McClintock, Barbara 31
medications 223, 224–225
medicine 222–235
meditation 200–201
medulla oblongata 57
meiosis 30–31
melanin 63, 64
melanomas 64, 65
melatonin 180, 182, 245
membranes (of cell) 12, 16–17, 110, 143
memory 160, 176–177, 178, 180, 181, 189
Mendel, Gregor 33
menstruation 204, 206, 214
mental well-being 179, 200–201, 217
minerals 44, 96, 112–113, 245
mitochondria 12, 14–15
mitosis 18–19
molecules 9
moles 63, 64
Montessori, Maria 212
mosquito bites 136–137
mouth 114–117, 190–191
movement 50–53, 168, 170, 172–173
MRI (medical resonance imaging) scans 161, 162–163, 226
mRNA (messenger ribonucleic acid) 26–27, 234
mucus 135, 140, 150, 188
muscle cells 49, 54, 55, 56
muscles 15, 38, 39, 48–57, 66, 69, 75, 93, 132, 196, 238
muscular system 25, 38, 48–57
mutations 36

nails 39, 60–61, 109
nerves 52, 53, 62, 132, 154, 170, 184–185
nervous system 25, 52–53, 154–158
neuromuscular junctions 52
neurons 154, 155, 164–165, 166, 171, 176, 177
neurotransmitters 164, 178, 185
Nightingale, Florence 111
nipples 69
nose 74–75, 135, 140, 150, 168, 188

255

nuclei (*sing.* nucleus) 12–13, 18, 19, 26
nucleic acids 10, 11, 26–27

olfactory bulbs 176, 188
organ systems 9, 24–25
organelles 12–13, 14–15, 27
organic molecules 10, 11
organs 9, 22–23
osmosis 16, 17
ovaries 182, 204, 206, 207
oxygen 10, 14, 15, 16, 54, 70, 72–73, 78–79, 80, 82, 84, 90, 92, 93, 107, 208
oxytocin 182–183, 237

pacemakers 230, 247
pain 53, 169, 175, 195, 224, 225
pancreas 98, 123, 128–129, 182, 238
Pasteur, Louis 246
penicillin 224, 247
penis 205
periods 204, 206, 214
PET (positron emission tomography) 226
phagocytosis 143
physicians 222, 223, 224
pineal gland 22, 180, 182
pituitary gland 25, 182, 183, 205
placenta 208, 210
plasma 88–89, 90
platelets 88, 89, 127, 152
pneumonia 136
polio 234–235
poop *see* feces
pregnancy 206–210
proprioception 196–197
prostheses 84, 230–231
proteins 10, 11, 19, 26, 27, 102, 108–109, 144–145
protozoa 136, 144
puberty 202, 204, 205, 214
pulmonary circulation 82
pulse 93, 210

rectum 96, 121
red blood cells 15, 71, 80, 88, 89, 90–91
reflexes 53, 174

relaxation 217, 237
reproductive system 25, 202–211
respiration (cellular) 14–15
respiratory system 24–25, 70, 72–79, 92
ribonucleic acid (RNA) 26–27, 35, 138, 234
ribosomes 12, 27
rituals 214, 220
Röntgen, Wilhelm 40, 247

saliva 114, 115, 174
salt (table) 94
scabs 152
scans 208–209, 223, 226
seeing *see* sight
senses 53, 162, 168–169, 170, 186–197, 211
serotonin 185, 245
sex chromosomes 29, 31, 204, 205
shivering 66
sight 56, 169, 170, 173, 175, 186–187, 211
sinuses 68
skeletal muscles 48–55, 132
skeletal system 25, 38, 40–47
skin 23, 39, 62–67, 109, 133, 134, 136, 137, 152, 194–195, 221
skull 43, 46, 157
sleep 175, 180–181, 236, 244–245
smallpox 234, 246
smell 168, 176, 188–189, 190, 191
smoking 95
smooth muscle 48, 56, 132
sneezing 76, 140–141, 143, 174
snoring 245
speech 68, 168, 198–199, 212
sperm 30, 204, 205, 206, 207, 209
sphincters 118, 132
spinal cord 50, 51, 155, 174, 184
spleen 123, 126–127, 146
starches 106, 115
stem cells 13, 45, 74, 152, 153, 230–231
stethoscopes 222, 246
stomach 98, 100, 118, 119
sugars (in diet) 103, 106, 107, 116
sunburn 64, 65
surgery 47, 69, 84, 124, 125, 228–229, 231, 247, 248
swallowing 114, 174
sweat 62, 67, 133, 150–151

synovial fluid 47
systemic circulation 82
systems (body) 24–25

taste 169, 190–191, 211
tears 135, 178, 179, 187
teeth 42–43, 68, 115, 116–117, 198, 212
temperature 66, 111, 151, 182, 195
tendons 50, 51, 196, 226–227
thalamus 160, 161
thinking 154, 158, 164, 166–169
thymus gland 146, 182
thyroid gland 24, 182
tissues 9, 20–21, 152, 153
tongue 115, 190, 198
tonsils 69, 146
touch 53, 169, 191, 194–195, 211
transfusions 89, 232
transplants 231, 247
twins 34, 209

ultrasound scans 208–209
umbilical cord 208, 231
urea 127, 130
urinary system 25, 130–133, 137
urine 67, 130, 132–133, 137
uterus 204, 206, 207, 208, 209, 210

vaccinations 65, 136, 145, 150, 234–235, 246
veins 80–81, 82
vertebrae (*sing.* vertebra) 41
Vesalius, Andreas 48
vesicles 17
vestibular system 196–197
vestigial organs 68–69, 124–125
viruses 138–139, 144–145, 150, 151, 234
vitamins 65, 111, 112–113
vomiting 140, 174

water 10, 16, 65, 67, 79, 130, 132–133, 140, 151
Watson, James 27
white blood cells 16–17, 69, 88, 89, 134, 135, 142–143, 144–145, 146, 148, 182
windpipe (trachea) 74
womb *see* uterus

X-rays 40, 152–153, 223, 226, 247